Hahn and Economic Methodology

Frank Hahn maintained a relentless critical attitude to economic methodology throughout his career, regarding it effectively as a fruitless activity that should be avoided. Yet, paradoxically, this did not inhibit Hahn from propounding a prescriptive approach to economic theorizing and the role and status of economic theory. In *Hahn and Economic Methodology* we provide the first book-length study of Hahn's overall position on methodology, including his strident critique of certain methodological positions, and his positive methodological prescriptions and their rationale.

Hahn and Economic Methodology addresses two fundamental questions: (1) what is distinctive about economic theorizing; (2) what is the cognitive value of the outcome of this activity of economic theorizing? i.e. economic theory? We will argue that, for Hahn, economic theorizing is distinctive with respect to four dimensions. First, the aim of economic theory is neither to describe nor to explain the real economic world, as in the physical sciences. Rather, the aim is to achieve objective, but non-scientific, understanding. Second, the central question for economic theory remains, for Hahn, how to understand, but not to predict as in physics for instance, how decentralized choices interact and perhaps get co-ordinated. Third, Hahn identifies 'three commitments,' without which, he argues, economic theorizing for him is not possible. Finally, economic theorizing has a distinctive approach, which Hahn calls its 'grammar of argumentation.'

The two fundamental questions and these four dimensions of economic theorizing constitute both the holding frame of our investigation, and the central subject matter of this book, at the end of which readers should have a clearer overall view of Hahn's reflections on economic methodology, which are always subtle, at times tantalizingly elusive, but always intriguing.

Thomas A. Boylan is Personal Professor of Economics at the National University of Ireland, Galway.

Paschal F. O'Gorman is Personal Professor of Philosophy at the National University of Ireland, Galway.

Both Professors have collaborated over the last 20 years and have co-written and co-edited a number of books (all with Routledge), and they have published extensively in an array of international journals.

Routledge frontiers of political economy

1 **Equilibrium Versus Understanding**
Towards the rehumanization of economics within social theory
Mark Addleson

2 **Evolution, Order and Complexity**
Edited by Elias L. Khalil and Kenneth E. Boulding

3 **Interactions in Political Economy**
Malvern after ten years
Edited by Steven Pressman

4 **The End of Economics**
Michael Perelman

5 **Probability in Economics**
Omar F. Hamouda and Robin Rowley

6 **Capital Controversy, Post Keynesian Economics and the History of Economics**
Essays in honour of Geoff Harcourt, volume one
Edited by Philip Arestis, Gabriel Palma and Malcolm Sawyer

7 **Markets, Unemployment and Economic Policy**
Essays in honour of Geoff Harcourt, volume two
Edited by Philip Arestis, Gabriel Palma and Malcolm Sawyer

8 **Social Economy**
The logic of capitalist development
Clark Everling

9 **New Keynesian Economics/ Post Keynesian Alternatives**
Edited by Roy J. Rotheim

10 **The Representative Agent in Macroeconomics**
James E. Hartley

11 **Borderlands of Economics**
Essays in honour of Daniel R. Fusfeld
Edited by Nahid Aslanbeigui and Young Back Choi

12 **Value, Distribution and Capital**
Essays in honour of Pierangelo Garegnani
Edited by Gary Mongiovi and Fabio Petri

13 **The Economics of Science**
Methodology and epistemology as if economics really mattered
James R. Wible

14 **Competitiveness, Localised Learning and Regional Development**
Specialisation and prosperity in small open economies
Peter Maskell, Heikki Eskelinen, Ingjaldur Hannibalsson, Anders Malmberg and Eirik Vatne

15 **Labour Market Theory**
A constructive reassessment
Ben J. Fine

16 **Women and European Employment**
Jill Rubery, Mark Smith, Colette Fagan and Damian Grimshaw

17 **Explorations in Economic Methodology**
From Lakatos to empirical philosophy of science
Roger Backhouse

18 **Subjectivity in Political Economy**
Essays on wanting and choosing
David P. Levine

19 **The Political Economy of Middle East Peace**
The impact of competing trade agendas
Edited by J.W. Wright, Jr

20 **The Active Consumer**
Novelty and surprise in consumer choice
Edited by Marina Bianchi

21 **Subjectivism and Economic Analysis**
Essays in memory of Ludwig Lachmann
Edited by Roger Koppl and Gary Mongiovi

22 **Themes in Post-Keynesian Economics**
Essays in honour of Geoff Harcourt, volume three
Edited by Claudio Sardoni and Peter Kriesler

23 **The Dynamics of Technological Knowledge**
Cristiano Antonelli

24 **The Political Economy of Diet, Health and Food Policy**
Ben J. Fine

25 **The End of Finance**
Capital market inflation, financial derivatives and pension fund capitalism
Jan Toporowski

26 **Political Economy and the New Capitalism**
Edited by Jan Toporowski

27 **Growth Theory**
A philosophical perspective
Patricia Northover

28 **The Political Economy of the Small Firm**
Edited by Charlie Dannreuther

29 Hahn and Economic Methodology
Thomas Boylan and Paschal F. O'Gorman

30 Gender, Growth and Trade
The miracle economies of the postwar years
David Kucera

31 Normative Political Economy
Subjective freedom, the market and the state
David Levine

32 Economist with a Public Purpose
Essays in honour of John Kenneth Galbraith
Edited by Michael Keaney

33 Involuntary Unemployment
The elusive quest for a theory
Michel De Vroey

34 The Fundamental Institutions of Capitalism
Ernesto Screpanti

35 Transcending Transaction
The search for self-generating markets
Alan Shipman

36 Power in Business and the State
An historical analysis of its concentration
Frank Bealey

37 Editing Economics
Essays in honour of Mark Perlman
Edited by Hank Lim, Ungsuh K. Park and Geoff Harcourt

38 Money, Macroeconomics and Keynes
Essays in honour of Victoria Chick, volume one
Edited by Philip Arestis, Meghnad Desai and Sheila Dow

39 Methodology, Microeconomics and Keynes
Essays in honour of Victoria Chick, volume two
Edited by Philip Arestis, Meghnad Desai and Sheila Dow

40 Market Drive and Governance
Reexamining the rules for economic and commercial contest
Ralf Boscheck

41 The Value of Marx
Political economy for contemporary capitalism
Alfredo Saad-Filho

42 Issues in Positive Political Economy
S. Mansoob Murshed

43 The Enigma of Globalization
A journey to a new stage of capitalism
Robert Went

44 The Market
Equilibrium, stability, mythology
S.N. Afriat

45 The Political Economy of Rule Evasion and Policy Reform
Jim Leitzel

46 **Unpaid Work and the Economy**
Edited by Antonella Picchio

47 **Distributional Justice**
Theory and measurement
Hilde Bojer

48 **Cognitive Developments in Economics**
Edited by Salvatore Rizzello

49 **Social Foundations of Markets, Money and Credit**
Costas Lapavitsas

50 **Rethinking Capitalist Development**
Essays on the economics of Josef Steindl
Edited by Tracy Mott and Nina Shapiro

51 **An Evolutionary Approach to Social Welfare**
Christian Sartorius

52 **Kalecki's Economics Today**
Edited by Zdzislaw L. Sadowski and Adam Szeworski

53 **Fiscal Policy from Reagan to Blair**
The left veers right
Ravi K. Roy and Arthur T. Denzau

54 **The Cognitive Mechanics of Economic Development and Institutional Change**
Bertin Martens

55 **Individualism and the Social Order**
The social element in liberal thought
Charles R. McCann Jr

56 **Affirmative Action in the United States and India**
A comparative perspective
Thomas E. Weisskopf

57 **Global Political Economy and the Wealth of Nations**
Performance, institutions, problems and policies
Edited by Phillip Anthony O'Hara

58 **Structural Economics**
Thijs ten Raa

59 **Macroeconomic Theory and Economic Policy**
Essays in honour of Jean-Paul Fitoussi
Edited by K. Vela Velupillai

60 **The Struggle Over Work**
The "end of work" and employment alternatives in post-industrial societies
Shaun Wilson

61 **The Political Economy of Global Sporting Organisations**
John Forster and Nigel Pope

62 **The Flawed Foundations of General Equilibrium Theory**
Critical essays on economic theory
Frank Ackerman and Alejandro Nadal

63 **Uncertainty in Economic Theory**
Essays in honor of David Schmeidler's 65th birthday
Edited by Itzhak Gilboa

64 **The New Institutional Economics of Corruption**
Edited by Johann Graf Lambsdorff, Markus Taube and Matthias Schramm

65 **The Price Index and its Extension**
A chapter in economic measurement
S.N. Afriat

66 **Reduction, Rationality and Game Theory in Marxian Economics**
Bruce Philp

67 **Culture and Politics in Economic Development**
Volker Bornschier

68 **Modern Applications of Austrian Thought**
Edited by Jürgen G. Backhaus

69 **Ordinary Choices**
Individuals, incommensurability, and democracy
Robert Urquhart

70 **Labour Theory of Value**
Peter C. Dooley

71 **Capitalism**
Victor D. Lippit

72 **Macroeconomic Foundations of Macroeconomics**
Alvaro Cencini

73 **Marx for the 21st Century**
Edited by Hiroshi Uchida

74 **Growth and Development in the Global Political Economy**
Social structures of accumulation and modes of regulation
Phillip Anthony O'Hara

75 **The New Economy and Macroeconomic Stability**
A neo-modern perspective drawing on the complexity approach and Keynesian economics
Teodoro Dario Togati

76 **The Future of Social Security Policy**
Women, work and a citizens' basic income
Ailsa McKay

77 **Clinton and Blair**
The political economy of the third way
Flavio Romano

78 **Marxian Reproduction Schema**
Money and aggregate demand in a capitalist economy
A.B. Trigg

79 **The Core Theory in Economics**
Problems and solutions
Lester G. Telser

80 **Economics, Ethics and the Market**
Introduction and applications
Johan J. Graafland

81 Social Costs and Public Action in Modern Capitalism
Essays inspired by Karl William Kapp's theory of social costs
Edited by Wolfram Elsner, Pietro Frigato and Paolo Ramazzotti

82 Globalization and the Myths of Free Trade
History, theory and empirical evidence
Edited by Anwar Shaikh

83 Equilibrium in Economics
Scope and limits
Edited by Valeria Mosini

84 Globalization
State of the art and perspectives
Edited by Stefan A. Schirm

85 Neoliberalism
National and regional experiments with global ideas
Edited by Ravi K. Roy, Arthur T. Denzau and Thomas D. Willett

86 Post-Keynesian Macroeconomics
Essays in honour of Ingrid Rima
Edited by Mathew Forstater, Gary Mongiovi and Steven Pressman

87 Consumer Capitalism
Anastasios S. Korkotsides

88 Remapping Gender in the New Global Order
Edited by Marjorie Griffin Cohen and Janine Brodie

89 Hayek and Natural Law
Eric Angner

90 Race and Economic Opportunity in the Twenty-First Century
Edited by Marlene Kim

91 Renaissance in Behavioural Economics
Harvey Leibenstein's impact on contemporary economic analysis
Edited by Roger Frantz

92 Human Ecology Economics
A new framework for global sustainability
Edited by Roy E. Allen

93 Imagining Economics Otherwise
Encounters with identity/difference
Nitasha Kaul

94 Reigniting the Labor Movement
Restoring means to ends in a democratic labor movement
Gerald Friedman

95 The Spatial Model of Politics
Norman Schofield

96 The Economics of American Judaism
Carmel Ullman Chiswick

97 Critical Political Economy
Christian Arnsperger

98 Culture and Economic Explanation
Economics in the US and Japan
Donald W. Katzner

99 **Feminism, Economics and Utopia**
Time travelling through paradigms
Karin Schönpflug

100 **Risk in International Finance**
Vikash Yadav

101 **Economic Policy and Performance in Industrial Democracies**
Party governments, central banks and the fiscal–monetary policy mix
Takayuki Sakamoto

102 **Advances on Income Inequality and Concentration Measures**
Edited by Gianni Betti and Achille Lemmi

103 **Economic Representations**
Academic and everyday
Edited by David F. Ruccio

104 **Mathematical Economics and the Dynamics of Capitalism**
Goodwin's legacy continued
Edited by Peter Flaschel and Michael Landesmann

105 **The Keynesian Multiplier**
Edited by Claude Gnos and Louis-Philippe Rochon

106 **Money, Enterprise and Income Distribution**
Towards a macroeconomic theory of capitalism
John Smithin

107 **Fiscal Decentralization and Local Public Finance in Japan**
Nobuki Mochida

108 **The 'Uncertain' Foundations of Post-Keynesian Economics**
Essays in exploration
Stephen P. Dunn

109 **Karl Marx's *Grundrisse***
Foundations of the critique of political economy 150 years later
Edited by Marcello Musto

110 **Economics and the Price Index**
S.N. Afriat and Carlo Milana

111 **Sublime Economy**
On the intersection of art and economics
Edited by Jack Amariglio, Joseph W. Childers and Stephen E. Cullenberg

112 **Popper, Hayek and the Open Society**
Calvin Hayes

113 **The Political Economy of Work**
David Spencer

114 **Institutional Economics**
Bernard Chavance

115 **Religion, Economics and Demography**
The effects of religion on education, work, and the family
Evelyn L. Lehrer

116 **Economics, Rational Choice and Normative Philosophy**
Edited by Thomas A. Boylan and Ruvin Gekker

117 Economics Versus Human Rights
Manuel Couret Branco

118 Hayek Versus Marx and Today's Challenges
Eric Aarons

119 Work Time Regulation as Sustainable Full Employment Policy
Robert LaJeunesse

120 Equilibrium, Welfare and Uncertainty
Mukul Majumdar

121 Capitalism, Institutions and Economic Development
Michael Heller

122 Economic Pluralism
Robert Garnett, Erik Olsen and Martha Starr

123 Dialectics of Class Struggle in the Global Economy
Clark Everling

124 Political Economy and Globalization
Richard Westra

125 Full-Spectrum Economics
Toward an inclusive and emancipatory social science
Christian Arnsperger

126 Computable, Constructive and Behavioural Economic Dynamics
Essays in honour of Kumaraswamy (Vela) Velupillai
Stefano Zambelli

127 Monetary Macrodynamics
Toichiro Asada, Carl Chiarella, Peter Flaschel and Reiner Franke

128 Rationality and Explanation in Economics
Maurice Lagueux

129 The Market, Happiness, and Solidarity
A Christian perspective
Johan J. Graafland

130 Economic Complexity and Equilibrium Illusion
Essays on market instability and macro vitality
Ping Chen

131 Economic Theory and Social Change
Problems and revisions
Hasse Ekstedt and Angelo Fusari

132 The Practices of Happiness
Political economy, religion and wellbeing
Edited by John Atherton, Elaine Graham and Ian Steedman

133 The Measurement of Individual Well-Being and Group Inequalities
Essays in memory of Z. M. Berrebi
Edited by Joseph Deutsch and Jacques Silber

134 Wage Policy, Income Distribution, and Democratic Theory
Oren M. Levin-Waldman

135 The Political Economy of Bureaucracy
Steven O. Richardson

136 The Moral Rhetoric of Political Economy
Justice and modern economic thought
Paul Turpin

137 Macroeconomic Regimes in Western Industrial Countries
Hansjörg Herr and Milka Kazandziska

138 The Political Economy of the Environment
Edited by Simon Dietz, Jonathan Michie and Christine Oughton

139 Business Ethics and the Austrian Tradition in Economics
Hardy Bouillon

140 Inequality and Power
The economics of class
Eric A. Schutz

141 Capital as a Social Kind
Definitions and transformations in the critique of political economy
Howard Engelskirchen

142 Happiness, Ethics and Economics
Johannes Hirata

143 Capital, Exploitation and Economic Crisis
John Weeks

144 The Global Economic Crisis
New perspectives on the critique of economic theory and policy
Edited by Emiliano Brancaccio and Giuseppe Fontana

145 Economics and Diversity
Carlo D'Ippoliti

146 Political Economy of Human Rights
Rights, realities and realization
Bas de Gaay Fortman

146 Robinson Crusoe's Economic Man
A construction and deconstruction
Edited by Ulla Grapard and Gillian Hewitson

147 Freedom and Happiness in Economic Thought and Philosophy
From clash to reconciliation
Edited by Ragip Ege and Herrade Igersheim

148 Political Economy After Economics
David Laibman

149 Reconstructing Keynesian Macroeconomics Volume 1
Partial perspectives
Carl Chiarella, Peter Flaschel and Willi Semmler

150 Institutional Economics and National Competitiveness
Edited by Young Back Choi

151 **Capitalist Diversity and Diversity within Capitalism**
Edited by Geoffrey T. Wood and Christel Lane

152 **The Consumer, Credit and Neoliberalism**
Governing the modern economy
Christopher Payne

153 **Order and Control in American Socio-Economic Thought**
U.S. social scientists and progressive-era reform
Charles McCann

Hahn and Economic Methodology

Thomas A. Boylan and
Paschal F. O'Gorman

Routledge
Taylor & Francis Group
LONDON AND NEW YORK

First published 2012
by Routledge
2 Park Square, Milton Park, Abingdon, Oxfordshire OX14 4RN
Simultaneously published in the USA and Canada
by Routledge
711 Third Avenue, New York, NY 10017
First issued in paperback 2014
Routledge is an imprint of the Taylor and Francis Group, an informa business

British Library Cataloguing in Publication Data
A catalogue record for this book is available from the British Library

Library of Congress Cataloging in Publication Data
Boylan, Thomas A.
Hahn and economic methodology / Thomas A. Boylan and Paschal F. O'Gorman.
p. cm.
1. Economics–Methodology. 2. Economics–Mathematical models. 3. Equilibrium (Economics) 4. Hahn, Frank. I. O'Gorman, Paschal F. (Paschal Francis), 1943– II. Title.
HB131.B696 2011
330.1–dc23
2011034594

ISBN 978-0-415-21348-6 (hbk)
ISBN 978-1-138-81065-5 (pbk)
ISBN 978-0-203-12734-6 (ebk)

Typeset in Times
by Wearset Ltd, Boldon, Tyne and Wear

Contents

Acknowledgements

The gestation period of this book was singularly protracted for a variety of reasons, which included the usual demands of academic administration, heavy teaching loads, participation on national boards and committees, to the altogether more serious matter of non-trivial health issues. All conspired to intrude, deflect and delay the completion of this work. But happily it has been completed, albeit after many delays, and missing a number of promised delivery dates. The patient and kind people in Routledge, which included Thomas Sutton and Gemma Walker, must have quietly despaired of ever receiving the final manuscript, but to their eternal credit they never gave up on us. To all of those at Routledge we offer our venal apologies but sincere thanks for their quiet persistence and encouragement.

There are also a small number of people who we would like to single out for mention and particular thanks. First, to Frank Hahn, the subject matter of this book, who in his own inimitable style, felt 'immensely flattered' with being the object of our study. But that was as good as it got. His reply to us opened with the phrase, 'I hope you know what you are doing!' and ended with the hope that we were 'sober people who can evaluate the risks of spending time possibly fruitlessly.' If that wasn't enough, in the middle of his correspondence, he felt that this particular project was 'not the route to fame, or indeed anything much else.' But fame was the farthest thought from our minds. It was an altogether more old-fashioned idea of intellectual curiosity as to what exactly was Hahn's position on methodology. But he did wish us well and coupled with his 'sober' admonitions, we are indeed grateful to him.

We would like to single out Tony Lawson, who on the first occasion we mentioned the project to him, in a small restaurant somewhere outside Cambridge, what feels like aeons ago, was immediately enthusiastic and supportive of the project. In this, as in all our work, Tony has been extraordinarily helpful, supportive and positively disposed, even when we differed from his position. For his friendship and intellectual support over many years we are deeply grateful and appreciative. In Galway, our very good colleague, Dr Ashley Piggins, a former student of Frank Hahn in Cambridge, has provided us with fascinating insights and anecdotes of Hahn's lecturing style and personality. Ashley has been immensely supportive and is looking forward to reading the finished product. We hope he likes it!

Finally, there are two women centrally involved in the production of this volume. One is Claire Noone of the Economics Department in Galway, who has typed, and re-typed, corrected and electronically managed this project from start to finish. The sheer efficiency, cheerfulness and professionalism of Claire, under increasingly pressurized working conditions, have been truly astounding. For this, our sincere thanks. Second, there is Louisa Earls of Routledge who arrived at the end of a long line of people who dealt with this project. But Louisa was the person who had to extract the final manuscript from us, which she did with an exquisite balance of charm and tactful insistence, which would be the envy of any professional diplomat. Louisa was a pleasure to work with, and for her understanding, kindness and encouragement, sometimes in difficult circumstances for us, we wish to convey our most sincere gratitude.

1 Introduction

A book on Frank Hahn's contribution to economic methodology requires a brief account by way of rationale for undertaking this project. If the project has an identifiable genesis, it arose from the teaching, by one of the authors, of a course on General Equilibrium to senior undergraduates at the National University of Ireland, Galway in the late 1970s and early 1980s. Although this course engaged the substantive economic issues, it became increasingly clear that, surrounding Hahn's contribution to this field of economics, there was a methodological 'ghost at the table' to which Hahn appeared deeply committed. The methodological comments by Hahn were duly noted and placed in that ever-expanding file of 'topics to be examined in the future.' In the course of time, however, Hahn's reflections and writings became altogether more explicit and indeed paradoxical. He began to emerge as a relentless critic of methodological preoccupations within the discipline, and proceeded to excoriate all those involved in it, exhorted young academics to avoid it like the plague as essentially a waste of time, and lost no opportunity to convey his dislike for methodology. But it wasn't Hahn's negative disposition towards methodology (in this he is hardly unique) that caught our attention, though it was difficult not to miss it. Rather, it was Hahn's insistence on the correctness of his commitment to certain tenets as to how the pursuit of understanding in economics should be pursued. So, the file on 'topics to be examined' was resuscitated and the element of paradox, as we perceived it, became the philosophical lens that would influence our approach to 'reading' Hahn on methodology. Clearly his methodological writings began to reflect two threads of thought. His negative disposition identified dispositions that he indefatigably opposed as being seriously flawed and unacceptable in the pursuit of understanding in economics, whereas his positive contributions began to articulate a subtle and sophisticated philosophical and methodological position. This book addresses both aspects of Hahn's contributions, the negative and the positive, and concentrates on the philosophical and methodological issues raised in Hahn's writings on these topics. It does not address nor attempt to evaluate his contributions to substantive economic theory during the course of his extended and productive career.

From the perspective of methodological writing in economics, Hahn can be viewed as part of that post-war generation of economists, who at particular stages in their careers engaged in or reflected on the methodological foundations of the discipline. The contributions of Friedman, Samuelson, Harrod, Hicks, Coase and many others can be cited in this genre. In the case of Friedman and Samuelson, their methodological writings became immensely influential within the post-war methodological literature, whereas in the case of others their works were less influential. In the case of Hahn, however, apart perhaps from interesting and perceptive comments by Tony Lawson, Roger Backhouse and Terence Hutchison, among others, his methodological writings have not been addressed in any comprehensive manner, and certainly not a book length study.

It must be noted, however, that addressing Hahn's methodological writings has a historical specificity, which clearly exerted immense influence on the topics engaged by Hahn in his later intellectual trajectory. Hahn was clearly committed to the neo-Walrasian framework, which culminated for him in the Arrow–Debreu contribution on the issue of existence. This was certainly a starting point for him, but could not be the finishing point. Hahn could arguably be termed a 'post neo-Walrasian,' a term with some ambiguity, not to mention a certain linguistic awkwardness. In any event, labels in this context may not be particularly enlightening. But Hahn was acutely aware that the neo-Walrasian framework would not perhaps be the presiding framework for economic theorizing in the twenty-first century, and this topic is addressed in our study. After all, as correctly noted by Düppe (2010), 'general equilibrium (GET) is the economics of yesterday,' and he goes on to observe that, although 'GET had mirrored most analytic advances in economic theory before Debreu, after Debreu most theoretical innovations came as alternatives to GET (from game theory to complexity theory)' (Düppe 2010: 3). Nevertheless, the historical specificity of Hahn's methodological contributions must involve their interrogation in relation to his contemporaries whom he engaged with respect to methodological issues. These included such contemporaries as Kaldor, Friedman and, later, Hausman, as a philosopher of economics. These engagements will feature centrally in this study as the intellectual sites in which Hahn expounded both his negative and positive positions on methodology. He also invoked celebrated names in twentieth-century philosophy such as Moore and Wittgenstein, but never developed the implications of their influence on his methodological reflections. While remaining a staunch defender of the neo-Walrasian approach to economic theorizing, an intriguing aspect of his methodological position, we will argue, is his distinctive position within the orthodox school of neoclassical economics, which is cogently but subtly argued. But there is much more involved in addressing Hahn's contribution to methodological issues than the excavation and identification of his position, in either their negative or positive guise. Central to Hahn's agenda, we would argue, is his deep-seated concern with the integrity of economic theorizing or, what more figuratively might be called, 'the heart and mind' of the discipline. And this concern exerted considerable influence on us as the project developed, to the extent that we discerned this preoccupation in Hahn's own methodological writings. In the remainder of this introduction, we provide an overview of the issues and agenda that informed our approach to this study.

This work is structured around two central questions: (1) what, according to Hahn, is distinctive about economic theorizing? and (2) what is the cognitive value of the outcome of this economic theorizing? By way of introduction, we suggest that economic theorizing, according to Hahn, is distinctive along four lines. First, contrary to what is frequently assumed, the aim of economic theory is neither to describe nor explain the real economic world, as that is done in the physical sciences. Rather, its aim is to achieve objective, but non-scientific, understanding of events and happenings in the real economic world. Second, the central question of economic theory concerns the intellectual agenda set by Adam Smith's invisible hand: to understand, but not predict *à la* physics, how decentralized choices interact and perhaps get co-ordinated. Third, he identifies 'three commitments' on the part of theoreticians, namely rationality, equilibrium and individualism, which are indispensable for economic theorizing. Finally, economic theorizing has a distinctive approach, which Hahn calls its 'grammar of argumentation.' In a sense, these four themes constitute the subject matter of this book.

Many will, perhaps, be surprised that Hahn, in his defence of orthodox economic theorizing, places theoretical economics outside the pale of the empirical sciences. For our contemporary scientific mindset, this location could be read as placing theoretical economics in some rather obscure or highly subjective domain where critical scrutiny is not at a premium. Such a reading would be utterly unfair to Hahn, for whom the commitment to critical scrutiny is absolutely indispensable. Hahn is well aware that numerous economists either explicitly or implicitly claim that economic theorizing is scientific. Nonetheless, he emphatically rejects that claim. In this connection, we critically engage his reasoning for rejecting that claim. This entails a detailed analysis of his rejection of Friedman's and Hausman's defences of orthodox economic theory – both of which insist that economic theory is scientific.

In particular, Hahn argues that economic theory is not concerned with prediction. Neither is it concerned with scientific laws. Any reading of economic theory along these lines utterly misrepresents the authentic cognitive value of neoclassical theorizing. If economic theory is neither in the business of predicting the future nor of discovering economic laws, what is its objective or cognitive value? According to Hahn, economic theory makes an indispensable contribution to the rational, objective understanding of the economic world. This rational, objective understanding, as we have just noted, is not scientific. Neither is it to be identified with the kind of understanding emphasized by those social scientists who adopt a hermeneutical approach to all of the human sciences, in which the correct understanding of human action is modelled on the understanding of a foreign text, as distinct from the scientific understanding of a complex physical system, like the brain. In this connection, we explore Hahn's rationale for rejecting this *geisteswissenschaften* approach to economic understanding. Given that economic understanding furnished by the best theorizing of orthodox economics is neither scientific nor hermeneutical, the onus is on Hahn to elucidate his pivotal concept of understanding. Throughout his methodological/

philosophical writings, Hahn addresses this challenging task. In this book, the first systematic study of Hahn's philosophy of economics, we excavate Hahn's concept of understanding. As one would expect, this concept is complex, penetrating and sophisticated. This excavation takes us through what Hahn considers to be the best practice of economic theorizing to his references to developments in philosophy, notably Moore's contribution to ethics and to what is known as the linguistic turn in philosophy, associated with Wittgenstein. These philosophical developments, synergized with the best theoretical practice of economists, are key components in Hahn's concept of economic understanding. In this respect, Hahn requires us to engage philosophers not commonly addressed in economic methodology.

The central question of economic theory for Hahn is neither to describe nor explain, *à la* physics, real economies. Rather, the central question concerns the intellectual agenda set by Adam Smith's invisible hand: 'to understand how decentralized choices interact and perhaps get co-ordinated' (Hahn 1991(a): 49). The first objective and rigorous response to this central issue was furnished by Debreu. According to Hahn, Debreu's response gave rise to a new dawn of economic theorizing, with its distinctive grammar of argumentation. In this connection, Hahn is insistent that genuine theoretical work of this new dawn should not be confused with the misguided attempts by orthodox economists who advocate 'a theory according to which an economy is to be understood as the outcome of the maximization of a representative agent's utility over an infinitive future' (Hahn 1991(a): 49). In Hahn's view, the latter approach is theoretically barren and symptomatic of a discipline in decay. Whether or not one agrees with Hahn, his position clearly points to the battle for the heart of economics in orthodox economics and its methodology. In this connection, we critically engage Hahn's unique strategy in this battle. Among other issues, this entails a detailed discussion of Hahn's interpretation of Debreu's revolutionary contribution to theoretical economics, especially the economic analysis of the notion of equilibrium.

This brings us to Hahn's 'grammar of argumentation.' This distinctive mode of economic theorizing, which is inextricably linked to the economic quest for objective understanding, is another indispensable pillar in Hahn's philosophy of economics. In the first place, this economic mode of theorizing has a unique, logically impeccable starting point, namely Debreu's existence proof. In this connection, Hahn is at pains to point out that existence in the context of Debreu's proof has a very specific meaning, namely freedom from contradiction. It does not mean empirical existence. Neither does it mean socio-historical existence. Other steps in Hahn's grammar of argumentation presuppose Hahn's emphatic distinction between economic axioms and assumptions. In this connection, we explain Hahn's insistence on this distinction by contrasting his approach to an axiomatic system with Debreu's Bourbaki, purely formalist approach on the one hand and Hausman's implicit definitional approach on the other. By recourse to a detailed analysis of his grammar of argumentation, we show how Hahn justifies his central claim that economic theory – which is both abstract and mathematical, and which neither describes nor explains the mechanisms of real economies – makes an indispensable contribution to the rational, objective understanding of the real economic world.

This study is not confined to a sympathetic exposé of Hahn's unique and challenging defence of orthodox economic theory. We are also concerned with the question of whether or not, or to what extent, Hahn's novel defence stands up to critical scrutiny. According to some methodologists, neoclassical economics is in crisis. The source of this crisis resides in its methodological commitment to mathematical formalism, as exemplified in the research of Arrow, Debreu, Hahn and their likes. Hahn dismisses these claims of crisis by vigorously defending theoreticians' recourse to sophisticated mathematics in their economic theorizing. In this connection, Hahn distinguishes between the unwarranted claims of crisis, on the part of those methodologists who view economic theory solely through the lens of their favourite methodology borrowed from the philosophy of the physical sciences, and the more serious claims by major post-war economists, such as Kaldor, who argues that orthodox theory is barren, irrelevant and a hindrance to economic progress.

Hahn took Kaldor's critique seriously, and in this connection we critically engage Hahn's response to Kaldor. As noted by Hahn, a central issue in the divergence between himself and Kaldor hinges on the use of mathematics in economic theorizing. Moreover, as we noted in the preceding paragraph, Hahn resolutely defends the sophisticated mathematics used by Debreu in his famous existence proof. According to Kaldor, this sophisticated mathematics is the problem. It fails to establish economic, as distinct from mathematical, existence. We critically evaluate this crucial methodological conflict between Kaldor and Hahn by recourse to developments in the history of and in the philosophy of twentieth century mathematics. Such recourse, in our view, is the most fruitful, rational way of evaluating this conflict. We show how, in the course of the twentieth century, under the influence of Brouwer, mathematicians developed a different, but equally sophisticated, mathematics to that exploited by Debreu. Brouwer's alternative mathematics is called intuitionist mathematics. By recourse to Dummett's philosophical analysis of the differences between these two kinds of mathematics, especially their divergent notions of existence, we buttress Kaldor's rejection of Debreu's proof. In addition to buttressing Kaldor's negative assessment of the economic, as distinct from the mathematical, value of Debreu's proof, we show how intuitionist mathematics could offer economic theoreticians a host of novel mathematical tools that may prove both original and fruitful in their efforts at modelling rational economic actions and their consequences. In short, intuitionist mathematics, not the mathematics used by Debreu and Hahn, could enable theoretical economists to accomplish the Hahnian task of gaining a rigorous, deeper and more accurate understanding of economic rationality and of real economies.

Clearly, Hahn's conception of orthodox economic theorizing is very much influenced by the 'new dawn' of theorizing, which broke on the theoretical landscape with the creative research of Arrow and Debreu. Hahn, however, is well aware that, with the passing of the decades since that dawn, this mode of theorizing has reached its dusk. The reasons for its decline are internal to developments within that theoretical framework: its mode of theorizing gave rise to new challenging questions. Unfortunately, the theory lacked the resources to answer these issues. 'Instead of theorems we shall need simulations, instead of simple transparent axioms there looms the likelihood of psychological, sociological and historical postulates' (Hahn 1991(a): 47). In view of this decline, clearly acknowledged by Hahn, what is the contemporary methodological relevance of Hahn's philosophical reflections? In terms of the history of economic methodology, one surely must admire the sheer creativity and complex architecture of Hahn's defence of this mode of theorizing. By exploiting his concepts of understanding and of a dynamic grammar of argumentation, Hahn has developed a consistent, unique and challenging defence of this mode of theorizing, which merits its place in the history of economic methodology – a place which, to date, has not been properly acknowledged.

Moreover, in our opinion, Hahn's philosophical–methodological reflections are also relevant in the following sense: a number of the issues which he opens up for consideration will remain on the methodological agenda, at least, for the foreseeable future. Among the central issues raised by Hahn is the question: what is distinctive about economic theorizing in comparison with theorizing in physics and the other empirical sciences? Hahn's answer is not strikingly original: economic theoreticians, at the most fundamental level, are concerned with persons who engage in economic actions and transactions in complex, interrelated economies. For Hahn, our economic world is populated with human agents, such that, as of now, despite all the achievements of neurophysiology and neuropsychology, the intentional domain of the mind is not reducible to the neurophysiological domain. Hence, the economic world, the outcome of the intended and unintended consequences of billions of human actions, is a unique, highly complex system. Following on from that, Hahn's next central issue is: what are economists attempting to achieve when theorizing in this distinctive domain? He correctly insists that methodologists should not automatically assume that theoretical economists are doing what theoretical physicists and other empirical scientists are doing in their theorizing. In this connection, given the unique complexity of our economic system, the central issue for Hahn is its intelligibility. Is it possible to make objective sense of the global economic system, or, given its unique complexity, should theoreticians acknowledge their conceptual limitations and concede that the system is beyond comprehension? In this connection, Hahn is committed to the enlightenment philosophical tradition, which holds that the quest for objective understanding is legitimate. Thus, economists are obliged to theorize about their unique complex system.

Arising from this obligation, the issue of how economists are to theorize cannot be ignored. Hahn is correct in pointing out that, in most economic theorizing to date, economists have recourse to the concepts of rationality and of equilibrium. These are distinctive organizing concepts in the domain of economics. However, at the common sense level, there is no consensus on the precise usage of these terms. In light of this, how are economic theoreticians to proceed? According to Hahn, if they use these concepts without rigorous examination, their theories will, in all probability, be either wooly or highly subjective. To avoid these dangers, theoreticians have no choice. They are obliged to espouse the Platonic tradition which, negatively, is absolutely hostile to unexamined opinions, however well intentioned, and which, positively, demands consistency and coherence in our thinking. Thus, for Hahn, economic theoreticians, in the interests of avoiding a lack of rigour or uncritical opinion, and in the interests of attaining objective understanding, are engaged in the logico-conceptual task of constructing a consistent and coherent theory of rationality and of equilibrium, in which the economic premium is on explicitness and rigour. In particular, Hahn's Platonic virtues of rigour, explicitness, clarity, consistency and coherence oblige the economic theoretician to use advanced mathematics. This is Hahn's challenge to those post-modern methodologists and others who object to the formalization of economic theory. More generally, Hahn focuses our attention on a crucial methodological question: namely, given the centrality of rationality and of equilibrium to their discipline, how are economists to proceed with their theorizing?

As we have emphasized, according to Hahn, economic theoreticians cannot avoid recourse to sophisticated mathematics. In light of his hostility to unrigorous thinking and subjective opinions combined with the paucity of non-mathematical theorizing relative to the richness of general equilibrium theorizing, Hahn opts for mathematical theorizing. Moreover, in his view, the theoretical success of Debreu over Walras lay in the fact that the sophisticated mathematics used by Debreu was not available to Walras. In this connection, the Hahn–Kaldor debate about the economic usefulness of this sophisticated mathematics is certainly relevant to contemporary economic methodology. It raises a crucial issue for those concerned with economic modelling: namely, will the economic constraints, as identified by Hahn, require economic theoreticians to use a different kind of mathematics to that used by Debreu? What is the most appropriate mathematics for the task of theorizing economic decision making? Does the fact that economic agents are historically located persons, with limited information and limited cognitive, linguistic and rational capacities, imply that economic theoreticians need to use an alternative mathematics to that which has, to date, dominated the discipline in theorizing rational economic decision making?

Clearly, this book is not claiming to be the definitive study of Hahn's novel and challenging defence of orthodox economic theory. Rather, our intention is twofold: First, to introduce the reader to the principal motives for Hahn's defence of orthodox theory. Not least because he rejects the widespread view that economics is scientific, Hahn's motives require us to introduce philosophical themes that are not familiar in mainstream methodology. Second, we wish to critically evaluate Hahn's defence. In general, critique is either internal or external. This divide frequently breaks down into critique by orthodox economists on the one hand and heterodox economists on the other. For the most part, our evaluation falls into the internal kind of critique. This means that assumptions or positions that heterodoxy may wish to critically interrogate are not challenged. For instance, one could argue, contrary to Hahn's assumption, that rationality is constrained irrationality, such that the constraining is effected in quite different ways in different regions of real economies. This would imply that Hahn's search for one unified theory of rationality does not stand up to critical scrutiny. Addressing such issues with due sensitivity and care would require a detailed investigation into philosophical positions ranging from Putnam to Davidson, which in turn would require an extended study in its own right. Despite this limitation, our hope is that this work will constructively add to the ongoing debate in economic methodology.

2 Hahn in context

An overview

> I am not an intellectual historian, although some of my best friends are.... I want to get on with the business of understanding the world rather than with the understanding of the manner someone else understood it.
>
> (Hahn 2005(a): 6–7)

Introduction

In this chapter we provide an outline of Hahn's biographical details. This is followed by an account of what he termed his 'journeyings through economic theory,' and, finally, we give a very brief account of the methodological environment that Hahn would have encountered at the very outset of his academic career. The purpose of the chapter is to provide a short overview of the context of Hahn's work and preoccupations, along with his methodological concerns, which are the subject of detailed analysis in the subsequent chapters of the book. Hopefully this will provide a helpful framework for readers who may be unfamiliar with the range of Hahn's interests, his intellectual background and the emergence of his methodological agenda over the course of his career in economics.

Hahn: a biographical profile

In his own words, Hahn was 'not much in the habit of reflecting on [his] life, let alone on so weighty a matter as [his] philosophy of life' (Hahn 1993(b): 160). This was in the context of Hahn's contribution to Michael Szenberg's engaging book on *Eminent Economists: Their Life Philosophies* (1993). Were it not for this contribution to Szenberg's book, followed in 1994 by 'An Intellectual Retrospect' in the *Banca Nazionale Del Lavoro Quarterly* (Hahn 1994), our insight into Hahn's background and academic trajectory would be singularly sparse. However, when the opportunity arose, 'an opportunity for self-indulgence' as he described it, Hahn was happy to avail of it.

Hahn was born into 'an intellectual Central European family' in Berlin in 1925: the 'son of a famous German philosopher and mathematician,' according to Blaug (1985: 78). Hahn, however, describes his father as a chemist by profession, who decided early on that chemistry was less than compelling as a life-long career, since, as Hahn adds rather mischievously, chemistry 'involved exposure to unpleasant smells' and his father was 'a notable hypochondriac' (Hahn 1993(b): 160). Hahn's father, by the time 'that I came to know him' (ibid.: 160) had become something of a literary figure, producing novels and poetry, along with popular science books. He was clearly a man of wide learning and reading, who was anxious to impart the same characteristics to his two sons, an aim in which he appeared to have been successful, since his parents' influence left the young Frank Hahn 'with a voracious appetite for reading and intellectual speculation' (Hahn 1993(b): 161). This early education included, among other things, German classics, Greek mythology and the Bible. Hahn left Berlin at the age of six and the family settled in Prague, but by 1938 they had left that city and moved to England.

England was agreeable to the young Hahn and clearly exerted a very formidable influence on his formation, and notwithstanding a number of caveats on his part, he can overwhelmingly declare that 'England made me' (Hahn 1993(b): 161). The English attributes that Hahn 'fell in love with' included, not only 'the English countryside and the wonderful purity of understatement of early English Gothic,' but also 'the intellectual tone of the place.' This intellectual tone was 'serious without being frantic,' and reflected a 'fastidiousness of expression,' which was 'not so much "understatement" as avoidance of pomposity and of extremes.' Although this made a deep impression on Hahn, age has brought qualification in that 'now that I am older I am no longer an unqualified admirer' (ibid.: 161). These culturally imbued values of English intellectual tonality arguably provided Hahn with the intellectual bulwark against intellectuals of a particular ilk, since he admits to having become somewhat wary of intellectuals, 'especially when they are French or educated above their intelligence.' But, notwithstanding his invective against particular species of intellectuals, he does admit that 'I am of that ilk,' and tellingly admits to finding himself 'irritated when so many of my economist friends whose work I admire turn out to have no appetite for anything but economics.' This latter aptitude for interests outside economics, in particular the outreach to philosophy, is clearly reflected in Hahn's methodological work, as we will demonstrate in the later chapters of this book.

Hahn thought of pursuing a career as a chemist, as in his father's case, even though his 'real love' was mathematics. He chose the latter. However, the Second World War intervened and Hahn found himself in the air force for the duration of the war. It appears that Kalecki, who knew his parents, urged Hahn to read economics, and after the war this was the path he chose to pursue at the London School of Economics (LSE). At the LSE, Hahn's contemporaries included many who were to become influential figures in the discipline: William Baumol, Lionel Robbins, Nicholas Kaldor, Ronald Coase and Friederich von Hayek. Two of these, Kaldor and, later, Robbins, were to act as supervisors of his PhD at the LSE. During his period at the LSE, Hahn heard Harrod deliver his celebrated lectures on growth theory in the famous LSE seminars. Hahn's laconic comment on Harrod's contribution was that, at the time, 'it seemed less momentous that it turned out to be' (Hahn 1993(b): 162).

Hahn provides an interesting insight into the pivotal texts in economics that exerted a profound and influential impact on his understanding of economics and the orientation his career followed. One of the first books in economics that he read, and one that 'made a deep impression' on him was Hick's *Value and Capital* (1939), and this for both methodological and substantive reasons. Methodologically, Hahn's attraction to Hick's book arose from the 'reductionist project,' which Hahn deciphered to be its central principle of organization, i.e. of 'going from the "atom" to the whole.' What was later to be termed the micro-foundations of macroeconomics, as if Hahn observes 'this were a new insight,' was for Hahn a fundamental methodological principle, which his 'early Hicksian experience had never led me to think otherwise' (Hahn 1993(b): 162).

Hahn notes that his 'later absorption in General Equilibrium Theory' was a direct consequence of his early Hicksian experience, and he can claim, with some justification arising from his later career, that Hicks was indeed 'a lasting influence' (Hahn 1993(b): 162). But Hicks wasn't the only influence. Hahn and his contemporaries at the LSE were 'inspired' by a small number of books that were appearing at this time: Samuelson's *Foundations of Economic Analysis* (1947), whom Hahn regarded as 'by far the cleverest and most versatile economist' he had ever met; Lange's *Price Flexibility and Employment* (1944); and Arrow's *Social Choice and Individual Values* (1951). Hahn is of the opinion that no 'comparable coincidence of great books in economic theory has occurred since that time' (ibid.: 162). It was these texts, rather than Keynes's *The General Theory of Employment, Interest and Money* (1936) that 'set the agenda for some of us young theorists' (ibid.: 163). Hahn's predilection for the orientation and influence of these unquestionably seminal texts, rather than that of Keynes, would be compatible with his own admission that he lacked 'some of the attributes of an economist that Keynes thought necessary,' in particular his 'weak interest in the practical end of the subject' (ibid.: 161), which he regarded as a failing, since questions of economic policy would never engage him in the same way that theoretical questions could and would throughout his career. Lange's book steered him to 'a lifelong concern with monetary theory in a general equilibrium context,' and Arrow's work 'set a standard of rigour and elegance' that was clearly to be aspired to (Hahn 1993(b): 163).

The completion of his PhD at the LSE represented the culmination of his formal education, after which he moved to his first teaching position as an Assistant Lecturer in Economics at Birmingham in 1953, where he felt his 'real education in economics began.' Birmingham was important to Hahn for two reasons. First, Birmingham was, at this time, one of the forerunners among the British universities in which mathematical methods in economics was nurtured and developed, and, in his view, it actually 'flourished.' This was because of, in large part, the disposition of Gilbert Walker, the then head of the department of economics, who facilitated the teaching of mathematical economics. The second contributing factor, and clearly the motive force of his 'real education,' was his 'great good fortune' to have as a colleague the Irishman Terence Gorman, who in Hahn's estimation was 'touched by genius' (Hahn 1994: 249). Gorman, an accomplished mathematician, has produced a number of important results, including the duality theory of the consumer. Gorman pursued an ascetic attitude to his own academic work, resisting the publication of his work apart from a small number of papers that met his own demanding standards of rigour and credit-worthiness of publication. Clearly, Hahn was very impressed by Gorman, and was very taken by his 'unworldly' disposition, and a lifelong friendship ensued.

Hahn was to remain in Birmingham until 1960, but during his period of teaching there he received an invitation to take up a Visiting Professorship at the Massachusetts Institute of Technology (MIT). This was the beginning of a lifelong relationship with America and American economists, and frequent visits to America became essential for him, since it was there 'that one can find the best practitioners of the kind of economic theory that interests me' (Hahn 1993(b): 163). Not that Hahn found everything in America compatible to his intellectual commitments; he discovered issues of fundamental differences from a number of American economists. However, he does describe his initial exposure to American economists as the beginning of 'the second phase of my economics education' (ibid.: 163). Friendships with Solow, Samuelson and Arrow, along with collaboration with Solow and Arrow, were to follow. But Hahn never moved to America on a permanent basis. After his stay at Birmingham, he moved in 1960 to the University of Cambridge and, among his other activities, became Managing Editor of the *Review of Economic Studies*. In 1967 he was appointed Professor of Economics at the LSE, but in 1972 he moved back to Cambridge as Professor of Economics. Following his retirement from Cambridge in 1992, he spent several years at the University of Siena. During the course of his academic career he has held numerous positions, including President of the Econometric Society in 1968, among others, along with Visiting Professorships at Harvard, MIT and the University of California, Berkeley.

Hahn's 'journeyings through economic theory'

Hahn's career, which covers the second half of the twentieth century and beyond, represents one of the most vibrant periods of theoretical developments in the history of the discipline. This period witnessed not only the growth of the discipline with respect to membership and institutional expansion, but more significantly a number of landmark intellectual achievements. The post-war period was characterized by the search for unifying conceptual frameworks in the light of major theoretical and policy developments. Not that this search process for such unifying structures was unique to this period. To take a longer perspective, two such 'classical situations' in the history of the discipline were identified by Schumpeter (1954). The first occurred at the end of the eighteenth century, and centred on Adam Smith's *Wealth of Nations* (1776), which represented the seminal attempt to provide something approaching an integrated framework for the discipline at this time. Even if Smith did not deliver on this mammoth task in all its details, his achievement was fundamental and pivotal for the future development of the discipline. Hahn acknowledges Smith's achievement and notes that his impact 'lies in his influence on his successors who grasped what they thought was the big picture and were not too concerned with its particulars or even whether it was indeed painted by him' (Hahn 2005: 6). For Hahn, the central question was indeed posed by Smith, in that the 'invisible hand' was a metaphor 'for self-organization and the latter I have always regarded in the case of economics the intellectually most challenging and interesting notion of the subject' (ibid.: 6). Accordingly for Hahn, the project of economics and, more particularly, of general equilibrium theorists 'from Walras onwards was to describe decentralized order. That is to show that the self-regarding choices of agents could be consistent with "spontaneous" order' (ibid.: 6).

The second 'classical situation,' in Schumpeter's sense, emerged from the combined, but independent, contributions of Jevons, Menger and Walras in the so-called 'Marginalist Revolution' of the 1870s (Black *et al.*, 1973). This followed the protracted methodological disputes of the *Methodenstreit* between the German Historical School and the Austrians: a dispute that found its way to Britain and produced its own local variant (Koot 1987). When the intellectual dust had settled on this dispute, the major contributions of Jevons, Menger and Walras exhibited for Schumpeter 'a large expanse of common ground and suggest a feeling of response, both of which created, in the superficial observer, an impression of finality' (Schumpeter 1954: 754). This was a perceptive comment with respect to both the expanse of the 'common ground' of these writers and, more particularly, the premature 'impression of finality,' albeit to the 'superficial observer!'

Historians of more recent developments in economics, which are relevant to providing a context for Hahn's work, have suggested that the period from 1960 represents a third 'classical situation' in Schumpeter's use of that term (Backhouse 2002). For the next 25 years, following the Second World War, what became known as the 'neoclassical synthesis' became the presiding framework within which a synthesis between the macroeconomic theory of value and Keynesian macroeconomics was pursued and implemented within the discipline. Running parallel with this development, a host of post-war theorists, including among others, Hicks, Samuelson, Arrow and Debreu, developed the macroeconomic dimension of the discipline within the framework of what has been termed the neo-Walrasian programme (Weintraub 1983, 1985).

The intellectual context in which Hahn's academic career began in the 1950s can be conceptually located between the twin pillars of the 'neoclassical synthesis' on the one hand and the 'neo-Walrasian' programme on the other. The emergence of the neoclassical synthesis is an involved story, but Hoover (1988) provides a succinct and perceptive account that will suffice for our purposes here. Keynes's macroeconomic theory in his *General Theory* was quickly encapsulated by Hicks (1937) in his celebrated IS-LM model, which emerged as the canonical textbook version of Keynes's theory; the IS curve (Investment equal to savings) represents equilibrium in the goods market, and the LM curve [the demand for money (L) equals the supply of money (S)] represents equilibrium in the money market. Keynes's macroeconomic theory, and its reformulation into the IS-LM model, was, as Hoover points out, 'welcome because it seemed to fill the yawning gap between economic analysis and the real-world problem of the Great Depression' (Hoover 1988: 9). It also offered 'a plausible explanation and a feasible course of action' (ibid.: 9). But the discipline was unhappy, committed as it was to a pre-Keynesian theory of value which was the presiding theoretical framework, and launched what Clower (1965) later, somewhat bizarrely, called the 'Keynesian counter-revolution.' The initial positions in the counter-revolutions came from Leontief (1936), who argued that Keynes' theory was a 'special' case in which the labour market participants suffered from 'money illusion,' and Hicks (1937), who also viewed Keynes's contribution as a 'special case' in which the economy was caught in a liquidity trap. Hicks' famous dictum was that the '*General Theory of Employment* is the Economics of Depression' (ibid.: 138). Underlying both Leontief and Hicks' position was a conceptual commitment that a thoroughly general theory should be a general equilibrium theory. Leontief was quite clear that this would imply a disaggregated Walrasian theory, even if Hicks was prepared to work with a more aggregated version of a general equilibrium model.

The counter-revolution culminated in the neoclassical synthesis, which Hoover correctly notes 'became the standard textbook approach to macroeconomics' (Hoover 1988: 9). The term 'neoclassical synthesis' was first used by Samuelson in the third edition of his famous textbook, *Economics*, published in 1955, although Blaug (2003) contends that Weintraub is right in claiming that it was Patinkin who truly 'created the neoclassical synthesis as we understand it' (Weintraub 1991: 123–4). The idea behind the neoclassical synthesis, according to Hoover, was that the Keynesian analysis explained unemployment and provided remedial action to be undertaken to rectify it. However, once

> full employment is established… the classical analysis of resource allocation, income distribution and welfare economics, all of which are grounded in microeconomics become relevant. The neoclassical synthesis was a schizophrenic approach to economics – a way of subscribing to both Keynesian and classical analysis.
>
> (Hoover 1988: 9–10)

A pivotal figure in post-war economics who attempted to overcome the 'schizophrenic approach,' and in so doing contributed to the creation of the neoclassical synthesis, was Don Patinkin, to whose work Hahn was to provide major qualifications. Patinkin's *Money, Interest and Prices*, published in 1956, was a veritable *tour de force* which, in Blaug's estimation, 'should have brought Patinkin the Nobel Prize twice over' (Blaug 2003: 407). In this work Patinkin attempted to integrate money and value theory. One of Keynes's critique of the 'classics' was their failure to provide an account of the interdependence of production and consumption decisions. Keynes's provided a reduced form of an aggregated general equilibrium system, certainly as reflected in the IS-LM model of his original theory. But beginning with the very early critique of the *General Theory*, the consistency of the Keynesian macroeconomic model with the microeconomic general equilibrium model was questioned.

Patinkin started from the standard Walrasian model, which is essentially one of barter. Patinkin noted that the same economic activity could be carried on irrespective of the level of absolute prices and with any supply of money. Walras had introduced money as an aggregate in a familiar quantity equation. This treatment of money did not provide a basis to account for the behaviour of individuals with respect to money, comparable to the other supply and demand relationships in the Walrasian model. But for Patinkin, money was not without value, and was therefore held for the services it could provide. Its value depended on what it could buy, which was determined by the price level. So in order to turn money and other financial assets, denominated in money, into the equivalent of other goods within the Walrasian system, Patinkin divides them by the price level. Following from this, Patinkin entered real money balances [M/P, where money (M) is adjusted by the price level (P)] into the individual utility functions of the Walrasian model.

According to Hoover (1988), Patinkin believed that this framework represented an integration of monetary and value theory, for two reasons. First, it was argued that the demand for real money balances was now incorporated into economic theory under the influence of utility, which was similar to the analysis of the demand for every other good in the system. Second, the level of absolute prices was determined jointly with the set of all relative prices, arising from the selection of a 'standard' which was derived from setting the price of a real good, e.g. gold, or of fiat money to a constant. Furthermore, Patinkin believed he had 'a microeconomic foundation for macroeconomics – particularly, for real balance effects' (Hoover 1988: 90). Since if there is 'an exogenous increase in the supply of money or a fall in the level of prices, there will be an excess supply of real money balances and an excess demand for commodities' (ibid.: 90). If, however, the equilibrium is stable, 'prices will respond by rising to a new level in the one case or returning to their old level in the other' (ibid.: 90).

If the neoclassical synthesis, embodied in the pivotal figure of Patinkin, represented one of the two major developments in post-war economic theory which shaped the intellectual milieu of Hahn's academic career, the neo-Walrasian programme and its development was its counter-part in the microeconomic domain that would arguably play an even larger role in Hahn's academic career. But, although general equilibrium theory and macroeconomics, and within the latter monetary theory in particular, were the principal domains of interest to Hahn throughout his career, his academic career did not begin in either general equilibrium or monetary theory per se, but with the theory of distribution within a macroeconomic framework. After the Second World War, Hahn returned to the LSE and, 'instead of turning at once to General Equilibrium analysis,' and being motivated by the desire 'to have a new and fairer world,' Hahn decided to write his 'Ph.D. on the Theory of Distribution' (Hahn 1994: 248). Kaldor was his first supervisor. After seeing Kaldor only twice, Robbins took over the role of supervisor. The thesis was completed in 1951, which involved the oral examination that was conducted by Hicks and Robbins, and, as Hahn recounts, without elaboration unfortunately, 'much of the discussion was about Wiesser and his tombstone!' (ibid.: 249). The thesis was published in book form 20 years later as *The Share of Wages in the National Income: An Inquiry into the Theory of Distribution* (Hahn 1972). Hahn thought it was 'not a bad thesis,' in which he 'proposed and developed a theory that had similarities with Kaldor's.' But any similarity between the two theories ended 'with the common assumption which we made that workers and capitalists had different marginal propensities to consume' (Hahn 1994: 248). As he points out, he was not 'fighting marginal productivity doctrines and developed the analysis almost entirely in a short period disequilibrium context.' But, for the long run, 'I had to assume imperfect competition (*à la* Kalecki) and suppose that somehow the degree of monopoly, and so the distribution of income, adjusted to bring about the equality between the "warranted" and "natural" rate of growth' (ibid.: 248). On balance, however, he thought that the long run part of his analysis in the thesis was not very convincing.

Among his earliest publications, two chapters of the thesis were published (Hahn 1950, 1951), and these led 'to the first of my communications from Joan Robinson, who seemed to approve of the line I was taking' (Hahn 1994: 248). In retrospect and by 'today's standards the analysis' in this 'youthful work' was 'somewhat crude and ad hoc although it was an attempt to take formal note of the role of uncertainty in determining investment in an imperfectly competitive world' (ibid.: 248). A later assessment, some 40 years after its completion, in a volume of essays in honour of Hahn's work and referring to the published version of the thesis, described the theory that Hahn developed as being 'remarkable for giving a central role to the distribution of income (in this, it anticipates the Kaldor–Passinetti theory of distribution and for incorporating a number of recent theoretical advances, such as expected-utility theory that were quite novel at that time in the mainstream of macroeconomic theory' (Dasgupta *et al.*, 1992: ix). In the same volume, Solow, in what is in fact a short methodological essay entitled 'Hahn in the Share of Wages in National Income,' draws attention to the move from the macroeconomics of the early Hahn to his more mature period of his preoccupation with the pronounced reductionist emphasis on modelling individual behaviour in the quest for microfoundations of macroeconomics. In this review, Solow provided a perceptive and spirited defence of Hahn's earlier style of macroeconomic theorizing (Solow 1992).

The development of the neo-Walrasian programme, which we have suggested was the second major pillar of the intellectual environment in which Hahn's career can be located, and to which he made important contributions, is an involved and complex story. We do not propose to rehearse this story, beyond outlining a number of the principal milestones involved.

The story of the emergence of the neo-Walrasian programme has been analysed in detail by Weintraub (1983, 1985), which has become the conventional narrative for this major episode in twentieth-century economics. Notwithstanding the fact that general equilibrium theory began with Walras in the 1870s, the Weintraub narrative takes Gustav Cassel's *The Theory of Social Economy* (1918) as its starting point. This work was first published in 1918, with the first English translation appearing in 1923, followed by a second English translation in 1932. Unique to Cassel's approach was his argument against the use of marginal utility and 'value.' Rather, Cassel put prices at the centre of his theory of allocation, with demand being treated as a primitive concept. Cassel set out clearly the divisions between consumers and producers, and he analysed the interaction between these players in both product and factor markets. For Weintraub, what is important 'is to recognize that Cassel's statement of the pricing problem, or the determination of prices by a system involving interrelated supply and demand in product and factor markets, was textbook knowledge before 1930, especially in those European countries where written German could be understood' (Weintraub 1985: 62). The significance of Cassel's book, in Weintraub's view, was not the fact that he considered Cassel's book to be analytically superior to Walras or Pareto. Rather, he states that

> the significance of *The Theory of Social Economy* was as a text, as a book that, like Marshall *Principles* could, and was, used by teachers and students... [and] that Cassel's presentation of the Walrasian general equilibrium system, modified by the exclusion of utility considerations, was available for study by any interested economists immediately before the early 1930s.
>
> (Weintraub 1985: 62)

It was, in the event, 'Cassel's formulation that spurred developments in the 1930s' (ibid.: 62).

Development of the neo-Walrasian programme – focused on the issue of existence, uniqueness and stability of a general equilibrium – centred initially around Karl Menger's Vienna Colloquium during the 1930s. This involved a dazzling array of economists and mathematicians who addressed the Cassell system of equations, originally derived from Walras's work. Problems with the Cassell model were noted early on by a number of the economists, including Zeuthen, Neissar, von Stackelberg and others. This included the possibility of negative prices in the proposed solution. Karl Schlesinger, a banker and economist, made highly original contributions arising from his work in 1914 and later in the 1930s, when his work, according to Menger, led to 'modifications of the original equations of Walras and Cassel' (Menger 1952: 18).

Schlesinger is an interesting figure within the Vienna Colloquium, in that he never held an academic position, but was, in Morgenstern's words, 'an active and highly respected member of the Vienna Economy Society,' whose banking business must have been conducted 'frequently at odd hours in coffee houses' (Morgenstern 1968: 509, 510). Morgenstern's assessment of Schlesinger pointed to the fact that 'Schlesinger's *Theorie der Geld-und Kreditwirtschaft* (1914) made him the only immediate follower of Walras, other than Wicksell, to advance Walras's theory of money,' and that he 'derived an excess demand equation for money that is virtually identical with the one commonly ascribed to Keynes. He was also probably the first to develop the notion of the equilibrium rate of interest' (Morgenstern 1968: 509). Interestingly, Schumpeter commented that Schlesinger's book was a 'striking [instance] of the fact that in our field first-class performance is neither a necessary nor a sufficient condition for success' (Schumpeter 1954: 1082n). The young mathematician, Abraham Wald contributed a proof of general equilibrium using inequalities, and John von Newmann, who was to have a distinguished career, introduced the use of fixed-point theorems into economics, which would play an important role in the development of existence proofs in general equilibrium. However, the invasion of Austria in 1938 led to the break-up of the Vienna Colloquium, and the members were forced to flee Vienna to either the United Kingdom or America.

The work on general equilibrium, and in particular on the proof of existence of a competitive equilibrium, continued in America, in the Cowles Commission, which was originally located in Chicago but later moved to New Haven. The general equilibrium agenda attracted a young generation of talented American economists, such as Arrow, Koopmans and McKenzie, among others. The European influence on the work of the American economists was reflected in the methodological domain with a shift in the mathematical techniques employed in the analysis of the existence proofs. The techniques deployed by the Cowles economists were based on the axiomatic approach and the use of set theory, rather than the calculus method of Hicks and Samuelson. The new mathematical methods were those of the Vienna Colloquium, as they were of von Newmann and Morgenstern's seminal work, *The Theory of Games and Economic Behaviour* of 1944. Central to this work was the contribution of a young French economist, Debreu, who had migrated to America and whose training and intellectual commitment was to the application of the axiomatic approach to economic theorizing.

By the mid-1950s, proofs for the existence of general equilibrium had been achieved by Arrow and Debreu (1954) and McKenzie (1954). In this context, mention must also be made to Gale (1955) and Nikaido (1956). In these proofs, the existence of competitive equilibrium was demonstrated using the axiomatic approach and fixed-point theorems that were related to the fixed-point theorem introduced into economics by von Newmann in the 1930s. These results were comprehensively, if succinctly, brought together in Debreu's *Theory of Value: An Axiomatic Analysis of Economic Equilibrium* (1959). An interesting insight into the methodological basis of the new approach was provided by Koopmans in his *Three Essays on the State of Economic Science* (1957). A comprehensive account of the emergence and development of the general equilibrium research programme from both historical and methodological perspectives is provided in Ingrao and Israel (1990), a work that covers the period from the diffusion of Newton's ideas and the works from the scientific culture of eighteenth-century Europe to the end of the twentieth century.

The demonstration of proofs for general equilibrium, in particular the existence theorem, did not, however, provide a demonstration of either uniqueness or stability. These latter aims of the general equilibrium agenda had been addressed earlier by Hicks and Samuelson and by later writers in the axiomatic tradition such as Koopmans (1957) and Scarf (1960, 1967). As Rizvi (2003) points out, 'important concerns' were not engaged in the work on the existence proofs. One such concern was the issue of comparative statics, which needed to address the question as to what would be the effects of changes in the underlying components of the model, such as preferences, endowments or technology, on the equilibrium, and in what direction. This critical question was closely linked to the uniqueness issue, which had not been delivered in the course of this work. But Rizvi identifies a host of additional questions that quickly emerged: could the existence of general equilibrium be proved for imperfectly competitive economies; could the general equilibrium framework identify econometric equations; could general equilibrium integrate theories of money, and macroeconomics in general; and what of the role of capital and economic growth (Rizvi 2003: 382)? Having identified these crucial issues, he notes that 'the demonstration of existence raised more questions than it answered' (ibid.: 382).

It is against this intellectual background of the post-war work in economics, namely the emergence of the neoclassical synthesis on the one hand and the development of the neo-Walrasian programme on the other, that Hahn's career was to be shaped by virtue of his reaction to the former and his many contributions to the latter. As Dasgupta *et al.* (1992) correctly point out, Hahn's career 'has intersected six decades of economics,' which 'was an exceptionally lively period for economic theory,' and that Hahn 'was active in many of the most exciting episodes.' This is clear from their comment that Hahn's 'research interests are broad, and he made contributions to a variety of fields: monetary theory, macroeconomics, general equilibrium, the economics of information, economic dynamics, and capital theory' (Dasgupta *et al.*, 1992: ix). His many positive and most significant contributions could be broadly divided into his concerns with general equilibrium, brought together in his book with Arrow (Arrow & Hahn 1971), the *ta tonnement* and *non-tâtonnement* stability of multi-market equilibrium (Hahn 1958, 1962(a), 1962(b), 1970, 1982(a)), the theory of money in sequence economies (Hahn 1965, 1971, 1973(b)), the theory of growth, money and heterogeneous capital (Hahn 1966, 1968, 1969, 1973(c), 1973(d); Hahn and Matthews 1964) and conjectural equilibria (Hahn 1977). In addition to these contributions, Hahn provided insightful criticisms of many of the major systems of economic thought that emerged in the course of his academic career, including Monetarism (Hahn 1980, 1984), neo-Ricardianism (Hahn 1982(b)) and New Classical Economics (Hahn and Solow 1995; Hahn 2003), along with a number of edited works and his extensive contributions to book reviewing in the leading economic journals.

A closer examination of Hahn's theoretical contribution, in particular to the neo-Walrasian programme, of which he remained a committed and articulate defender, would take us too far afield from our principal aim in this book, namely an in-depth analysis of the philosophical and methodological commitments underlying his economic theorizing. In any event, readers can glean considerable insights into his thinking, motivation and his own sense of achievement from his 'Intellectual Retrospect' of 1994, with respect to his contribution to economic theory, in particular general equilibrium and monetary theory (Hahn 1994). But, with respect to his contribution to economic theory, it is instructive to reflect on Hahn's own retrospective assessment of his achievements and that of his generation of theorists – an assessment of which is both realistic and lacking the distortions of illusion, characteristics that are easily imported into retrospective recollections.

Hahn believed 'that much of the theorizing post war was eminently worthwhile and required,' but he always 'took it to be in the nature of an overture. I am disappointed that I, and others, have found it so difficult to make a start on the opera. I am even more disappointed that so few realise that a start has yet to be made' (Hahn 1994: 347–8). If this conveys an overly pessimistic impression, he does concede that there have 'been impressive gains in knowledge.' There is, he feels, no 'doubt that game theory transformed our approach to many old problems,' but quickly adds that '[game] theory itself has probably got off on the wrong foot by continuing with assumptions designed to give answers which, on further consideration, turned out to be questions' (ibid.: 238). Notwithstanding this assessment of game theory, Hahn felt that it was one 'branch of our subject which is making genuine attempts to get to grips with some of the issues I have raised (learning, for instance),' and for this 'one can be hopeful,' even if 'an economy-wide picture still seems in the far future' (ibid.: 238). Overall, however, Hahn concluded that 'the task which we set ourselves after the last war, to deduce all that was required from a number of axioms, has almost been completed, and while not worthless has only made a small contribution to our understanding' (ibid.: 238).

The concept of 'understanding' is, in our view, the central integrating and organizing principle of Hahn's philosophical thinking as reflected in what we call his methodological writings – a central focus of our analysis in the following chapters. In the next section, we provide a very brief account, by way of contextual background, of the emergent methodological perspective at the outset of Hahn's career. This was a perspective that was to achieve very considerable influence within economics in the post-war period. This was, of course, Milton Friedman's 'positive' methodology of economics, against which Hahn would later provide a relentless and stringent critique. It is arguable that Hahn's encounter with Friedman's 'as if' methodology may well have motivated his vociferous hostility to methodology in general, particularly in the light of what was pivotal to his underlying philosophy for economics, namely the achievement of understanding through the medium of rigorous economic theorizing.

The methodological environment

Hahn's entry into the economics profession in the early 1950s coincided with the publication of Milton Friedman's essay on 'The Methodology of Positive

Economics' (Friedman 1953), which Wade Hands has described as 'clearly the best-known work in twentieth-century economic methodology' (Hands 2001: 53). For Caldwell it was 'a marketing masterpiece' (Caldwell 1982; 173), about which it has been claimed that almost a half-century after its publication, it remains 'the only essay on methodology that a large number, perhaps majority, of economists have ever read' (Hausman 1992(a): 162).

Friedman, who had little or no interest in fundamental philosophical issues, did not perceive himself as contributing to this domain of study. He was, rather, responding to issues that had arisen within economics that concerned both the status of orthodox economic theory and the role of theory in relation to actual economic practice. The 1930s and 1940s were periods of intense change in economics, including the emergence of Keynesian economics, the resuscitation of Walrasian general equilibrium in the form of the neo-Walrasian programme, along with the application of stochastic methods to economic relationships which were increasingly formulated in mathematical models. Notwithstanding the disruption of the Second World War, the 20-year period before the publication of Friedman's 1953 paper was a spectacularly vibrant period of development for economics, an idiom that was well captured in the title of Shackle's excellent study of this period, *The Years of High Theory* (Shackle 1967).

Wade Hands has identified three developments, which, in his interpretation, 'seemed to bear most directly on Friedman's methodological views' (Hands 2001: 53). The first concerned the status of 'marginal analysis' in microeconomics, arising from the work of Hall and Hitch (1939) and Lester (1946); they argued that firms did not, in fact, maximize expected returns as formulated in the standard marginalist analysis of orthodox economic theory. The second concerned the implications of the 'imperfect competition' theories contained in the independently produced work of Chamberlin (1933) and Robinson (1933), which challenged the assumption of perfectly competitive markets that had occupied a central position in orthodox economic theory over an extended period. The third development identified by Hands was the intriguing 'measurement without theory' debate, conducted between members of the Cowles Commission (Koopmans 1947) and the Chicago school of economics, which included Friedman (Vining 1949). The debate was concerned with a specific topic, i.e. the appropriate place of theory and empirical observation in the study of business cycles. However, more fundamental differences between the Cowles Commission approach and that of the Chicago school quickly surfaced. Friedman sought to steer a path, as argued by Hands, between 'the abstract Walrasian theorizing of Cowles on one hand and the more – broadly – social theorizing of certain Institutionalists on the other' (Hands 2001: 54). The Marshallian partial equilibrium approach advocated by Friedman sought to achieve a number of other methodological, and political, objectives, which need not detain us here. As Hands perceptively remarks, 'Keeping all of these balls in the air at the same time was not an easy job' (ibid.: 54).

Irrespective of Friedman's dexterity in keeping all the balls 'in the air,' the substantive argument in Friedman's 1953 paper was that the truth of the assumptions in economic theory, as used in positive economics, was not an issue of concern in theory evaluation. The principal criterion in differentiating between theories was the predictive capacity of a theory, and in particular the prediction of *novel facts*. The theory, in other words, that provides the most accurate predictions with respect to the phenomenon under analysis is considered to be the best theory, and the fact that it is based on 'unrealistic' or even 'false' assumptions does not in any way diminish its acceptability as a successful positive scientific theory. In Friedman's own words:

> Viewed as a body of substantive hypotheses, theory is to be judged by its predictive power for the class of phenomena which it is intended to 'explain.' Only factual evidence can show whether it is 'right' or 'wrong' or, better, tentatively 'accepted' as valid, or 'rejected'... the only relevant test of the *validity* of a hypothesis is comparison of its predictions with experience.
>
> (Friedman 1953: 8–9, italics in original)

The above statement of Friedman catches the essentials of what was to be a very influential contribution to economic methodology, an approach that Hahn would later reject totally in what he variously referred to as the 'Chicago position' or in other contexts the 'Chicago School.' Hahn would later criticise other approaches and 'schools of thought' that emerged in later decades, but his steadfast critique of the 'as if' methodology of Friedman was consistent and relentless throughout his career. Through the course of Hahn's career, economic methodology was to experience a major revival of attention and research by an expanding community of scholars within economics. This led to the emergence of plurality of methodological positions and perspectives. In the midst of this very vibrant revival in economic methodology, Hahn began the process of forging his own methodological perspective, notwithstanding his intensely critical disposition towards methodology in general. The articulation of his methodological commitments and their formulation around a number of pivotal organizing concepts was the product of both a critical reaction to a number of influential methodological positions, at the centre of which was Friedman's 'Chicago position,' along with the increasing articulation of his own particular perspective. Hahn's contribution in this domain has gone largely unnoticed and unexamined from a philosophical and methodological perspective.

We do not propose to rehearse the array of methodological positions that have emerged over the last forty years. These have generated a vast literature that has been excellently surveyed in works such as Caldwell (1982) and Hands (2001). In the remaining chapters of this book, our aim is to examine Hahn's reactions and critique of a number of methodological positions that he chose to engage. In addition, we will critically examine Hahn's particular methodological commitments along with their implications. Although clear and consistent about his methodological commitments, we will argue that Hahn may not always have appreciated the philosophical implications of his methodological arguments.

When critically examined, Hahn's methodological reflections present an intriguingly challenging and even novel perspective, and that from someone deep within the orthodox fold, who remained at once both a 'perennial renegade' but always a staunch defender of the neo-Walrasian programme, if not always of its contents, then certainly of its intellectual virtues of rigour and mode of theorizing.

3 Hahn's hostility to economic methodology

I hate methodology.

(Hahn 2005: 17)

Introduction

A quick preliminary survey of Hahn's extensive output could reveal a picture of a brilliant theoretical economist who is utterly antagonistic to economic methodology. In his 'Reflections,' written in 1992 on his retirement from Cambridge, he is emphatic and unequivocal in his advice to those taking up economics, suggesting they should 'give no thought at all to methodology' (Hahn 1992(a): 5). When Backhouse challenged Hahn by pointing out that economists who castigate methodology are nonetheless making methodological claims (Backhouse 1992), Hahn conceded that while he 'put matters a little too dogmatically.... Nonetheless I am largely unrepentant' (Hahn 1992(b): 5). Basically his advice to young economists is to avoid spending much time reflecting on methodology. 'As for them learning philosophy what next?' In Hahn's view philosophers have debated the same problems for thousands of years without linear progress. Philosophers form schools. 'Schools of economics are bad enough. Add to that schools of economic philosophy and we can pack in (There is no reason of course why one should not read philosophy for recreation)' (Hahn 1992(b): 5).[1]

While Hahn is certainly not being politically correct, neither is he being flippant. Writing in 1996 he concluded; 'But I am left wondering what good methodology can do to the practice of economics. So far it has only done harm' (Hahn 1996: 194). In view of this uncompromising belief that the methodology of economics has not accomplished anything positive, indeed it has been damaging, clearly Hahn is consistent in advising young economists to avoid it. Perhaps he should advise all economists, both young and old, to disown it. But Hahn, like Darwin when he published his *Origin of Species*, looks to the youth as the future practitioners of his beloved discipline of economics.[2] Aside from the misrepresentation of economic theorizing in Friedman's 'as if' methodology, which we will discuss in a separate section, what harm has methodology done? In this connection we discuss a number of methodological issues that, in Hahn's eyes, are either a waste of time or utterly misleading.

Crisis in neoclassical economics?

In the first place, some methodologists present an erroneous picture of economics as a discipline in crisis. In this connection, Hahn does not name specific methodologists. Indeed, it should be noted that not only methodologists but also eminent economists brought up in the neoclassical tradition have argued that orthodox economics is in crisis. Kaldor, who was Hahn's first supervisor – he saw him only twice as Kaldor left for Geneva – and who later gave seminars attended by Hahn at the LSE, is one such economist.[3] In this connection, Hahn is quite emphatic. 'The second most important reflection leads me to advise everyone to ignore cries of "economics in crisis" ' (Hahn 1992(a): 5).

Hahn maintains that the claims of crisis are based on a wrong diagnosis of the facts. He willingly concedes that 'some outstanding problems of importance seem to defy analysis' (ibid.: 5). In no way does this concession imply that economics is in crisis. On the contrary, from Hahn's perspective, 'There has been spectacular progress' in post war economics (ibid.: 5). This research progress is extensive, for instance game theoretic approaches, missing markets, information theory, and history-dependent equilibria. In short, 'neoclassical economists (however) have not been slouches' (Hahn 1996: 187). They have been exceptionally creative and innovative in their research theorizing. 'Indeed the questioning of almost everything, for instance the rationality postulate, is not a sign of crisis but of vigorous endeavour' (Hahn 1992(a): 5). Those methodologists advocating crisis are misdiagnosing the situation; neoclassical economics is not a fixed static doctrine conveyed in elementary textbooks. Rather, a crucial key to neoclassical economics is evident in its dynamic mode of research theorizing which responds to the radical questioning of the basic concepts of neoclassical textbooks. Crisis methodologists utterly misrepresent the true and progressive mode of economic theorizing evident in the vast research domains of neoclassical economics, and thereby cause harm.

In this connection, it is useful to refer to a canonical methodological text on claims of crisis in the physical sciences, namely Kuhn's *Structure of Scientific Revolutions*. Not least because Hahn does not view neoclassical economics as a science concerned with the discovery or use of scientific laws, we will tailor Kuhn's account to economics. One can legitimately claim that neoclassical economics is a body of disciplined and serious research based on past economic achievements taken as the source of its further practice. These achievements were accomplished by Walras and others at the turn of and the early part of the twentieth century, and by Arrow and Debreu in the 1950s. These achievements, however, are not summed up in a complete and closed system. On the contrary they were sufficiently open-ended to leave various problems on the books so-to-speak, which subsequent researchers identified and engaged.

Thus, neoclassical economics became a successful problem solving activity. It raised and enabled economists to clearly formulate specific problems that otherwise would very likely not be raised, and it contained within it the resources to solve these problems. The specific resources for Hahn include its mode of theorizing, its partial grammar of argumentation, its definitions and its language (Introduction to Hahn 1984). When these resources are creatively brought to bear, numerous problems are solved, and thereby there is linear progress in neoclassical economics.

However, neoclassical economics, as with the physical sciences, does not come to us unblemished: it has its own anomalies. Here an anomaly is identified by the fact that, *prima facie*, the existing parameters of neoclassical economics fail to accommodate truths or well grounded beliefs about existing economies. For instance, in the general equilibrium of Arrow and Debreu, increasing returns are anomalous. It should be noted that, unlike some Popperians, anomalies are not falsifiers: they do not falsify the theory. Rather, an anomaly is a source of challenge to the neoclassical theorist, and the hope is that the theorist will succeed in integrating the solution to the *prima facie* anomaly into the existing corpus, or at least integrate it by the minimum alteration possible of some parameter while retaining the others. Thus, as we already noted, Hahn correctly insists that neoclassical economists 'have not been slouches' (Hahn 1996: 187). For instance, vis-à-vis the anomaly of increasing returns, Hahn points out that 'Arrow has provided a rigorous general equilibrium with increasing returns' (Hahn 1973: 8).

However, if some anomalies resist resolution by the persistent efforts of the best experts, one may want to raise the possibility that the existing, hitherto successful, tradition should be re-examined, as it were, root and branch. In this way, the claim of crisis may be raised by some of the experts from within. In this neo-Kuhnian approach, if methodologists who are not accomplished economists and who come to neoclassical economics simply with a prescriptive methodology borrowed from another discipline, e.g. physics, and, by methodological argument alone, find neoclassical economics to be in crisis, then *à la* Hahn we may not be too impressed. However, when a number of sophisticated practitioners, such as Kaldor, claim neoclassical economics is in crisis, this is a different matter. In this neo-Kuhnian view, one cannot simply agree with Hahn that the claim of crisis is based on a misdiagnosis of the facts. One has to listen to both sides. Clearly, Hahn is hopeful that, with creative modifications, neoclassical economics will solve the problems that currently 'seem to defy analysis' (Hahn 1992(a): 5), whereas economists such as Kaldor do not share this optimism. We propose postponing the issues of crisis to our chapter on Kaldor and Hahn. For the moment, we concur with Hahn that purely external, prescriptive, philosophico-methodological claims for crisis are not compelling, but we keep an open mind when economists such as Kaldor claim the discipline is in crisis. This matter is not settled by Hahn's commitments. We need to critically examine how both sides diagnose the facts.

Mathematics and economics

We now turn to another methodological issue which, in Hahn's eyes, should be avoided 'like the plague:' namely, the role of mathematics in economics. Once again, Hahn does not explicitly identify the opposition. The extensive opposition, however, is not a figment of his imagination. As Caldwell points out in the symposium 'Has Formalization in Economics Gone too Far?' published in *Methodus* of June 1991, an earlier symposium of this topic appeared in *The Review of Economics and Statistics* in November 1954.[4] In the interim, the debate about mathematics continued to rage in methodological circles. Also, as with the crisis misdiagnosis, reservations about the role of mathematics in economics are not limited to philosophers. It is well known that famous economists, such as Marshall and Keynes, also had their misgivings. Contrary to what one would do in a court of law, Hahn (1992a) does not attempt to present the case of the opposition. He is brief and to the point: 'There is no point discussing the use of mathematics in economics' (Hahn 1992(a): 5). Rather, Hahn puts his 'faith in selection: if it turns out to be as futile as some believe then its use will wither, if not it will continue to grow' (ibid.: 5).[5] Despite the *prima facie* unbalanced appearance of his advice to completely ignore the debate on the role of mathematics in economics, Hahn's approach has some openness attached to it: he embraces 'the possibility of mathematics being driven out of economics.... Nothing is forever. We live in a stochastic world and also one in which the young must sooner or later revolt against the old if they are to live' (Hahn 1992(b): 5).

Hahn, moreover, is no methodological slouch. He is well aware that Marshall and Keynes had their reservations about the role of mathematics in economics. He initially dismisses these reservations as 'intellectually lazy *obiter dicta*' (Hahn 1985: 18). His point is that methodologists, by focusing on these lazy *obiter dicta*, fail to appreciate the genuine contributions of these pioneering economists. He is certainly correct in noting that the Marshallian advice to always translate mathematical equations into sentences of a natural language in order to ensure that they make sense is an exaggeration. For instance, nothing is to be gained by translating into English economic equations with complex roots. Moreover, with some humour, he notes that the same Marshall 'admitted that he first looked for a mathematical formulation before hiding it from the eyes of an 'intelligent businessman' whom he regarded as his customer' (Hahn 1994: 245). More seriously, Hahn concludes that 'he (Keynes) and other Cambridge economists were scornful of the mathematics their contemporaries employed – it was very simple' (Hahn 1992(a): 5). According to Hahn, their scorn was justified; the solution is more sophisticated mathematics.

Hahn recognizes two and 'only two possible coherent arguments' against the use of mathematical models in economics (Hahn 1985: 18). The first argument is based on the thesis that mathematical tractability has the opportunity cost of making theorists ignore relevant matters that cannot be captured in mathematical equations. For instance, as Joan Robinson pointed out, in connection with Keynes approach to investment, that, 'to understand the motives for investment, we have to understand human nature and the manner in which it reacts to the various kinds of social and economic systems in which it has to operate. We have not got far enough yet to put it into algebra' (Robinson 1970: 101). The second possible coherent argument is focused on the tension between the demands of mathematical rigour on the one hand and the requirements for creativity on the other. The tension is particularly evident in the initial phases of theory invention when creativity may outweigh the requirements of mathematical rigour.

Clearly, Hahn recognises that there are costs as well as benefits to the use of mathematics in economics. His thesis, however, is that the benefits far outweigh the costs. The benefits include 'definiteness and comprehension where there was flabby hand waving and how they have forced us to specify rather exactly the basis of any pronouncement' (Hahn 1985: 18). In this connection, it is interesting to note that in his 'Intellectual Retrospect' Hahn informs us that, from his earliest days in economics, he found the debates on the use of mathematics in economics 'of little interest or consequence' (Hahn 1994: 245). His fundamental reason for this position is that 'there simply is no corpus of non-mathematical economic theory to provide a countervailing paradigm' (Hahn 1994: 246). This seems close to the Popperian claim that no theory is rejected until as good a theory or a better one is available. Non-mathematical economic theory simply cannot, as yet, compete with mathematical economic theory.

Hahn in this same 'Intellectual Retrospect' does make an interesting concession to what he calls the 'anti-mathematics' lobby. 'But there is nonetheless a lesson which has only gradually been borne in on me which perhaps inclines me a little more favourably to the "anti-mathematics" group' (Hahn 1994: 246). This springs from what Hahn calls 'the great virtue of mathematical reasoning in economics' (ibid.: 246). This virtue is the explicit use of precisely formulated assumptions,[6] the usage of which enables everyone to 'see that we are not dealing with an actual economy' (ibid.: 246). These assumptions are usually introduced on the grounds of mathematical tractability, i.e. 'they enable certain results to emerge' (ibid.: 246). However, and this is the crucial point, these assumptions are not 'to be taken descriptively' (ibid.: 246). Because some of the assumptions, introduced primarily to facilitate the mathematical manipulation of the economic variables, are not descriptively adequate, and indeed in Hahn's view cannot be taken descriptively at all, 'it becomes crystal clear' that economic applications 'to the "real" world could at best be provisional' (ibid.: 246).

Mathematical economics, in so far as it uses assumptions, and these assumptions are indispensable, is not furnishing us with factual descriptions of actual economies. Here we see Hahn's challenging and intriguing methodological position emerging. 'Economic theory at its best is a powerful aid to thought about the world, *not because it provides a very satisfactory description*, but because it provides clear limits to understanding' (Hahn 1993(b): 164; italics added). Thus, Hahn tells his students 'everything I will teach you is in a certain sense false but useful' (Hahn 1996: 191). We will see in the next chapter how Hahn emphasizes and elaborates on this key notion of understanding. Here, we merely wish to note how he responds to the anti-mathematics group. They are correct in appreciating that economics via its assumptions is not a descriptive science like geology. However, this group fails to appreciate how economics enhances our understanding of the economic world, which is the topic of Chapters 4 and 8.

Although Hahn may have some good arguments for the use of mathematics in economic research, there is one related issue that needs to be addressed, namely the kind of mathematics to be used. Hahn is correct in pointing out that when Walras wrote he did not have at his disposal the mathematical developments available to Debreu and other later neoclassical economists. However, as we shall see in Chapter 7, other developments in twentieth-century mathematics and logic may be relevant to methodological debates on the existence proof of general equilibrium by Debreu. Nevertheless, one must remember that Hahn is, here, defending the role of mathematics in economics and is not addressing the issue of the kind of mathematics to be used.

Economics and the Weltanschauung of science

We have seen how Hahn dismisses methodological claims of crisis in economics, and how he finds methodological debates on the use of mathematics in economics of little consequence. According to Hahn, there is also 'a profound difference between the way American and European economists view their theories' (Hahn 1993(a): 86). Numerous American economists 'regard economics as a "science," and often refer to themselves as "scientists"' (Hahn 1993(b): 163).[7] In Hahn's opinion 'the claim that economics is a science is not only premature and not very honest but also, perhaps worse, pretentious' (Hahn 1993(b): 163). For Hahn, 'a profound difference' between American and European economists is best exemplified by a very influential methodological piece by Milton Friedman' (Hahn 1993(a): 86–7). Indeed, in Hahn's eyes, Friedman's methodology 'has been both influential and harmful' (Hahn 1996: 184). 'Friedman's methodology may be fine for Quantum theory (predictions confirmed to a high order of decimals), but only dangerous sloppiness and blinkered arguing can result from its use in economics' (Hahn 1996: 185).

There is little doubt that Friedman's classical methodological piece, 'The Methodology of Positive Economics,' published in 1953, had phenomenal influence in the domain of economic methodology. John Neville Keynes in his *The Scope and Method of Political Economy* of 1891 distinguished between 'a positive science,' 'a normative or regulative science' and an 'art.' In this context, Friedman explicitly introduces his own methodological reflections as a clear elaboration of how economics is a positive science. According to Friedman, economics, as a positive science, is 'a body of substantive hypotheses,' and that 'the only relevant test of the *validity* of a hypothesis is comparison of its predictions with experience' (Friedman 1953: 8–9).

Friedman readily conceded that economic hypotheses 'have not only "implications" but also "assumptions"' (Friedman 1953: 14). According to some economists and methodologists 'the conformity of these "assumptions" to reality is a test of the validity of a hypothesis *different from* or *additional to* the test by implications' (Friedman 1953: 14). To show that the test of the realism of assumptions is spurious, Friedman has recourse to his famous '*as if*' thesis. By means of three different analogies – a ball dropping as if it were falling in a vacuum, the density of leaves on a tree 'are positioned as if each leaf deliberately sought to maximize the amount of sunlight it receives...' and an excellent billiard player makes 'his shots as if he knew the complicated mathematical formulas' (Friedman 1953: 19–21) – he argues that

> individual firms behave *as if* they were seeking rationally to maximize their returns... *as if*, that is, they knew the relevant cost and demand functions, calculated marginal cost and marginal revenue from all actions open to them and pushed each line of action to the point at which the relevant marginal cost and marginal revenue were equal.
>
> (Friedman 1953: 21–2)

Friedman concludes 'that a theory cannot be tested by the "realism" of its "assumptions"' (Friedman 1953: 23).

As already noted, according to Hahn, Friedman's methodology is harmful and results in 'dangerous sloppiness' and 'blinkered argument' in economics (Hahn 1996: 185). The harm is to economics, as distinct from economic methodology. Here we have a skilled, eminent neoclassical economist being uncompromising in his negative evaluation of the very influential methodological legacy of another major figure in the neoclassical tradition. However, if, as Hahn suggests, one should completely ignore economic methodology, one would be completely ignorant of this conflict! Acting on Hahn's suggestion is not the way to deliberate on this conflict.

There are a number of layers to Hahn's critique of the legacy of Friedman's instrumentalist defence of neoclassical economics. The first layer lies in its claim that economics is a positive science: 'positive economics is, or can be, an "objective" science, in the same sense as any of the physical sciences' (Friedman 1953: 4). Hahn concludes that philosophers may be interested in this issue qua philosophers. For instance, the problem of demarcation, i.e. distinguishing science from other disciplines, is of interest to Popperians, and perhaps others. Hahn, however, as an economic theoretician, finds these philosophical discussions boring: arguments 'as to whether or not some branch of learning is or is not a science are intrinsically boring, although philosophers do not seem to have found it so' (Hahn 1996: 184).

In a sense the issue of whether or not economics is a science is a semantical one.[8] However, according to Hahn, there is more than semantics involved in the claim that economics is a science. Without explicitly noting that Friedman located his methodology in the context of John Neville Keynes' *Scope and Method of Political Economy*, Hahn correctly notes that behind the words 'science' and 'scientists' there 'is a *Weltanschauung*' (Hahn 1993(b): 163). This *Weltanschauung* includes 'the nineteenth-century view that what was achieved in the physical sciences can be achieved by the same means by the social sciences' (Hahn 1993(b): 163). In Hahn's opinion this general thesis concerning all the social sciences may turn out to be correct at some future time. 'What is striking, however, is that so far economics has provided no evidence that it is' (Hahn 1993(b): 163).

The harm resulting from the *Weltanschauung* of economics as a positive science lies along a number of dimensions. First, the erroneous view that the sole test of economic theory lies in its predictive success, misrepresents the role of prediction in economic theory. Second, this *Weltanschauung* leads one to misunderstand general equilibrium theory by giving it 'too empirical weight' (Hahn 2005: 9–10). Third, it encourages or facilitates economists in viewing their generalizations as laws. According to Hahn, there are no laws in economics. Fourthly, it is harmful when economists offer practical advice. Finally, the 'as if' methodology proposed by Friedman facilitates economists ignoring completely unrealistic assumptions and thus has a pernicious influence on economic theory, which aims at understanding and constructing a grammar of argumentation. We address these issues in the following sections.

Economic theory and prediction

In his 'Predicting the Economy,' published in 1993, Hahn opens with the rhetorical question 'How effectively in the 1990s can we predict the future course of a country's economy?' (Hahn 1993(a): 77). If we mean by predict, the manner in which physicists can successfully predict the future course of Haley's comet, the answer is obviously not very effectively. This, however, does not mean that economics in principle cannot predict. This erroneous thesis is frequently found in the methodological writings of those who distinguish between *Natur-Wissenshaften* and *Geistes-Wissenschaften* and locate economics in the latter. According to Hahn, 'there is not, in my view, anything unique and fundamental in the nature of the subject matter that inevitably makes economics intertemporarily non-predictive' (Hahn 1993(a): 94).

In this connection, Hahn addresses 'two frequently heard arguments' for the thesis that economics in principle is non-predictive, namely the argument from free will and the argument from the 'contamination of the predicted by prediction' (Hahn 1993(a): 88). Hahn unequivocally accepts the thesis that 'human beings are not physical objects. They are autonomous agents with their own projects, and their actions are by their very nature contingent on their will' (Hahn 1993(a): 90). We will see in the next chapter how this central thesis is inextricably related to Hahn's commitment to the rationality of economic agents. For the moment, Hahn unequivocally accepts that economic agents have free wills. What he wishes to deny is that the ability to predict an agent's action necessitates rejecting that the agent in question has free will. Hahn makes his case by elementary examples. Using probability theory, for instance, we can predict that a farmer who values her/his time will choose the most efficient, time wise, of two ways, one of which is twice as long as the other, of milking a cow. The farmer has free will and the prediction turns out to be correct because the farmer freely chooses to value her/his time. In Hahn's view, there is no question of some mechanical, law-like, force in operation. It is perfectly possible that the farmer would choose not to take the quicker method. The farmer makes this choice, not because she/he has to do so, but because she/he freely chooses to do so. Without getting involved in the complex relationship between philosophy of mind, the philosophy of action and economic decision making, we will give Hahn the benefit of the doubt and thereby concur with his thesis that free will and statistical probabilistic prediction are not necessarily incompatible.

The second objection is based on the so-called 'bandwagon effect' or the contamination of the predicted by prediction. We use Hahn's own example to illustrate this effect. In an election between two parties, say Labour and Conservative, a social scientist predicts that a fraction x of the electorate will vote Labour. When this prediction is widely published, it in turn will affect the proportion y who will actually vote Labour. Because of this bandwagon effect, in some countries the publication of such predictions for a specified number of days before an election is prohibited by law. From the bandwagon effect, it is inferred that, in principle, no correct prediction is possible. By recourse to elementary mathematics, Hahn demonstrates that this inference is invalid: prediction *in principle*, given the bandwagon effect, is possible. Of course what is *in principle* possible does not imply that 'we can predict correctly *in practice*. We would need to know the bandwagon function' (Hahn 1993(a): 90; italics added). In short, Hahn's objection to the Friedmanite view that the only test of an economic theory is the comparison of its predictions with experience is not grounded in any general philosophical thesis, to the effect that prediction is, in principle, impossible in economics.

We now turn to Hahn's analysis of prediction and, in particular, the issue of testing economic theory by its predictive success. In this connection Hahn makes a number of distinctions. First, he emphasizes the difference between predictions where 'the temporal aspect is not essential' and predictions which 'involve the future' (Hahn 1993(a): 77, 79). Vis-à-vis prediction in which time is not essential, Hahn starts with the philosophical truism that 'every non-tautological proposition concerning the world restricts what the world is like' (Hahn 1993(a): 77) and thus makes predictions. In this sense, economic theory is no exception. Indeed, 'a substantial part of economic theory is of this kind' (Hahn 1993(a): 77). For instance – this is Hahn's own example – if economists compare the equilibria of two economies that are identical in all but one respect; say one has a tax on tobacco and the other has not, economists may deduce something about the relative prices of tobacco and, say, beer in the two economies. In this case the economists are not predicting some future event – the temporal aspect is not essential. Rather, what they are predicting is 'what would be found if two actual economies satisfying the assumptions were to be compared' (Hahn 1993(a): 78).

Second, the methodological issue for Hahn is not deduction/prediction as such. All non-tautological disciplines, such as economics, geology, history, physics and sociology, to mention but a few, are deductive/predictive in this logical sense. The methodological issue is that of *testing* an economic theory by comparing its logical consequences to the results of controlled experimentations or other data. In general, the possibility of controlled experimentation 'is the possibility of putting the restrictions a theory imposes on the world to the test by ensuring that the conditions of the theory hold' (Hahn 1993(a): 78). Of course,

Hahn is not ruling out the use of controlled experimentation in economics. His point is that biologists, when using controlled experimentation in testing their theories, can have a great deal more certainty than economists in their results. For instance, experimental testing is frequently used in game theory and, according to Hahn, the results 'are useful and interesting' (Hahn 1993(a): 78). However, he concurs with those who claim that one may legitimately doubt whether people would act the same way in non-laboratory situations. For this reason he concludes that controlled, laboratory experiments provide 'insights but no certainty' (Hahn 1993(a): 78). In our opinion one should not put too much weight on Hahn's use of the word 'certainty' here, by assuming he is seeking the certainty which is only attainable in a purely formal system. His intention is clear from the context: experimentation in biology or physics is much more conclusive or decisive than in economics, and, consequently, one can be much more certain in biology or physics that their experimental results either confirm or reject their theories.

In relation to experimentation, Hahn also makes the point that the scope for laboratory experimentation in economics is much more limited than in either biology or physics – a point on which there appears to be a widespread consensus. Third, Hahn raises issues of how data in economics, outside of laboratory experimentation, are not as reliable as the data of physics. Again, he illustrates his point by means of an example. This time he takes Friedman's 'rather beautiful theory to the effect that out of given receipts, agents whose receipts were more variable would save a larger fraction than agents whose receipts were less variable' (Hahn 1993(a): 78). Friedman tested this theory by cross-sectional analysis, which enabled him to rule out the influence on savings by changes in interest rates and other factors relevant in a time-series test. Friedman's theory predicted that the saving ratio of farmers out of given receipts would generally be higher than that of doctors, and this was confirmed by the data. Does not this disprove Hahn's thesis? According to Hahn 'these tests could not be as conclusive as experiments in physics' (Hahn 1993(a): 79). He gives two reasons for this claim. First, one could argue that the variability of receipts was correlated with some other factor that, in reality, accounted for the observed difference in savings behaviour. Second, 'there are always endless doubts' concerning the reliability of the data (Hahn 1993(a): 79). For instance, do people correctly report their savings? Unlike physicists, 'economists have to live with such doubts, anticipate them, and try to resolve them as far as the nature of the subject allows' (Hahn 1993(a): 79).

In connection with such predictions, i.e. predictions not expressly concerned with predicting the future, Friedman would agree with Hahn that there is 'the inability to conduct so-called "controlled experiments" in economics' (Friedman 1953: 10). For Friedman, this inability 'does not, in my view, reflect a basic difference between the social and physical sciences' (Friedman 1953: 10). He gives two reasons for this view. First, this inability persists in some of the physical sciences, for example, astronomy. Second, 'the distinction between a controlled experiment and uncontrolled experience is at best one of degree' (Friedman

1953: 10). Moreover, like Hahn, he concedes that the evidence cast up by uncontrolled experience 'is far more difficult to interpret. It is frequently complex and also indirect and incomplete. Its collection is often arduous, and its interpretation generally requires subtle analysis, and involved chains of reasoning, which seldom carry real conviction' (Friedman 1953: 10–11).

In short, both Friedman and Hahn, by and large, agree on the methodological 'facts' concerning the limitations of controlled experimentation and the interpretative nature of other economic data, and yet they disagree on the diagnosis. In Friedman's eyes, economics is, nonetheless, a positive science *à la* physics. The differences are a matter of degree not of kind. Hahn, however, has no interest in the philosophical question of what constitutes a positive science, and thus is not interested in the issue of differences in kind. Again one recalls that, for him, both economics and physics, as non-tautological disciplines, make predictions. His claim is that the acknowledged differences between economics and physics noted above are of such a degree that, to claim economics is a positive science which is testable is unconvincing. In short, the predictions of economics, as such, are like those of physics or any other non-tautological discipline, but economists, when they attempt to test these by either controlled experimentation or other data, are at the other end of the spectrum of conclusiveness or decisiveness to physics or biology. Given that Hahn severs the umbilical cord between economic theory and predictive testing, he needs to develop an alternative account of the role of theory in economics. We will see in the next chapter how Hahn meets this challenge in an original and thought-provoking way.

Testing and the pragmatics of forecasting

We now turn to the prediction of future events in economics. This kind of prediction is 'of as much interest to economists as prediction without the time dimension' (Hahn 1993(a): 81). In this connection, Hahn insists that the desirability of predicting the future 'rests on two rather different considerations' (Hahn 1993(a): 84). On the one hand, there is the Friedmanite thesis, i.e. prediction is designed as a test for the theory. As with prediction without the time dimension, 'there are large difficulties' with predicting the future as a test for economic theory (Hahn 1993(a): 84). On the other hand, economic prediction, or forecasting, 'serves as an aid to action and decision' (ibid.: 84). For Hahn 'the surprise is not that we predict so badly, but rather that, in the relatively short term, we predict so well' (Hahn 1993(a): 94). This relative success, however, cannot be used to conclude that economists have thereby empirically tested and confirmed their theory. All that economists have is 'a *grammatical way* of peering into the future even if they do not always see it clearly. This is better than consulting entails' (Hahn 1993(a): 94; italics added).

What is the source of 'the large difficulties' in using successful forecasts as empirical tests to confirm economic theory? These reside in what we call the pragmatics of forecasting. In short, the pragmatics of forecasting is the open-ended range of things that economists do in making successful forecasts. This range includes, for example, econometric estimations, aggregation, errors of measurement, errors in estimation of functional forms, the possibility that the path of the exogenous variable may be stochastic, 'ad hoc doctoring of our theories' (Hahn 1993(a): 83) and so on. In Hahn's case, the pragmatics of forecasting are seen against the background of 'economists inability to experiment scientifically, that is adequately to control for the exogenous variable' and 'the intrinsic interrelatedness of economic phenomena' (Hahn 1993(a): 84). The pragmatics of forecasting constitute the source of the very large difficulties for taking successful forecasts in the domain of action and decision as empirical verifications of economic theory.

In this connection, Hahn gives us a concrete illustration of the pragmatics of forecasting – the things economists do in making a reasonable forecast.[9] He introduces his illustration with the truism that predicting the future, whether in physics or in economics, will invariably be conditional. However, 'in a subject like economics, conditionals require special care' (Hahn 1993(a): 81). Suppose an economist wants to forecast the British inflation rate for next year. The forecast is informed by what economists know or justifiably believe about inflation on the one hand and economic theory on the other. For instance, it is well known that the answer will partly depend on the course of interest rates. 'If interest rates are under the Chancellor of the Exchequer's control, then in giving his own forecast we may consider interest rates as a conditional of our forecast' (Hahn 1993(a): 81). However, it is also well known that, for instance, if current inflation were to force down exchange rates or put pressure on the balance of payments, interest rates may largely be outside the Chancellor's control. In that case, to predict inflation we must also predict interest rates; this, in turn, may require a prediction of exchange rates, and so on.

The conditionals of a forecast, strictly speaking, should be exogenous to the theory. 'But this is being very strict – indeed, one might argue, unmanageably strict' (Hahn 1993(a): 82). Economic theory has formalized the interdependence of economic variables. This theory leads to 'the view that in general the demand and supply of any good depends not only on its own price but also on the prices of everything else' and this 'everything else includes the prices of goods in the future' (Hahn 1993(a): 82). Thus, in our economic forecasts 'we must at each stage state what is assumed about the path of the exogenous variables and we must be sure, of course, that they are exogenous' (Hahn 1993(a): 83). Given the general interdependence of economic variables, including the prices of goods in the future, the economist makes some assumptions, such as that agents have correct expectations of future prices and, at every date, prices ensure that the amount of every good agents demand is equal to the amount of the good agents want to supply.

The upshot is that, if we know today's prices, we also know tomorrow's prices, and we can deduce the prices to clear markets the day after tomorrow, and so on. Now other aspects of the pragmatics of forecasting come into operation. For instance, we must know all the functional forms, but these are not accurately known. They are econometrically estimated. Moreover, as Hahn points out, 'there are reasons for arguing that this estimation must be simultaneous and not one at a time' (Hahn 1993(a): 83). Certainly, errors of estimation will occur, and in non-linear systems small errors may lead to widely different forecasts of the course of prices given the path of the exogenous variables. Much the same is true when we only know the prices inaccurately. Hahn's moral is that 'predicting from such a complex is therefore not easy' (Hahn 1993(a): 83).

In addition, and crucially, given the sheer complexity involved, to forecast 'we have to depart to some extent from what the theory demands.' In other words, 'we must recognize that it is simply beyond our capacity to proceed without *some more or less* ad hoc *doctoring of our theories* to make matters manageable' (Hahn 1993(a): 83; italics added). This ad hoc doctoring includes, for instance, reducing the dimension of the model by aggregation. Instead of one equation for each good separately, economists take one equation for bundles or aggregates of goods, e.g. consumer or investment goods. Furthermore, the methods of estimating excess demand functions are mostly linear. Also, in view of some inevitable errors in measurement and in the estimation of functional forms, the prediction will also be subject to error. Much more could be said about, for instance, challenges in short-run predictions and other compromises. Hahn feels, by means of his example which is only summarily presented here, he has 'said enough to show that there are very large difficulties with prediction *as a test for theory*' (Hahn 1993(a): 84; italics added).

Philosophers, reading through Hahn's example will, perhaps, hear Wittgenstein's warning bells ringing in their ears; 'A main cause of philosophical disease – a one-sided diet: one nourishes one's thinking with only one kind of example' (Wittgenstein 2000: 593). Is Hahn causing the methodological disease that economics is not a predictive science *à la* physics by means of his example? Predicting a country's inflation is a macroeconomic, not a microeconomic, problem. Partha Dasgupta gives philosophers a useful summary of macroeconomics as follows. Macroeconomics is

> the study of economics described in *aggregate* terms. Typical variables whose interrelationships are under investigation in macroeconomics are the level of employment, national output, the general price level, government deficit, the 'money' supply, the rate of inflation, government debt, the trade balance and so forth.
>
> (Dasgupta 2002: 72)

Clearly, lurking in the background of Hahn's example is the old methodological issue of whether or not macro theory requires microfoundations? Of course, the answer depends on how one understands the notion of foundations. Foundational programmes can range from strict, eliminative, reductionist ones in which all macro notions are eliminated in terms of micro ones to emergent programmes where, in Dasgupta's words, micro theory is foundational in the sense that 'the various pathways through which millions of decisions made by individual human beings give rise to *emergent* features' (e.g. rate of inflation, productivity gains, level of national income...), which in turn influence individual decisions, giving rise to 'mutual feedback over time' (Dasgupta 2002: 63).

Dasgupta sums up the conundrum of economists as follows:

> Macroeconomics is among the most problematic fields within economics because it is very very hard. Lord only knows why you should expect to be able to get things 'right' if you have to describe an entire economy in terms of nine or ten variables.[10] But then Lord only knows why you should expect to say much of practical moment if you were to work with models comprising thousands of commodities and millions of households.
>
> (Dasgupta 2002: 72–3)

Assuming that Dasgupta's summary is along the right lines, then the multifarious elements in the pragmatics of forecasting across this wide spectrum are such that Hahn's conclusion that successful forecasts in the domain of action are not genuine scientific tests of economic theory still stands: the Wittgensteinian alarm bells are not tolling for Hahn.

Economics without laws

The *weltanschauung* of science, at least in the eyes of numerous scientists and philosophers of science, puts a great deal of emphasis on the existence and discovery of the laws of nature. Moreover, once discovered, scientific laws are integral to the predictive success of science: since the laws of nature are true any logically valid deduction from them in conjunction with true initial conditions will also be true. This is very evident in the well-known Hempelian, D–N (Deductive–Nomological) model of scientific explanation. In the D–N model, the event requiring explanation is deduced, and thereby explained, from the law-like, i.e. nomological generalizations and the appropriate boundary or initial conditions. Thus, scientific laws for many philosophers of science are core to scientific understanding/explanation.

Two characteristics commonly ascribed to scientific laws, namely universality and necessity, are noted by Hahn. First, the laws of nature are universally true propositions. Second, laws of nature are more than contingently true generalizations. These methodological claims are clearly conveyed in the Hempelian distinction between accidentally true, universal statements that are not scientific laws and nomically true, universal statements that constitute scientific laws. For instance, 'all the chairs in my kitchen are brown' is an accidentally true, universal statement. Two points should be noted vis-à-vis this distinction. First, the domain of discourse of accidentally true, universal statements is frequently rather limited. This contrasts with nomic universals, such as copper expands on being heated, which applies to all copper, past, present and future. Second, an accidentally true universal expresses a contingent regularity: the situation could be otherwise. The nomic universal 'all copper expands on being heated' expresses more than a contingent regularity: the situation could not be otherwise.

It is not possible for copper to contract on being heated. I can correctly and confidently claim that, if I were to heat this piece of copper in forty years time it would expand, whereas I cannot claim that if I were to get a chair from my kitchen in 40 years time it would be brown. Philosophers of the physical sciences have devoted much time and energy in attempting to elucidate this nomic characteristic of scientific laws, ranging from various empiricists to realist analyses.

Such philosophical methodological analyses are of no concern to Hahn, for the simple reason that 'other than logical, that is tautological implications, economics has no laws' (Hahn 1996: 192). In his view, when economists lay claim to the mantle of science *à la* physics, 'they sooner or later babble about "the laws of economics" and begin to say much more than it is prudent to say. The subject gets a bad name' (Hahn 1993(a): 95). Of course, Hahn is not maintaining that contingent regularities or tendencies do not exist in the economic world. His point is that such contingent regularities are not laws of science *à la* physics. The so-called laws of economics are not nomic, universal truths *à la* physics. For instance, in the case of the law of supply and demand, Hahn insists that 'there is no such law which holds in *all* societies at *all* times' (Hahn 1993(a): 91; italics added). In particular, in Hahn's methodology, the so-called iron laws of economics do not refer to invariant, essential structures that have subsisted in all economies at all times. This, in part, results from Hahn's inference to the effect that, if one assumed that all economies were governed by nomic universal laws *à la* physics, then one assumes 'that we shall find a closed theory: that is one with no exogenous variables.'

However, 'in economic analysis we will always need to take account of exogenous variables such as history and social norms' (Hahn 1993(a): 91). Hahn, in his own unique style, supplies an elementary example. In accordance with what so-called economic laws would imply, 'when there was an excess supply of labour' in early eighteenth century Britain, 'there was indeed a tendency of wages to fall' (Hahn 1993(a): 91). Such a tendency, however, is not inevitable, i.e. is not necessary. For instance, given trade unions – an exogenous historico-social variable – such a tendency is by no means inevitable.

While one might conclude that so-called economic laws are not like the nomic universal laws of physics, perhaps economics is much more like meteorology than physics, where, in Mill's terminology, the effects of minor causes would be more influential than in general physics.[11] According to Hahn, economics is neither like physics nor meteorology. In the socio-economic world 'the law of large numbers does not self-evidently operate' because there 'the custom and views of some contaminate those of others' (Hahn 1985: 19). *Prima facie* there are more complex interactions in the socio-economic world in comparison with meteorology. Although that may be correct, the distinctiveness of economics resides in the fact 'that the constraints on what is possible seem much weaker than is the case with the physical processes studied in meteorology' (Hahn 1985: 19). In the terminology of philosophy of science, the regularities or tendencies of economics tend to the accidental rather than the nomic end of the spectrum of universal claims, whereas in meteorology numerous regularities are located at the nomic end. At the nomic end, the 'necessity' or nomicity imposes much stronger or limiting constraints on what is possible than at the accidental end. Thus Hahn concludes:

> A theorist then will be surprised if there are 'laws of economics' in the sense of propositions holding universally to be discovered. He will be surprised if deep knowledge of 'affairs' were to reveal some fundamental or invariant structure of an economy.
>
> (Hahn 1985: 19)

In this way Hahn distances himself from any essentialist/realist reading of economic theory as a discipline that successfully reveals the hidden essences of actual economic systems.

Hahn also addresses another set of reasons for not reading economic regularities and tendencies as nomic universals. This set of reasons is connected to his general, anti-reductionist or anti-physicalist philosophy of economic agents mentioned earlier. As we already noted, economic agents are autonomous human beings, free to make choices. When economists talk about their 'iron laws,' they erroneously create the impression that there are mechanical forces working their way inevitably through the system, the way, for instance, in which the laws of gravity necessitate the movement of the earth. Once again, according to Hahn, 'unlike the case of an object, there is no necessity here: there is no law' (Hahn 1993(a): 90). Economic agents are free to choose. Successful economic predictions do not imply the existence of nomic universal laws. Again Hahn illustrates his point by example. If profit can be made from arbitrage between two currencies, economists correctly predict that arbitrage would occur. However, there is no necessity here other than logical necessity. There is, for Hahn, no question of some mechanical, economic force necessitating the predicted outcome. Rather, the economic agent is free to choose. An agent takes advantage of the opportunity to make profit because the agent chooses to do so. The agent could choose not to take advantage of the arbitrage opportunity to make profit. In light of his overall case, Hahn concludes that 'we must expect very few laws of economics' (Hahn 1993(a): 91).

To sum up, according to Hahn, 'if science means the serious, disciplined study of observed phenomena it (economics) clearly is. If, however, science means uncovering "laws" and providing accurate inter-temporal predictions, I should say that it is not' (Hahn 1993(a): 95). The mantle of economics as a science gives the subject a bad name because it can be shown that it just does not succeed *à la* physics. Nevertheless, economics has 'cast much light and it can be a powerful weapon against nonsense. Certainly if it did not exist, it would urgently need inventing' (Hahn 1993(a): 95).

The harmful influence of Friedman's 'as if' methodology

We have already seen how Hahn portrays Friedman as a key player in the cultivation of the misleading view of economics as a positive, predictive science.

Moreover, we noted that Friedman methodologically defended his reading of economics by recourse to his famous 'as if' thesis. In this 'as if' approach, it does not matter how counter-intuitive economic axioms are, if their predictions are verified by observed events, then nothing else matters, since the economy is behaving as if it were so. Hahn totally rejects this Friedmanite methodology. Friedman's 'as if' methodology 'may be fine for Quantum theory... but only dangerous sloppiness and blundered arguing can result from its use in economics' (Hahn 1996: 185).

As we have already discussed, for Hahn, economics is not a science with a body of claims confirmed by controlled experiments. If it were, Friedman's 'as if' methodology would have something going for it; economics would be like quantum physics in being 'an implausible theory which delivers results – the very best support for "as if"' (Hahn 1996: 189). Hahn, however, is quite scathing about any favourable comparison between economics and quantum physics in terms of predictive success.

> To hang on the coattails of a theory of such seeming paradox as quantum mechanics, say, because 'it works' will be justified when economists' theories predict correctly to eight decimal places as quantum theory does. Until then the direct plausibility of our assumptions remains a test a theory applied to the 'real' world must pass.
>
> (Hahn 1994: 247)

Friedman, legitimated his 'as if' methodology, in part, by means of the three analogies mentioned earlier. The first analogy is rooted in classical mechanics. A ball dropped from a height 'behaves *as if* it were falling in a vacuum' (Friedman 1953: 16). In the eyes of someone like Hahn, this is not a very compelling analogy for economics. Controlled experimentation is very pertinent to the testing of this mechanical 'as if' claim, whereas economics is not similarly blessed. Friedman appears to be aware of this limitation, as he claims his second analogy 'is an analogue of many hypotheses in the social sciences' (Friedman 1953: 19). In response to the request for an explanation of the density of leaves on a tree, one is told that

> the leaves are positioned as if each leaf deliberately sought to maximize the amount of sunlight it receives, given the position of its neighbours, as if it knew the physical laws determining the amount of sunlight that would be received in various positions and could move rapidly and instantaneously from any one position to any other desired and unoccupied position.
>
> (Friedman 1953: 19)

Hahn, in his usual very brief style, addresses this analogy. The 'as if' hypothesis 'may well predict the orientation of leaves but it is *not* an account which we *understand*, precisely because we *know* that plants are not, as Friedman notes, capable of any calculations' (Hahn 1985: 15; italics added). In other words, despite its successful prediction, in light of what we know about plants, that 'as if' hypothesis fails to furnish us with any understanding of what is going on. But, according to Friedman's methodological stance, namely that the *only* test of a theory is its predictive success, the 'as if' hypothesis is all there is. Friedman's 'as if' methodology implies that economists should leave matters stand with successful 'as if' hypotheses. This is where the 'as if' methodology is harmful. It discourages economists' curiosity about matters they fail to understand on the grounds of lazy 'as if' reasoning. Friedman's 'as if' methodology unduly closes down genuine research problems that theoretical economists, striving for genuine understanding, as opposed to prediction, will seek to pursue. The 'as if' methodology has the potential to close down rather than open up genuine theoretical research.

For instance, as Partha Dasgupta points out, by the late 1970s 'a new direction in macroeconomic research began to take shape in the form of small-scale, piecemeal enquiries into separate markets, such as those for labour, credit, savings and skills' (Dasgupta 2002: 75). In particular, according to Hahn, a number of 'influential economists' held the view that the British labour market in 1984 was in continuous Walrasian equilibrium, or at least it was 'as if' it were. The 'as if' methodology in this case is harmful for at least two reasons. First, in insisting that all that economics should be concerned with is this 'as if' hypothesis, Friedmanite methodology removes issues crucial to the correct understanding of the British labour market in 1984 from the research agenda. Second, it leads to further and further rather futile econometric exercises in testing.

Hahn is at pains to point out that his objection is to the Friedmanite 'as if' methodological approach to the problem. The Friedmanite 'as if' methodological reading is not to be confused with the legitimate, and indeed very valuable, economic research programme that investigates or enquires 'how far *observed events are consistent with* an economy which is in continuous Walrasian equilibrium' (Hahn 1985: 15, italics added). This legitimate economic research programme does aid our understanding. For instance 'we might find that events that we had explained as due to disequilibrium or indeed to Trade Unions and monopolists could be accounted for without these. That surely would be valuable for understanding' (Hahn 1985: 15). In general this economic research programme would show that 'this and this is not inconsistent with an economy in perpetual Walrasian equilibrium and not that this and this is explained by such an equilibrium' (Hahn 1985: 15). Such a programme is not a Friedmanite 'as if' programme. For Hahn, it is carried out under the methodological quest for understanding that is at variance with Friedmanite 'as if' methodology. Clearly, we must get clarification on Hahn's notion of understanding, which for him is central to economic theorizing.

Conclusion: towards economic, as distinct from scientific, understanding

We opened this chapter with Hahn's blunt claim 'I hate methodology' (Hahn 2005: 17). In the course of the chapter we have seen how Hahn, despite his *prima facie* antagonism to economic methodology, makes rather bold methodological claims. We have seen why he is hostile to methodological claims that neoclassical economics is in crisis. Frequently, methodologists make such claims on the misunderstanding that neoclassical theory is scientific, buttressed with a methodology inappropriately borrowed from the physical sciences. These methodologists are dazzled by textbook accounts of neoclassical economics and ignore the frontiers of neoclassical research.

Hahn is equally hostile to methodological claims that neoclassical economics is too formalistic. While acknowledging that nothing is forever and that younger economists will eventually revolt, he defends the mathematization of economics on the grounds that non-mathematical economics has thus far failed to compete with mathematical economics as a rigorous, disciplined research programme with a dynamic grammar of argumentation.

In particular, he is unequivocally hostile to Friedman's 'as if' methodology. In Hahn's view, this methodology has actually damaged the discipline of economics. An integral part of this damage lies in the manner in which it curtails genuine economic curiosity and closes down genuine economic research endeavours. Unlike Friedmanite, 'as if' economists, Hahn insists that theoretical economists are engaged in the authentic task of understanding complex economic systems, a theoretical task which is quite distinct from the pragmatic economic task of forecasting. Indeed, as we will see in the next chapter, Hahn elaborates on how theoretical economists gain a specific understanding of complex economic systems which has little or nothing to do with scientific prediction.

In the physical sciences, explanation, and thus understanding, is inextricably linked to the discovery of scientific laws and their subsequent use in making successful predictions. According to Hahn, this methodological portrait of the physical sciences does not apply to theoretical economics. It gives a misleading account of the rigorous discipline of economic theorizing and analysis. As we have seen, according to Hahn, there are no economic laws. Thus, he rejects the claim that neoclassical economics is a 'study of the laws of motion of a capitalist society' (Hahn 1973(a): 39). Unfortunately, many methodologists incorrectly identify economic axioms or economic contingent regularities with scientific laws. These then face the issue as to why economics is not as successful as physics at making accurate predictions about future events. For Hahn, the business of predicting the future belongs to pragmatics. Undoubtedly, economic theory plays a role here. However, its central economic role is to enable us to gain a correct objective, though partial, understanding of complex economic systems where successful prediction is not the *sine qua non* of this objective understanding. Clearly, Hahn must face the methodological challenge of illuminating his concept of objective understanding. In the next chapter we examine how he meets this challenge.

4 In defence of economic theorizing

A line of first defence against madmen and witches.

(Hahn 1985: 4)

Introduction

In the previous chapter we engaged Hahn's negative assessment of economic methodology. In a sense, he would concur with Mäki's thesis that much of economic methodology is unsatisfactory. A reason for this view is the 'top-down' approach fashionable in economic methodology in which methodologists adopt a favoured philosophy of science and apply this to economics. According to Mäki, in this 'top-down' approach 'more often than not, the outcome of the exercise is the conclusion that economics appears to be in more or less bad shape as it does not meet the presumed criteria of good science' (Mäki 2002: 91). Indeed, we have seen how Hahn wishes to take economic theory out of the shadows of science and understood as an empirical, predictive, well-confirmed discipline or one engaged in the discovery and use of iron laws. In this context, Hahn constructs an alternative account of economic theory in which the triad of theory, prediction and explanation, so pervasive in much of philosophy of science, is largely redundant. In this chapter we explore how Hahn creatively achieves this alternative methodological project.

Economic theory and economic theorizing

Hahn delivered his Jevons Memorial Fund Lecture at the University of London in November of 1984. He titled his challenging address 'In Praise of Economic Theory.' However, in the opening paragraph he makes, in our opinion, a very telling aside. He suggested that a change of title to 'In Praise of Theorizing in Economics' would be more apt (Hahn 1985: 3). This shift of focus from economic theory to theorizing in economics, which for short we call economic theorizing, is not a piece of trivial semantics. It marks a key distinction for Hahn between the dynamic process or activity of theorizing in economics on the one hand and the end product or outcome, i.e. the emerging economic theory, on the other.

According to Hahn, a rigorous economic theory can be presented as an axiomatic system. He is well aware that this thesis is not universally accepted by practicing economists.

> To some economists axiomatic-logico deductive theory is anathema; for instance this is the case for Professor Kornai and Lord Kaldor. However, it seems to me that any coherent general propositions are decomposable into this form.... One of my first reasons for praising theory, at least in its modern mode, is that it comes clean on both its axioms and assumptions.
>
> Hahn 1985: 5

Indeed, arising out of the philosophical research of Mary Hesse, Max Black and others on the roles of analogy and of metaphor in science in general, some economic methodologists argue that economic theory is misrepresented when presented in axiomatic form. We have discussed some of these positions in an earlier work (Boylan and O'Gorman 1995). The point at issue here is neither the appropriateness nor the accuracy of the use of an axiomatic system in presenting an economic theory. Rather, it is much more elementary, namely that numerous philosophers and methodologists focus on economic theory in their methodological reflections. As such, there is nothing wrong with that. On the contrary it is legitimate, indeed necessary, to give the most rigorous possible formulation to an economic theory and, according to Hahn, this is best done in the form of an axiomatic system. Such a presentation serves our ideals of clarity and rigour, ideals that are absolutely central to Hahn. In short, philosophers and methodologists have every right to reflect on economic theory. However, and this is Hahn's point, if one ignores the activity of theorizing as distinct from the outcome of this activity, namely the theory, one's methodology will be incomplete.

The process or activity of theorizing puts the methodological spotlight on economic theorizing at the frontiers of economic research. In his view, theorizing in post-Second World War economics has witnessed 'spectacular success,' ranging over game theoretic developments to history-dependent equilibrium: 'the questioning of almost everything, for instance the rationality postulate, is not a sign of crisis but of vigorous endeavour' (Hahn 1992(a): 5). This kind of dynamic theoretical research must also be an indispensable dimension to any methodology that is claiming to do justice to economics.

In our opinion, Hahn's distinction between theory and theorizing is significant for economic methodology. Indeed, one could draw a boundary in the philosophies of the physical sciences and of mathematics along analogous lines. For instance, in the philosophy of mathematics, the works of Frege and of Russell in the foundations of mathematics furnish us with logical rigorous reconstructions of arithmetic, using the resources of axiomatic systems among others. Here, the focus is on the outcome of mathematical activity. On the other hand, Poincaré and, later, Wittgenstein focus on the activities of mathematicians in doing mathematics, thereby furnishing us with different philosophies of mathematics to those of Russell and Frege. Be that as it may, Hahn, in our view, is demanding that methodologists should not ignore either economic theory or theorizing in economics. In particular, Hahn is concerned with the erroneous view presented by methodologists who solely focus on economic theory as a corpus that is 'complete and secure' (Hahn 1996: 192) By putting the methodological spotlight on the activity of theorizing in economics, Hahn is insisting that methodologists resist the temptation of viewing post-war theory in economics as, in the phrase of Mary Hesse, some kind of 'static museum piece' (Hesse 1966: 4).

In the above paragraph we have emphasized the distinction between economic theory as an output or end product and the activity of theorizing, which, in the first instance, is a non-descriptive thought experiment. In our opinion, one could argue that the spirit of this distinction is indispensable for Hahn, but that its letter is misleading. Economic theory and the activity of economic theorizing are not independent of each other. There is a dynamic relationship between them. The theorizing is not carried out in a vacuum: economic theorizing, as a thought experiment, is concerned with some aspect or other of the theory. This is very evident in Hahn's claim that the activity of economic theorizing 'in the first instance is a large series of thought experiments most of which, as Hausman states, starts from some kind of constrained maximizing behaviour and appeal to some kind of notion of equilibrium' (Hahn 1996: 192). Most of economic theorizing starts with a notion of rationality and equilibrium – key notions of neoclassical economic theory. We will discuss the specifics of rationality and equilibrium later. The point here is more general, namely that economic theory and economic theorizing for Hahn are not totally independent of each other. These are separate but interrelated, and economic methodologists should address both their distinctiveness and their interrelations.

Theorizing in economics, understanding and Moore's naturalistic fallacy

According to Hahn, economic theorists are not 'slouches' (Hahn 1996: 187): they are forging innovations at the frontiers of research, theorizing that is neglected in much of the philosophy of economics. In Hahn's view, what is the point or objectives of this theorizing? Contrary to numerous realist readings of economics, the objective is not to attain the law-like explanation of real economies and, contrary to Friedmanite instrumentalists, the objective is not to predict. Hahn sums up the objective of economic theorizing as 'the undertaking to gain *understanding* of the particular by reference to generalizing insights and in the light of certain abstract unifying principles' (Hahn 1985: 3, italics added). Clearly, this summary needs analysis and development, which Hahn, in the course of his reflections, develops. The first notion he draws attention to in this analysis is the concept of understanding. Basically, theoretical economics is in the business of understanding and economic theorizing enhances this understanding.

By way of a preliminary introduction to the concept of understanding relevant to economic theorizing, he repeatedly insists that it is not to be confused with prediction. For Hahn, this is evident in the concept of understanding used in non-predictive domains. He correctly points out that geologists 'understand the cause of earthquakes but cannot at the moment predict them' (Hahn 1985: 3). Similarly, in economics 'we may be able to understand an allocation of resources as one of a number of possible equilibrium allocations without being able to predict which equilibrium will be observed in any one case' (ibid.: 3). Moreover, he explicitly maintains that 'understanding doesn't imply the ability to manipulate events' (Hahn 1985: 4). Again, Hahn gives us an example of what he has in mind here; economists may understand the causes of unemployment but this does not imply that 'they know how to cure it' (ibid.: 4).

The hard-headed pragmatist may respond that Hahn's notion of understanding is not much use to those making economic decisions in the real world. If economic theorizing does not give us some handle or other on the economy, how are we to distinguish it from speculative metaphysics? If one feels that is too harsh a criticism, at least Hahn's understanding, 'which does not facilitate manipulation, is a useless luxury' (Hahn 1995: 4). Such a critique, according to Hahn, is misguided. The kind of understanding achieved in economic theorizing 'can certainly aid us in recognizing futile or misdirected attempts at manipulation' (ibid.: 4). In other words, understanding furnished in economic theorizing serves a negative heuristic: it rules out certain strategies. For instance, as Hahn notes, we cannot change the orbit of the moon by praying to the sun! In this sense 'it (economic theory) is a line of first defence against madmen and witches' (ibid.: 4). Madmen and witches propose strategies that are incompatible with the correct, or at least our best rigorous, understanding of the economic world.

In his preliminary reflections on the concept of understanding required for economic theorizing, Hahn makes fleeting remarks to two towering figures in the history of Cambridge philosophy, namely Moore and Wittgenstein.[1] In this section we will attempt to decode his reference to Moore. When claiming that economics is a line of first defence against madmen and witches, he remarks that

> even if that were not so, I have never seen an argument to show that... understanding of the world needs, justification in terms of other things. G.E. Moore's chapter on the 'Naturalistic Fallacy' can easily be adapted to demonstrate the confusion of such a view.
>
> (ibid.: 4)

Moore's Naturalistic Fallacy is developed in his famous *Principia Ethica*, first published in 1905. According to Russell, it dominated discussion in Cambridge at the time, and, according to Keynes, it was better than anything produced by Plato. Moore's *Principi*a is based on a crucial distinction between ethical theorizing on the one hand and applied ethics on the other. What we, by analogy to Hahn's economic theorizing, call ethical theorizing – Moore calls this 'the business of the ethical philosopher' (Moore 1976: 3) – is critically concerned with the concept of good. Applied ethics is concerned with the subsidiary question 'what kind of actions ought we to perform' (Moore 1976: viii). If we do not get our philosophical theorizing about 'good' correct, we will end up confused in any attempt to answer the questions of applied ethics. Ethical theorizing is absolutely necessary to any systematic, rigorous study of ethics. In this sense, 'it is not the business of the ethical philosopher to give personal advice or exhortation' (Moore 1976: 3).

The hypothesis we wish to explore is that, in Hahn's methodology, the concept of understanding is to economic theorizing what the concept of good is to Moore's ethical theorizing. As we have seen, for Moore, ethical theorizing is indispensable to ethics, even though it does not, as such, give personal advice or exhort us to do anything specific. Anyone who is serious in applied ethics presupposes that this theoretical work has been correctly done. If it is not done correctly, confusion will be the order of the day. Similarly for Hahn, economic theorizing is indispensible for applied economics. Applied economists, in having recourse to the relevant aspect of economic theory, presuppose this work has been carried out to the best standards available. If economic theorizing is not done correctly, confusion will be the order of the day.[2]

In particular for Moore, the concept of 'good' is the key concept of ethical theorizing. More precisely, the 'question, how "good" is to be defined is the most fundamental question in all ethics' (Moore 1976: 5). Moore's answer to this question is that good 'cannot be defined and that is all I have to say about it' (Moore 1976: 6). The concept of good is absolutely basic to ethics, and hence is indefinable. Other notions are defined in terms of it. As pointed out by Russell, Frege and other logicians, there must be indefinables. In this vein for Moore, 'there is no intrinsic difficulty in the contention that "good" denotes a simple and indefinable quality' (Moore 1976: 10).

In Moore's eyes the indefinability of good is inextricably linked to his claim that good is a simple quality possessed by all good acts. According to Moore, we can, for instance, define a horse in terms of its component parts arranged in definite relations to one another. 'It is in this sense I deny good to be definable' (Moore 1976: 8). In other words good is not a complex property, rather it is simple and hence is indefinable; 'in this sense "good" has no definition because it is simple and has no parts' (Moore 1976: 9). Finally, Moore emphasizes the fact that 'good' is primarily an adjective that is distinct from the substantive use of the expression 'the good.' For Moore, the substantive use of the expression 'the good' is definable. 'It is just because I think there will be less risk of error in our search for a definition of "the good" that I am now insisting that good is indefinable' (Moore 1976: 9). This is the context of Moore's naturalistic fallacy.

The hypothesis which we are exploring is that the concept of understanding is to Hahn's economic theorizing what the concept of good is to Moore's ethical theorizing. If this is so, then understanding is basic to economic theorizing and this, for Hahn, is unquestionably the case. Moreover, just as in Chapter VI of his *Principia,* in which Moore has no difficulty with something that 'is good in itself in a high degree' (Moore 1976: 184), Hahn can allow his concept of understanding to range over an analogous spectrum from shallow to deep. In this sense,

Hahn speaks of deepening our understanding (Hahn 1985: 9). We have seen above that, for Moore, 'good' is not just basic or indispensable to his ethical theorizing, it is both simple and indefinable. If the above hypothesis were to hold, then we could see Hahn re-echoing Moore's famous claim that 'when I am asked "what is good?" my answer is that good is good and that is the end of the matter' (Moore 1976: 6). Thus, the hypothesis would have Hahn saying 'understanding is understanding and that is the end of the matter; understanding is indefinable.' Assuming that Hahn has not changed his mind between the time of his Jevons lecture and 1996, when responding to Hausman's challenging methodology of economics, we can categorically claim that, for Hahn, his concept of understanding is definable. He maintains 'I am not capable of settling on a precise definition of understanding and indeed such a definition may be context-dependent' (Hahn 1996: 192, footnote 6). Moreover, given that understanding is definable for Hahn, one can reasonably imply it is not simple. Thus, while understanding is basic to the activity of economic theorizing, it is neither simple nor indefinable. For this and other reasons we reject the hypothesis that understanding is to Hahn's economic theorizing what 'good' is to Moore's ethical theorizing. Let us now look more closely at Moore's naturalistic fallacy.

As we have already outlined, Moore introduces his naturalistic fallacy in the context of his thesis that good is simple and indefinable. He then presents the fallacy along the following lines. 'All things which are good are *also* something else' (Moore 1976: 10). Indeed, ethics aims at discovering those other properties that belong to all good things.

> But far too many philosophers have thought that when they have named those other properties they were actually defining good; that these properties, in fact, were simply not 'other', but absolutely and entirely the same as goodness. This view I propose to call the naturalistic fallacy.
>
> (Moore 1976: 10)

According to Moore, the naturalistic fallacy is quite specific, and should be distinguished from a related fallacy. He does not supply a name for this related fallacy, but he does give us an example. This fallacy arose when someone 'tried to define pleasure for us as being any other natural object' (Moore 1976: 13). More generally,

> when a man confuses two natural objects with one another, defining the one by the other… then there is no reason to call the fallacy naturalistic. But if he confuses 'good' which is not in the same sense a natural object with any other natural object whatever, then there is a reason for calling that a naturalistic fallacy.
>
> (Moore 1976: 13)

Our question is the following: is it Moore's naturalistic fallacy or the other fallacy noted above which is to be adapted by Hahn to demonstrate the confusion in the thesis that understanding needs justification in terms of other things? If one insists on using the naturalistic fallacy, one may end up claiming that understanding is very unique in that it does not belong to the range of cognitive activities in which, for instance, predicting is located. *Prima facie*, that is not plausible; understanding and predicting seem to belong to the same range of cognitive activities. This issue, however, does not arise with the second fallacy. When adapted, this fallacy shows the error in confusing two separate activities, predicting and understanding, which belong to the same range of activities.

Be that as it may, Hahn locates economic theorizing in a domain of understanding that is utterly unrelated to the philosophers' of science notion of explanation, where explanation and prediction are inextricably linked. Thus, despite his criticism of the *Geistes-Wissenschaften* philosophers outlined in the previous chapter, he concurs with their thesis that, understanding in the humanities and the social sciences has, in principle, nothing to do with successful prediction, at least as far as theoretical economics is concerned.

Economic theorizing and understanding

Hahn admits that his notion of understanding is not 'straightforward' and that he has not furnished a 'watertight definition' of it in terms of necessary and sufficient conditions (Hahn 1993(a): 85). For the moment, let us assume *à la* Wittgenstein that the concept of understanding is a family resemblance one which lacks necessary and sufficient conditions. How is one to deal with such a concept? One suggestion is that one presents clear cases to which the term applies along with clear counter cases.[3] This, indeed, is exactly what Hahn does. He furnishes clear examples of understanding without prediction and clear examples for which no understanding is achieved. Geologists have an adequate theoretical understanding of earthquakes in terms of plate movements and so forth, yet they cannot accurately predict the next earthquake. Similarly, evolution provides us with a theoretical understanding of *Homo sapiens*, but the theory does not, as such, predict 'the emergence of *Homo sapiens'* (Hahn 1993(a): 92). In elementary economics we gain an understanding of Giffen goods in terms of the distinction between substitution and income effects, or 'we can understand why two people are seen to exchange without being able to predict that they will exchange' (Hahn 1985: 3). More generally, 'Adam Smith provided an understanding of how an economy with self-interested agents could be orderly, an intellectual achievement of a high order. But ' "this understanding theory" does not allow us to predict that any actual economies will be orderly in practice' (Hahn 1993(a): 88).

We now turn to clear counter examples. Lack of understanding is evident in low-level generalizations that summarize empirical regularities. For instance taking aspirin relieves headaches. Regularities like these, in terms of understanding, 'have no bite... we do not understand why aspirin relieves headaches' (Hahn 1993(a): 87). 'Nonsense – correlations' are another set of examples for which no understanding is achieved. In this connection, Hahn points out that some of his colleagues found that the incidence of rickets in Scotland was better correlated with the price level than are money aggregates! If we were to use this correlation to predict the price level, 'we would be predicting without understanding' (Hahn 1993(a): 85). The upshot of this sequence of instances and counter instances is to show that, while the concept of understanding may be vague, it is not useless: it has bite.[4]

Hahn enumerates 'at least three necessary conditions for understanding an event or events' (Hahn 1985(a): 3). First, one must have a theory that comprises the event or events to be understood. Second, the event(s) must not contradict the theory. Third, the 'theory must be in the public domain' (ibid.: 3). The third condition, which requires that the theory be formulated in a public language, eliminates the worry, raised by Hahn, that many see 'an inevitable subjective element' in the notion of understanding (Hahn 1993(a): 88). It is instructive to compare these three necessary conditions for understanding an event with Hahn's two necessary characteristics of 'a theory which provides understanding' (Hahn 1993(a): 85). Any theory which provides understanding is such that '(a) its statement involves no logical error; and (b) it does not contradict – indeed it fits in with – other things we think we know' (ibid.: 85). According to Hahn (a) is not controversial. While this may well be the case, its full implications are certainly not spelled out. No logical error could mean any or some or all of the following: (1) the logical forms of each axiom and other propositions of the theory are correctly stated; (2) the rules of inference are explicitly and correctly stated; (3) the rules of inference are correctly applied; (4) the theory is shown to be consistent.[5]

Hahn concedes that his condition (b), i.e. that a good economic theory fits in with other things we know, is both loosely formulated and more difficult. He illustrates the difficulty with reference to quantum physics – it was, to say the least, very hard to reconcile quantum theory with what physicists thought they knew, namely classical mechanics and relativity theory. Hahn has no systematically worked out resolution of this difficulty. We suspect that any systematic resolution of this difficulty would be too prescriptive and thus unsatisfactory. On the one hand, Hahn does not want the concept of economic understanding to be too conservative in the sense that, if we give too much weight to the things we think we know, we will never broaden or deepen our understanding. On the other hand, economics is not like quantum physics in that some of its basic parameters are indispensable, e.g. economic agents are human beings who make choices. These put some limits on the notion of understanding – economic theory must not violate these.

Hahn readily admits his admiration for clear-cut concepts, i.e. ones that are clearly defined. His concept of understanding, however, has not been so defined. His wish is that philosophers would fill this lacuna.[6] In the meantime, he is insistent that his concept of understanding is methodologically indispensable to a correct analysis of economic theorizing. Finally, we are now in a better position to appreciate Hahn's uncompromising opposition to the Friedmanite 'as if' methodology. Just suppose that some Friedmanite 'as if' assumptions were successful, i.e. they enabled economists to make well-confirmed predictions. Hahn would still not be convinced. 'We want to understand why the "as if" assumptions are successful.' With a telling, rhetorical flourish, which would be admired by the great Roman orators of old, Hahn remarks that a Friedmanite 'as if' hypothesis 'does not allow one, for instance, to distinguish between agents who act on their preferences from those compelled to act on those of a hypnotist' (Hahn 1985: 6). In short, for Hahn, economic theorizing without understanding is like Hamlet without the Prince.

Axioms and economic understanding

In the previous sections we focused on Hahn's notion of understanding in general. The enterprise of economic theorizing, however, is more specific. It aims to gain 'understanding of the particular by reference to generalizing insights and in light of certain abstract unifying principles' (Hahn 1985: 3). Economic theorists are not alone in the search for correct understanding. Other academic researchers are similarly engaged. Thus, economic theorizing achieves a specific kind of understanding, i.e. that which is constrained by generalizing insights and abstract unifying principles.[7]

What are these abstract unifying principles that are indispensable to theoretical economic understanding? These are the axioms and the assumptions of theoretical economics. As we saw in an earlier section, according to Hahn, theoretical economics can, contrary to Kaldor and others, be formulated in an 'axiomatic–logico deductive' fashion (Hahn 1985: 5). One of Hahn's principal reasons for this requirement is its explicitness. To use Frege's metaphor, every link in any inference chain is thereby rendered explicit. In the case of theoretical economics, both the axioms and assumptions are clearly and explicitly stated. This may sound rather abstract. Hahn, in his concrete style, once again furnishes us with a pertinent example. He focuses on 'the best known and most important axiom,' the so-called rationality principle, which he formulates as follows: 'The rational agent knows what he wants and from among the alternatives available to him chooses what he wants' (Hahn 1985: 5).[8] This axiom is an abstract unifying principle of economic understanding. Economic understanding is governed by this and other such axiomatic principles.

It is crucial to appreciate that, unlike Friedman's 'as if' methodology, abstract unifying principles are not capricious, whimsical constraints imposed on economic understanding. Far from being arbitrary, these axioms

> are not plucked out of thin air and far from distancing the theorists from what somewhat mysteriously is called the 'real' world they constitute claims about this world so widely agreed as to make further argument unnecessary.
> (Hahn 1985: 5)

The thesis that economic axioms, like the rationality principle, constitute non-arbitrary claims about the world is central to Hahn's methodological position. These axioms, which are unifying principles of economic understanding, are not

Friedmanite 'as if' imaginative, implausible propositions. On the contrary, they are statements about the real world on which there is widespread consensus.[9] The claim that rational agents know what they want is a generalizing insight on which there is almost universal consensus. We might want to say that, when interpreted as the claim that economic agents have well-ordered preferences over a relevant domain, the rationality axiom is very close to the common sense belief that economic agents are persons.[10] In this sense, the rationality axiom refers to human agents and consequently is not a Friedmanite 'as if' hypothesis. The rationality axiom of economics, however, is not reducible without reminder to the claim that economic agents are persons. In Hahn's terminology, the axiom 'is stronger than that' (Hahn 1985: 6). The universal belief that economic agents are persons is transformed into the rationality axiom of economics by a process of idealization and strengthening. For instance, in the economic axiom of rationality, an agent's preferences are taken to be transitive. In some cases this may actually be false. Hence, the economic axiom is in this sense 'idealized and strengthened' (Hahn 1985: 7), and consequently is not reducible without remainder to the truism that economic agents are persons. The truth that rational agents are persons is not, as such, identical to the rationality axiom of neoclassical economics. To become that axiom, the truism must be sharpened into a precise statement, and in this sense it is strengthened or idealized.

An analogy may be useful here. The axioms of neoclassical economics are like the axioms of Euclidean geometry in that both are precise and clearly stated. They are also like Euclidean geometry in that our common sense perceptions of the spatial world are sharpened and strengthened into Euclidean axioms. For instance, perceptual space is not a mathematical continuum – no one can observe a mathematical continuum, but a continuum is integral to our definition of Euclidean space. Moreover, these Euclidean axioms are central to our mature understanding of space as expressed in, say, Newtonian physics. Finally, given their relationship to our primitive experience of space, Euclidean axioms are not arbitrary constructions. Hahn's axioms, though not reducible to universal or common-sense beliefs, are inextricably linked to such beliefs. Theoretical economists restructure these common sense beliefs into precise axiomatic idealizations. This brings us to Hahn's next point. In the process of idealization, the universal consensus about the common sense belief need no longer hold. In Hahn's terminology, an economic axiom is 'idealized and strengthened by theorists beyond the point at which it commands universal consent' (Hahn 1985: 7). The less than universal consent given to an economic axiom means that further argument about the formulation of that axiom is, in principle, possible. This appears crucial for a correct understanding of Hahn's methodology; in no way are economic theorists dogmatically committed to their economic axioms.

Let us briefly summarize or present a preliminary reconstruction of Hahn's position.[11] In this connection, we use the later Wittgenstein's notion of 'bedrock,' and we adjust Quine's notion of explication. We start with Hahn's basic truth that economic agents are persons. This is bedrock for Hahn. As the later Wittgenstein remarked 'if I have exhausted justifications I have reached bedrock and my spade is turned' (Wittgenstein 2000: 217). Hahn's justification of his choice of some economic axioms finally rests on the bedrock that economic agents are persons. The next step in formulating an economic axiom is taken by *explicating* this bedrock position, thereby transforming it into a rigorous or precisely formulated axiom. The notion of explication used here is Quine's notion of explication adjusted to Wittgenstein's bedrock position. According to Quine, in explicating a vague notion,

> we fix on particular functions of the unclear notion that make it worth troubling about, and then devise a substitute, clear and couched in terms of our liking, that fills these functions. Beyond those conditions of partial agreement, dictated by our interests and purposes, any traits of the explicans come under the head 'don't cares.' Under this head we are free to allow the explicans all manner of novel connotations never associated with the explicandum.
>
> (Quine 1969: 258–9)

An explication is not definition. It is not claiming that the explicans and explicandum are synonymous. Neither is it expressing hidden or subjective private meanings.

In this reconstruction, Hahn is taking the bedrock, common sense claim that economic agents are persons and is explicating it into a precise axiom of rationality. However, unlike Quine, he is explicating a bedrock position which imposes constraints on the head 'don't cares.' For instance, any suggestion that economic agents are infinitely lived agents contradicts the bedrock position and thus cannot be included in an economic axiom. Moreover, like Quine, there is, in principle, more than one way of explicating. Economic theorizing consists in, first, the rigorous mathematical exploration of specific explications and, second, a series of novel thought experiments exploring alternative explications in response to telling critiques of the original one. These new explications or axioms may replace the old ones in the range of 'abstract, unifying principles' used by economists in enriching their understanding.

In this connection, Hahn appears to assume that the changes in economic theory which result from altering its axioms do not result in a *new* theory – the outcome is not revolutionary in the Popperian sense, in which one theory replaces another. For instance, although Hahn is adamant that the earlier theory of rationality has been modified in light of the telling critiques of the transitivity axiom and other limitations, these changes do not justify the claim that a new theory has emerged which has replaced the older one. This position is suggested by his emphasis on 'richer' theories and by his conceptualization of such changes in terms of a 'deepening' rather than a change in our understanding (Hahn 1985: 9). However, one may wish to question this suggestion.

The point being made here may be illustrated by our analogy to Euclidean geometry used above. The changes in Euclidean axioms, when they are reshaped into Riemannian ones, do not deepen or enrich our understanding of Euclidean space. In other words, developments in geometry that resulted from altering the axioms of Euclidean geometry have resulted in a plurality of understandings, rather than a deepening or enrichment of the original Euclidean understanding. Moreover, in the geometrical case, the mode of dynamic theorizing remains the same, namely the reshaping of the axioms of an axiomatic-logico deductive theory. It could thus be argued that Hahn's defence of dynamic ongoing theorizing in economics is logically independent of his thesis that such development in theorizing deepen or enrich our current orthodox understanding, rather than changing that understanding. Hahn's defence of dynamic economic theorizing is logically compatible with the emergence of a new and different theory.[12]

Hahn is very aware of this issue. In his augural lecture as professor of economics in the University of Cambridge he responds by concurring with Einstein's view of the matter:

> Creating a new theory is not like destroying an old barn and erecting a skyscraper in its place. It is rather like climbing a mountain, gaining new and wider views, discovering new connections between our starting point and its rich environment. But the point from which we started still exists and can be seen, although it appears smaller and forms a tiny part of our broad view gained by the mastery of the obstacles on our adventurous way up.
>
> (Einstein, quoted by Hahn 1973(a): 42)

Although one may be sympathetic to this metaphor, one may suspect that Einstein would still want to mark the differences between classical mechanics and relativity theory. Relativity theory is, as implied in the above quote, a *new theory* and deserves to be identified as such.

Assumptions and economic understanding

As we have already seen, the understanding furnished by theoretical economics is dependent on 'abstract unifying principles' that include both axioms and assumptions. 'Whatever it is a theory suggest that we understand, that understanding is contingent on both axioms and assumptions' (Hahn 1985: 11). Hahn is emphatic on this distinction between axioms and assumptions. In this section we focus on how he draws this distinction and its implications for what it is that one understands via economic theory.

In connection with the distinction between axioms and assumptions, Hahn gives us some examples of both. The proposition 'managers have preferences' is an axiom, while it is assumed that these preferences are linear in expected profit. In this case, the assumption is serving the interests of tractability: it facilitates the mathematical exploitation of the issue. According to Hahn, it also 'encapsulates a sort of casual empiricism' in that 'it seems not implausible in light of experience' (Hahn 1985: 11). This example suggests that, although axioms are constrained by what we called 'bedrock' or widespread consensus truths, assumptions are not so constrained. Rather some assumptions are explications of beliefs of 'casual empiricism.' Thus, there is some plausibility to them: they are 'not capriciously imposed' (Hahn 1985: 11).

Another example is that the proposition 'agents have preferences and try to satisfy them' is an axiom, whereas 'universal perfect competition' is an assumption. Hahn's reason for identifying universal perfect competition as an assumption as distinct from an axiom is that 'neither introspection nor observation make it self-evident up to an acceptable margin of error that agents are price takers in all markets' (Hahn 1985: 10–11). Like the previous example, this assumption is too far removed from bedrock truths to make it an axiom.

Let us now turn to what Hahn, in the 1980s, called 'a fashionable example,' namely rational expectations theory. He insists that the proposition 'an agent whose forecasts of future events are systematically disappointed will change his forecasts' is an axiom (Hahn 1985: 11). That proposition is semantically very close to the truism that rational people will not persist in an erroneous belief; hence it is an axiom. On the other hand, the proposition 'agents have rational expectations' is an assumption. *Prima facie* one may feel that Hahn is engaged in esoteric hair-splitting. However, Hahn is insistent that this distinction is crucial. His reason for insisting that the proposition 'agents have rational expectations' is an assumption and not an axiom is that 'there are great difficulties in understanding' how an agent could acquire such expectations' (Hahn 1985: 11). The assumption presupposes that economic agents have learned to make forecasts that are not systematically disappointed, with no understanding of how that state is achievable. In other words, according to Hahn, identifying a proposition or propositions as assumptions, in cases like this example, is signalling to economists that there are gaps in our understandings which do not exist in the case of axioms, and that these gaps are challenges which must be addressed by economic theorizing.

Moreover, in this particular case, i.e. rational expectations theory, the gap is not satisfactorily filled by Rational Expectations econometrics with good fits. His reason for this is that 'we cannot understand why it should fit well' (Hahn 1985: 11). Rational expectations econometrics with good fits does not enhance our understanding. In Hahn's eyes 'the evidence for miracles at Lourdes is stronger than is this econometrics' (ibid.: 11). Those who claim that rational expectations econometrics with good fits suffices to fill the gap in that the assumption is verified may, under the influence of Friedman's methodology of economics, be tempted to exclude genuine economic challenges from their research agenda, thereby imposing unnecessary limitations on economists' efforts at understanding.

Before turning to the issue of what it is we understand via economic theory, we revisit our preliminary reconstruction of the role of axioms in economic theorizing, outlined in the previous section. In that reconstruction we underlined the fact that, in principle, there is more than one way of explicating, and we implied that economic axioms are open to a plurality of explications. This reconstruction was motivated by Hahn's claim that economic axioms are 'strengthened' and 'idealized' versions of basic, bedrock truths, combined with his claim that, in theorizing at the frontiers of research, 'the questioning of almost everything, for instance the rationality postulate, is not a sign of crisis but of vigorous endeavour' (Hahn 1992(a): 5). However, in light of the manner in which he draws the distinction between axioms and some assumptions, especially his claim of the semantical proximity of some economic axioms to bedrock truths, the scope for explication would appear to be rather limited. Given this, and in view of the thesis that economic understanding is contingent on both axioms and assumptions, one may suggest that the scope for alternative explications largely rests with the assumptions. This suggestion is plausible in view of the thesis that some assumptions are explications of beliefs informed by what Hahn calls 'a casual empiricism,' but pragmatic considerations, such as simplicity, govern the introduction of others. Thus one has much greater latitude with the content of assumptions vis-à-vis the content of axioms. On the one hand, assumptions are not governed by the constraints of bedrock truths – the hallmark of axioms. On the other hand, they are not capriciously imposed. There are good reasons for using them, ranging from casual empiricism to tractability and simplicity.

In so far as a casual empiricism constrains the content of assumptions, economic understanding by means of a theory based on such assumptions is, in some sense, about the real world. Economic assumptions, however, may be much more informed by tractability–simplicity considerations. In this connection, Hahn notes that the mathematical ability to simplify may well lead to the introduction of quite unrealistic assumptions. Thus, he advises 'circumspection in praising simplicity in economic theorizing' (Hahn 1994: 250). He re-echoes the famous, early Wittgensteinian thesis enunciated at the end of the *Tractatus*: 'what we cannot speak about we must pass over in silence' (Wittgenstein 1963: 151). Hahn puts it this way, 'If at a certain stage of knowledge, nothing can be said without drastic simplifying falsification, then perhaps we should keep quiet' (Hahn 1994: 251). In this connection, while expressing 'considerable impatience when silly models[13] are defended by virtue of their simplicity' (Hahn 1994: 251), he admits that he himself has not always adhered to his own advice. For instance, he concedes that 'a good deal' of his work is based on the simplification of perfect competition and the absence of increasing returns. Indeed in his view, 'the perfect competition simplification has had rather disastrous effects on macro-economics' (Hahn 1994: 252). Be that as it may, to sum up, in Hahn's view, economic assumptions are introduced on considerations ranging from specific beliefs of casual empiricism to simplicity, with many occupying the simplicity end of the spectrum. Vis-à-vis the latter, the price is eternal vigilance.

We now turn to the issue of what it is we understand by means of economic theory. In general, because of economists' acknowledgement of the role of assumptions in their reasoning 'it becomes crystal clear that application to the 'real' world could at best be provisional' (Hahn 1994: 246). This, for instance, applies to his own work on the assumption of perfect competition. He insists that he 'never took the results as applicable economics,' unlike many macroeconomists (Hahn 1994: 252). Rather, with this assumption one is 'a good many stages removed from actual economies' (ibid.: 252). Similarly, in connection with rational expectations theory, what is provided is 'an understanding of an *imagined* economy which satisfies the assumption' (Hahn 1985: 11, italics added).

We are now in a position to *begin* to complete Hahn's picture of economic understanding. It is 'contingent on both axioms and assumptions' (Hahn 1985: 11). Economic understanding is achieved by deductively deriving the logical consequences of the axioms subject to the constraints of specific assumptions, and, by refining the axioms or weakening the assumptions, we facilitate 'an orderly and coherent deepening of our understanding' (Hahn 1985: 9). In this connection, it is worth noting Hahn's own formulation of his central thesis: '*whatever it is a theory suggest that we understand*, that understanding is contingent on both axioms and assumptions' (Hahn 1985: 11, italics added). This formulation, *prima facie* at least, suggests a shift in, or qualification of, Hahn's initial account of economic understanding outlined in the previous sections. The aim of economic understanding, as outlined earlier, is, in Hahn's terminology, directly focused on the 'understanding of the particular,' which he immediately instances as the understanding of 'an event or a series of events' (Hahn 1985: 3). In other words, and as one would expect, economic theorizing is primarily concerned with understanding actual economies, events in these economies, actions of economic agents and so on. This is clearly achievable within the parameters of Hahn's methodology, if we confine understanding to economic axioms.

However, when assumptions are added to the constraints on economic understanding, what we appear to understand is not actual economies, but imagined ones that satisfy the specified assumptions. Hahn is well aware of this. To put it concisely and bluntly, when economic assumptions are introduced, as they invariably are, we shift to what would be found if actual economies *were* to satisfy the stated assumptions. The cognitive process of understanding has shifted from the actual to the counterfactual conditional,[14] and, as Hahn notes, this shift 'leaves us with a whole set of possible worlds' (Hahn 1993(b): 164). Moreover, since 'the basic assumptions of much of our theory are often of low descriptive merit' (Hahn 1993(b): 163), one might be tempted to conclude that any theoretical understanding contingent on such assumptions cannot contribute very much to our understanding of actual economies. How can the enterprise of economic theorizing, which results in a 'construction' that is neither 'descriptive' nor 'immediately applicable,' enhance our correct understanding of actual economies? If 'everything I will teach you (in economic theorizing) is in a certain sense false' (Hahn 1996: 191), is not this contributing to our misunderstanding of real economies? What we gain an understanding of is not a real economy; rather, all we succeed in understanding is an idealized fiction.

The imagined, idealized economy of good, as distinct from bad, economic theorizing, is not, for Hahn, a pure fiction. It lies somewhere between a purely fictitious picture and 'the messy reality' (Hahn 1996: 193) of actual economies. We have already seen that both the axioms and assumptions of good economic theorizing are not capriciously imposed. They are not poetic works of unconstrained imaginations. They are serious attempts at imposing precision on the messy reality of actual economies. Moreover, by responding to a legitimate critique of its axioms or by weakening its assumptions, economists can move somewhat closer to the messy reality of actual economies.

In short, economic theorizing neither furnishes us with purely fictitious speculations nor with pure descriptions of actual economies. In this connection, it should be noted that, while the understanding gained is of imagined economies which satisfy the assumptions – and thus what one understands may be a relatively long way removed from actual economies – a theory based on such assumptions 'may be of great use' (Hahn 1985: 11). For instance, in connection with rational expectations theory, if one were to dismiss it on the grounds of its assumptions, this would be a 'vulgar misunderstanding of theory and its aims' (Hahn 1985: 11). As we have already seen, in view of its basic assumption, this theory is not a description. Indeed, for Hahn, the situation is much worse; even if the theory is understood as a 'thought experiment,' it is still, from the theoretical point of view, 'pretty shaky' (Hahn 1985: 12). Nonetheless, it cannot be dismissed as useless. It, for instance, allows one 'to study pathologies which cannot be traced to expectational mistakes.... Or yet again it allows us to grasp the informational disturbances introduced by an unknown monetary policy' (Hahn 1985: 11). In these ways, it may contribute to our understanding. In short, the imaginary economies of theoretical economics, while neither describing nor explaining in the sense of revealing the fundamental or essential mechanisms operating in a real economy, are useful in various ways; from highly intellectual issues at one end of the range to the study of pathologies et alia at the other end, we gain in understanding. However, for Hahn, the constant challenge is to enrich and deepen these partial understandings.

Economic theory and a grammar of argumentation: Wittgensteinian waters

As we have already seen, neoclassical theorizing does not furnish us with a descriptively adequate account of real economies, and neither is it exceptionally good at predicting the future. Rather, what we gain is understanding of imagined economies which meet the specified assumptions. Thus, applied economics is not like engineering. Nonetheless, economics 'is both useful and important' (Hahn 1993(b): 163). One of its central uses is as 'a line of first defence against madmen and witches' (Hahn 1985: 4). A crucial reason for this success lies in Hahn's insight that economic theory is 'a kind of grammar – a way of speaking coherently about complex social events' (Hahn 1994: 247). What economic theory 'delivers at present is a route for grammatical argument and methods for usefully summarizing such economic data as there are. The "grammar" I take very seriously' (Hahn 1993(b): 163). Despite the fact that he, time and again, refers to economic theory as a grammar, and despite his assertion that he takes this claim very seriously, he does not explicitly and systematically elaborate on this claim. We suggest that his thesis that economic theory is a grammar contains a constellation of methodological claims, and we address some of these here.

The first claim in this methodological constellation is the thesis that economic theory supplies economists with a sophisticated language, and that this language has a public sense. There are a number of philosophical–methodological layers to this claim. With his emphasis on language, we take it that one may legitimately locate Hahn's methodology in what has been called 'the linguistic turn' in twentieth century philosophy. This linguistic turn marks a paradigm shift in philosophy that was effected by Frege, the early Wittgenstein and others at the end of the nineteenth and beginning of the twentieth century. This shift was initially dominated by a logical analysis of language. The later Wittgenstein and others took this paradigm shift down additional roads to those explored in strict logical analysis.

From the seventeenth century up to the linguistic turn, epistemology, in both rationalist and empiricist approaches, was largely conducted in the domain of individual, mentalist psychology. The epistemological primacy was given to cognitive psychology, while language was given a subsidiary role. For instance, in a quasi-Humean epistemology,[15] knowledge began with individual perceptions, e.g. I look and I see a tree. The next step is that I close my eyes and form an image of the tree. The next step lies in the formation of my idea of a tree which is merely a less clear image. Thus my concept of a tree is a vague image. Finally, my concept of a tree is, if I am a native English speaker expressed by the word 'tree' or if I were a native French speaker it would be expressed by the word 'arbe.' In this epistemology, knowledge has a large subjective, private basis.

The linguistic turn fundamentally changes this epistemological approach. After the linguistic turn, having an idea or concept has nothing to do with psychological images or indeed private mental states. Having the idea or concept of a tree, for instance, is having the ability to use the word 'tree,' as it is used in English. Conceptual ability is linguistic ability. Frege launched the linguistic turn with his famous principle 'always to separate sharply the psychological from the logical, the subjective from the objective' (Frege 1968 (1884): x). For instance, cognitive psychologists are legitimately interested in the issue of the psychological origin of the concept 'number.' Their results, however, are of no help to mathematics teachers in teaching the mathematical continuum to their pupils. What is important here are the logical relationships, not the psychological origins.

Moreover, by means of his famous distinction between sense and reference, Frege demonstrated how sense is always public. The reference may be public or private, e.g. the reference of the term 'cow' is public, while the reference to the term 'pain in my tooth' is private and the term 'leprechaun' has no reference. However, in all cases the sense is public – the sense for the later Wittgenstein is given by the correct usage of these terms and expressions. The sense or meaning of numerous terms is grasped when one grasps how to use these terms in their appropriate settings. For instance, if we want to know whether the child has the concept of, say, 'sheep' we engage the child in conversation to see how he is using the word 'sheep': we cannot look into his head and see his innermost mental processes.

Let us now return to Hahn's methodology. First, given this linguistic turn, we can say that Hahn's central notion of understanding is liberated from the chains of inner privacy or subjectivity. The sense of the expression 'understanding' is public. In, for instance, much of nineteenth century hermeneutics understanding was taken to be inherently subjective, being identified with some private inner state or process. In the linguistic turn the focus is on the 'grammar' of the term 'understanding,' which is public. Second, take the economic term 'equilibrium.' Numerous methodologists focus on the origins of that concept in the domain of classical mechanics. For the historian of economic thought, professional research into, say, how Walras was influenced by Poincaré's *Science and Hypothesis* in developing his views of equilibrium would be an invaluable contribution to historical scholarship. However, such scholarship will not be of much help to anyone who wants to understand the notion of equilibrium in, say, the Arrow–Debreu general equilibrium theory, or indeed in Hahn's theoretical development of that theory. Rather, *à la* the later Wittgenstein, economists demonstrate their understanding of the latter notion of equilibrium when they have *mastered its usage* in that theory. The focus shifts to *mastery of use*, away from psychological or historical origins. In this Wittgensteinian, gramatico-linguistic context, one can appreciate Hahn's claim that the history of economic thought is not a discipline 'which either greatly pleases me or engages my deepest interests. I want to get on with the business of understanding the world rather than with the understanding of the manner someone else understood it' (Hahn 2005(a): 6).

Furthermore, for Hahn, economic theory has the *linguistic* capacity to add to the resources of natural language, and thereby to add to economists' linguistic 'tools' when dealing with the messy reality of real economies. Contrary to numerous realist philosophers of economic theory who insist that economic theory *must* or *should* furnish us with *the explanation* of the path of real economies by revealing their generative mechanisms, economic theory is a grammar of argumentation. One important task of such a grammar is to extend our conceptual tools beyond the rather limited resources of what was bequeathed to us by our natural languages. Economic theory extends our conceptual resources by its linguistic innovations, especially by its use of the sophisticated language of mathematics. These extensions are indispensable in economic analyses of complex social events. Again, there is no contamination by anything subjective: these innovations are public, i.e. are publicly understood.

The thesis that the sense of economic theory is public has another significant methodological implication for Hahn. This implication concerns the issue of Kuhnian incommensurability, where economists in espousing different theories or paradigms end up failing to communicate with each other, i.e. 'speaking past each other' (Hahn 1993(b): 163). Certainly, Kuhn's thesis of meaning variance across theoretical divides is very plausible in a Wittgensteinian context. Given that the meaning of a term is intimately related to its usage within a theory or a paradigm, then there is meaning variance across theoretical divides. To take Hahn's own example, the term 'rational' is used in different ways in the neoclassical theory of rationality and Simon's theory of bounded rationality – there is meaning variance across the divide.

According to Hahn, however, in these circumstances 'economic theorists can speak to each other and not past each other' (Hahn 1993(b): 163). This is because, First, 'Simon's argument gains what force it has by the existence of the pure theory which he finds wanting' (Hahn 1985: 8). Hahn, *prima facie*, has a good point here. Given that Simon is criticizing neoclassical theory, there cannot be complete incommensurability, unless of course one assumes Simon is criticizing 'a straw man' of his own making. Hahn's second reason for denying incommensurability is that neoclassical theory 'provides the language in which proposals, like Simon's, can be discussed' (Hahn 1985: 8). This reason, *prima facie*, prejudices the issue in favour of neoclassical theory. Presumably Simon would want to maintain that his theory also provides the language for discussing and criticizing the neoclassical theory. Hahn, however, would challenge this retort. He remarks 'who can deny that Simon has a good point? But who also can deny that 'satisfying' does nothing much to meet it?' (Hahn 1985: 8).

The language of Simon's 'satisfying' theory is rather primitive relative to the sophisticated, mathematically regimented language of neoclassical theory. Indeed, Simon's critique can be integrated into the language of neoclassical theory 'to deepen our understanding of what we already have' (Hahn 1985: 8). Once again, Hahn gives us a clear example of what he has in mind. If a consumer buys a good at a higher price than the price of the same good somewhere else, this is puzzling because neoclassical theory does not, *prima facie*, account for that event. Simon, however, enables the neoclassical economist to address this puzzle by proposing that the consumer may not know about the cheaper good and 'that he would have to expend effort to find out. He will spend that effort if his aspirations not to be taken for a ride are seriously impaired, i.e. when he believes the gain from search is large enough' (Hahn 1985: 9).

There are two distinct methodological issues at play here. The first is the issue of incommensurability. We concur with Hahn that there is not a complete breakdown in communication between neoclassical economists and Simon. Our reasons for this, however, are different to Hahn. Both Hahn, as the representative of neoclassical theory, and Simon share the pre-theoretical notion of rationality in that both subscribe to the bedrock truth that economic agents are persons. This offers some guarantee that communication across the theoretical divide will not completely break down. Our second reason is much more philosophical: it hinges on what philosophers of science call the principle of charitable translation, or the principle of charity for short. This principle is used in the context of two conflicting theoretical languages for which there is no neutral third language available into which the rival languages could be translated, and thereby their respective merits objectively, i.e. neutrally, assessed. This, *prima facie*, is the case with Simon and Hahn. In this connection, we will enunciate a prescriptive version of the principle, adapted to the situation in economics. The principle demands that neoclassical economists should charitably translate Simon's theory into its own by maximizing the plausibility of as many as possible of Simon's claims in neoclassical theory and *vice versa* for Simonite economists. In that manner the meaning variance is overcome without misguided recourse to what does not exist, i.e. a neutral language. After that, one is in a better position to evaluate the merits of each side. We will return to this issue in Chapter 8 when we address Velupillai's computable economics, which he develops in the shadow of Simon.

We now turn to another methodological implication of Hahn's view of economic theory as a grammar. This concerns what he himself calls his own 'excessively cerebral approach to economics' (Hahn 1993(b): 164), which we will argue, is much more concerned with logico-grammatical problems at the theoretical end of the spectrum of economic research than the empirical end, including the issues of economic policy. He acknowledges that he was stirred on his first reading of Keynes by the promise of more sensible policies. 'But what in the end proved most exciting was the prospect of studying whether the claims *could* be made true and under what assumptions' (Hahn 1993(b): 164, italics in original). In general, since the linguistic turn, the 'cerebral' task of identifying the conditions under which various complex propositions *could* be true or false, is a logico-grammatical, and not an empirical, issue. Indeed, this 'cerebral' task is inextricably linked to the notion of understanding in the context of the linguistic turn. We already noted how, in the Fregian–Wittgenstein approach, the sense of a term is public. Frege, however, was not only concerned with the sense of terms, he was also concerned with understanding the sense of complex propositions. He proposed the thesis that *to understand a complex proposition* is to grasp its truth conditions, i.e. the conditions under which it *could* be true or false.

To illustrate this we take a very elementary example from truth–functional logic – the logic of propositions developed by Frege and Russell. Take the proposition 'Gordon Browne did not blink his left eye on the morning of the third of January, 1981, at 8.23 a.m.' In truth–functional logic, this is a complex proposition constructed from *the negation* of the more elementary proposition 'Gordon Browne blinked his left eye on the morning of the third of January, 1981 at 8.23 a.m.' (The negation makes the opening example complex). In the Fregian context, I understand that complex proposition because I grasp its 'truth conditions,' even though I have no way of empirically verifying it (and we hope the reader will be sufficiently charitable to assume it is not verifiable. For the more critical reader we take the example of 'the leaves of the tree in my garden are not green even when no one is observing them'). The truth conditions of the Gordon Browne example are schematically presented in the following truth table.

Table A

P	Not P
T	F
F	T

Negatively, if, for instance, a child does not grasp these truth conditions then the child does not understand the proposition 'Gordon Browne did not blink his left eye on the morning of the third of January, 1981, at 8.23 a.m.' In short, integral to the correct understanding of any complex proposition is grasping the conditions under which it *could* be true or false; logicians call this grasping its truth conditions. Specifying these truth conditions is, in the logical sense, a grammatical task, not an empirical one.

Once we move out of the domain of truth–functional logic and quantification theory into other domains, the specification of truth conditions proves to be a very challenging and difficult task. This is very evident in, for instance, the 'grammatical' work of the philosopher Donald Davidson. In Hahn's methodology, economic theorizing, as a grammar of argumentation, is attempting to accomplish this challenging task. Thus, Hahn insists that 'what in the end proved most exciting was the prospect of studying whether the claims made could be true and under what assumptions' (Hahn 1993(b): 164). For instance, when we read the pioneering work of Arrow and Debreu in this grammatical way, it becomes quickly evident that its truth conditions are such that the theory leaves us a good many stages removed from actual economies, and thus it 'does not describe the world' (Hahn 1985: 14). The aim of the theory is not to describe the actual world – 'there is nothing here (in general equilibrium theory) to tell us that any given economy will be in that state or that it tends to that state' (Hahn 1985: 12). In short, while general equilibrium is like rational expectations in that neither can be read as a description, Hahn insists that 'if we did not have Arrow–Debreu theory it would be priority number one to construct it. For while it does not describe the world it is a solid starting point for the quest for understanding it' (Hahn 1985: 14).

There is, *prima facie*, a puzzle here. Both are based on a 'lack of realism' but general equilibrium is 'the ideal reference point' in economists' search for understanding (Hahn 1985: 13). The question is what privileges general equilibrium theory such that it is a solid starting point in economic understanding? We will return to this issue in the next section. In the meantime, our concern is to emphasize that, for Hahn, this theory clearly specifies its truth conditions. For instance, to take Hahn's own example (Hahn 1993(b): 163, 164), the claim that the American economy is in competitive equilibrium may be in dispute. However, both sides *understand the meaning* of this claim by reference to its *truth conditions* as articulated in general equilibrium theory. This common understanding is guaranteed because the conditions under which the theory could be true or false are explicitly and clearly stated – no mean 'cerebral' achievement.

Hahn appears to be aware of the possibility of locating his approach to understanding in the linguistic turn. In the opening paragraphs of his 'In Praise of Economic Theory,' he remarks 'I am aware that these are deep Wittgensteinian waters into which however I do not propose to splash or drown' (Hahn 1985: 3). In this section, we have merely paddled in these Wittgensteinian waters in order to further buttress the non-subjective dimension of economic theorizing as a grammar of argumentation. When we come to the proof of existence in general equilibrium, we will have to venture further into the deep where other Wittgensteinian currents may prove much more threatening.

Neoclassical economics and Hahn's commitments

In the opening section of this chapter we focused on the dynamic relationship between the activity of theorizing and the outcome of that activity, i.e. the emerging theory. In the subsequent sections we have largely concentrated on Hahn's account of economic theorizing. In this section we look at some of his constraints on the content of economic theory in the neoclassical tradition. He is aware that, in the eyes of some, e.g. neo-Ricardians, he is perceived as 'a dyed-in-the-wood neo-classical who considered Arrow–Debreu adequate for all of economics' (Hahn 1984: 18). Naturally, he rejects this characterization. Nonetheless, he reluctantly accepts being labelled a neoclassical economist and specifies in what sense this term can be correctly applied to himself. In this connection he identifies three 'commitments' (Hahn 1984: 2). These are:

> 1 I am a reductionist in that I attempt to locate explanations in the actions of individual agents.
> 2 In theorizing about the agent I look for some axioms of rationality.
> 3 I hold some notion of equilibrium is required and that the study of equilibrium states is useful.
>
> (Hahn 1984: 1–2)

Hahn tells us that he is 'not equally comfortable' with these commitments. Vis-à-vis point 1, his conviction is 'pretty strong' (Hahn 1984: 2). If we distinguish between a strong and a weak form of reductionism by defining strong reductionism as the programme whereby all references to macro notions and to institutions must be eliminated in terms of individual parameters, then Hahn is not a strong reductionist. He is willing to accept that 'the whole may differ from the sum of its parts,' but in his view such claims make sense only 'when one starts at the level of the individual' (Hahn 1984: 2). In line with this, a weak reductionist starts with the individual and denies that there are laws governing the movement of social structures which work independently of human agency. In this connection, Hahn admits to not knowing the extensive literature by holistic philosophers in depth. Nonetheless, 'what I have read and what I have heard argued leaves me faithful to (1)' (Hahn 1984: 2).

In relation to point 2, one may be surprised to see Hahn maintaining that 'I can also be *wrong* in the acceptance of (2) and as I have already said I hold to it because I can see no other alternative of comparable power and appeal' (Hahn 1984: 2, italics added). These claims are, *prima facie*, quite different from his analysis and defence of rationality outlined earlier. In that defence, Hahn starts with the thesis that economic agents are persons, and he idealized and strengthened that truth into the rationality axiom in such a way that it would be highly improbable to claim that he could be wrong in accepting that axiom. In light of what he maintains here, however, one might be tempted to say that his earlier defence of the rationality axiom is merely a matter of looking at it in theory. *In practice*, the rationality axiom is not like that. 'In practice an axiom of rationality postulates a complete preordering of alternatives and a choice which is not dominated (in preference) by another available one' (Hahn 1984: 2). In this context, i.e. in practice, Hahn emphasizes 'its dangers' and 'its weakness,' but defends it on the grounds of its 'theoretical fruitfulness' (Hahn 1984: 2).

In short, Hahn has two different rationality axioms: one which holds in theory and the other which holds in practice. Indeed, he expressly admits to this when he insists that 'the real danger is this: one is tempted to confuse the narrowed formulation with the axiom of rationality itself' (Hahn 1984: 3). The 'axiom of rationality itself' is what we are saying holds in theory, whereas the narrowly formulated one is the axiom which holds in practice. What are philosophers and others interested in methodology to make of this distinction, especially the status of 'the rationality axiom itself?' Certainly Dasgupta's remarks come to mind. When addressing 'internal' attacks on economics (i.e. attacks by economists rather than methodologists) he locates them in a 'lineage which often operates at an Olympian height of generality,' and which 'usually works round what modern economists *say* in their "literary" moments rather than what they actually *do* in their technical work' (Dasgupta 2002: 58). Surely, what is sauce for the goose is sauce for the gander: the same lineage applies to defences as well as attacks. Is Hahn's axiom of rationality in theory to be located as part of the largely irrelevant 'literary' discourse of methodologists living in a remote Mount Olympus totally cut off from economic practice?

In our opinion, such a suggestion does not do justice to the situation; the situation is the internalist dispute among reputable economists about whether or not neoclassical economics has the necessary resources to adequately solve the major economic problems facing the profession. In such a dispute, each side displays the advantages of its own position and the disadvantages of its opponents' position. As we have already argued, in an ideal rational discussion, each side should use a principle of charity in translating the opponent's position, even when the aim is to show its disadvantages. In displaying the advantages of one's own position, the situation in economics is analogous to 'crisis' disputes, which occur in the physical sciences from time to time when the experts there disagree. As Kuhn points out, in that situation physical scientists behave *professionally* in continuing with their research projects and also they behave *like philosophers* in defending their framework by recourse to methodological analyses. Similarly, in a dispute about the future direction of economics, both research activity and methodological argumentation are relevant to the merits of the case being made. In relegating the methodological dimension to 'literary moments,' one fails to do justice to the nature of the dispute.

Hahn's methodology is thus core to his defence of neoclassical economics, and cannot be dismissed on the grounds that one should look at what he does in his research, rather than looking at what he says he is doing. Both are indispensable to the defence of neoclassical economics when challenged by other reputable economists. In particular, his distinction between the narrowly conceived rationality axiom used in practice and what we called the rationality principle 'in theory' is significant. Although these axioms are not identical, they are not utterly unrelated. The narrower axiom of rationality used in practice is, in principle, analysable into the core axiom, i.e. the axiom in theory, and assumptions. Most of the difficulties reside with the assumptions, and these are open to radical review in economic theorizing. The core axiom, however, is not similarly open to criticism. This analysis is a key argument for Hahn in his defence of neoclassical economics. This key argument is buttressed by the other argument on the grounds of fruitfulness for the narrower axiom. In short, Hahn's rationality axiom in theory cannot reasonably be banished to a mythical Mount Olympus with no relevance to the discipline of economics. If one condemns it to such an exile, one is betraying the heritage of rationality, which has been defended by philosophers over the centuries and which is indispensable to any well-argued case addressing the issue at hand, i.e. the correct direction economics *should* take.

We now turn to his third commitment, the indispensability of some notion of equilibrium. Like his commitment to point 1, Hahn is equally secure with it. This commitment, however, is very general, one might say vague: the commitment is to some notion or other of equilibrium, not to a specific one. Clearly, the commitment presupposes a multiplicity of concepts of equilibrium. In this connection, Hahn is very explicit: time and again he draws our attention to the distinction between the multiplicity of concepts of equilibrium on the one hand and the concept of multiple equilibria on the other (Hahn 1973(a): 11). Among the range of equilibrium concepts encountered in economics, we have, for instance, long-run equilibrium and short-run equilibrium, stochastic equilibrium and steady-state equilibrium (Hahn 1996: 189). This open-ended range of equilibrium concepts should not be confused with the notion of multiple equilibria, i.e. the non-uniqueness of a specific equilibrium state. For instance, as Hahn notes, the Arrow–Debreu equilibrium concept does not imply uniqueness; there is the possibility of 'many states which are Arrow–Debreu equilibria' (ibid.: 11).

In his inaugural lecture 'On the Notion of Equilibrium in Economics,' Hahn opens with 'wherever economics is used or thought about, equilibrium is a central organizing idea' (Hahn 1973(a): 1). The term 'equilibrium' is, for instance, to be found in popular analyses of an economy by economic journalists, in speeches by ministers of finance and among theoretical economists. Clearly, Hahn's focus is on the latter, i.e. its use in theoretical economics, especially the Arrow–Debreu general equilibrium theory. The Arrow–Debreu equilibrium has a long lineage going back to Adam Smith's famous metaphor of the invisible hand. From the common sense point of view, this metaphor has very little going for it. Hahn calls it 'astonishing.' This astonishing claim maintains that 'it is logically possible to describe an economy in which millions of agents, looking no further than their own interests and responding to the sparse information system of prices only, can still attain a coherent economic disposition of resources' (Hahn 1982(a): 114).

According to Hahn, Arrow and Debreu provided the first essential step in any serious discussion of the invisible hand. They 'wrote down precise, and beyond the power of misunderstanding of a normal person, what state of an economy was to be designated as an equilibrium' (Hahn 1985: 12). Thus, in place of the various usages of the terms 'equilibrium' and 'invisible hand' found in the history of economic thought, Arrow and Debreu introduce a very precise formulation of an equilibrium that is readily understandable to normal persons. Perhaps one should add, to normal persons with extensive mathematical training. Be that as it may, given this precise formulation, the next step was to prove that such a state could exist. In doing this, 'it became clear that without certain assumptions it would always be possible to describe an economy of the kind which they considered for which no equilibrium existed' (Hahn 1985: 12). Hahn continues:

> No ambiguity of what it is that is being done is possible. We are concerned with the existence of a particular state of the economy in which the best choices of individuals are mutually compatible when these choices are entirely determined by preferences, technology endowments and market prices. There is nothing here to tell us that any given economy will be in that state or that it tends to that state.
>
> (Hahn 1985: 12)

In other words, on the basis of very restrictive assumptions, the existence proof establishes 'the logical possibility' of this equilibrium state (Hahn 1982(a): 114). No claim is being made about actual economies. The Arrow–Debreu results merely show that, under certain assumptions, a specific invisible hand state is logically possible. Clearly, general equilibrium is neither a description of an actual economy nor is it serving any explanatory role in terms of specifying the hidden mechanisms of real economies.

According to Hahn, this general equilibrium 'is the crown of Neo-classical theory' (Hahn 2005(a): 8). Moreover, in a rather rare Popperian vein, he maintains that the Arrow–Debreu general equilibrium is 'a vastly superior theory to preceding theories' (Hahn 2005(a): 7). Indeed, in an explicitly '*ex cathedra*' manner, he asks us to 'recall that the "classics" and their followers… were theorists hook, line and sinker, and G.E. has made it clear that they were bad theorists' (Hahn 2005(a): 8). Thus, as we already noted, Hahn, as a theoretician, dismisses the history of economic thought. He sums up his attitude: 'let the dead bury the dead and let us get down to real questions' (Hahn 2005(a): 8). One may wonder what principle of charitable translation Hahn is using in his *ex cathedra* dismissal of the classicists as bad theorists? We can't imagine an Einstein or a Heisenberg dismissing classical physicists as bad theorists. For the moment, we will leave Hahn's '*ex cathedra*' claims aside and focus on his thesis that general equilibrium is the crown of neoclassical theory.

In particular, 'Arrow and Debreu are 'the giants of equilibrium theory' (Hahn 1985: 12). Later, he remarks that 'if we did not have Arrow–Debreu theory it would be *priority number one* to construct it. For while it does not describe *the world* it is a solid starting point for the quest for understanding *it*' (Hahn 1985: 14, italics added). On the one hand, Arrow–Debreu equilibrium is neither a description nor the explanation of the economic world – the assumptions under which it could exist are such as to leave us a long way from the actual economic world. On the other hand, it is 'a solid starting point' in economists' quest for understanding the real world. This brings us back to our puzzle at the end of the last section; Arrow–Debreu equilibrium theory is like rational expectations in that both, given their assumptions, are a long way from the real world. However, general equilibrium, not rational expectations, constitutes 'a solid starting point' in understanding the world.

The starting point in general equilibrium has numerous advantages. First, 'it is precise, complete and unambiguous' (Hahn 1973(a): 3). In these respects, there is nothing to match it in neoclassical economics. In this sense, it is 'the crown' of neoclassical economics. Second, it is 'extraordinary fertile' in generating new questions and answers (Hahn 2005(a): 11). For instance, Arrow–Debreu worked out their theory on the assumption that markets are complete. 'The next question' was 'what happened if they are not?' (Hahn 2005(a): 12). This gave rise to further theorizing. Third, 'it is possible to pinpoint with great accuracy where change is required if a change is made in the economic circumstances it is asked to illuminate' (Hahn 1973(a): 3). For instance, it is unquestionably clear that 'increasing returns are a telling objection' to Arrow–Debreu equilibrium (Hahn 1973(a): 12). In view of this objection, economists engaged in further theorizing.

After some research, the following result emerged. 'If in a precise sense increasing returns are small relative to the scale of the economy there is an Arrow–Debreu equilibrium which is an approximate equilibrium for the increasing returns economy' (Hahn 1973(a): 13). Obviously, this result is a significant addition to our understanding. However, this result implies, as Hahn correctly states, 'the whole theory (Arrow–Debreu) is at risk if there are increasing returns which are large relative to the size of the economy' (Hahn 1982(a): 116). Hahn does not flinch in spelling out the consequence. 'So even in the world of pure theory, the invisible hand may falter and such market outcomes as appear may be unsatisfactory, since they may have to involve monopolistic elements' (Hahn 1982(a): 116). This, again, is a considerable addition to the correct understanding of the invisible hand. 'The invisible hand is likely to be unsure in its operation and occasionally downright arthritic' (Hahn 1982(a): 129), a point often not properly understood by those who unquestionably invoke this hand for their own political purposes. In short, by starting with Arrow–Debreu equilibrium, we gain a better understanding of aspects of real economies on the one hand and also a better understanding of the invisible hand from a purely theoretical point of view, on the other.

Nonetheless, Hahn acknowledges that 'every feature of *an actual economy* which Keynes regarded as important is missing in Debreu' (Hahn 1973(a): 34, italics added). Thus, an indispensable part of economic theorizing is concerned with constructing a 'more "feet on the ground" Keynesian' notion of equilibrium' (Hahn 1973(a): 16). Indeed, he says that the Arrow–Debreu notion 'gives way to the "more feet on the ground" Keynesian one' (ibid.: 16). If we take this notion of 'giving way to' in a strong sense, then the Arrow–Debreu conception of equilibrium would be consigned to the history of economic thought, which, according to Hahn, can be ignored by practising economists engaged in understanding the real world. Hahn, however, does not appear willing to go that far. He asks us to 'think of externalities, of imperfect competition, of increasing returns and many other 'realistic' phenomena and ask how we could fit them into our comprehension *without the ideal reference point* provided by Arrow–Debreu' (Hahn 1985: 13, italics added). On the one hand, Arrow–Debreu equilibrium 'gives way to the more 'feet on the ground' Keynesian one and, on the other, it is *the ideal* reference point in our understanding of these realistic Keynesian insights. In short, is the Arrow–Debreu equilibrium a dispensable or an indispensable starting point in our understanding *the economic world?*

If one takes the Einstein metaphor of theory change seriously, as noted earlier, then Arrow–Debreu equilibrium is an indispensable starting point. We repeat the quote here:

> Creating a new theory… is rather like climbing a mountain, gaining new and wider views, *discovering new connections between our starting point and its rich environment.* But the point from which we started still exists and can be seen, although it appears smaller and forms a tiny part of our broad view gained by mastery of the obstacles on our adventurous way up.
>
> (Hahn 1973(a): 42, italics added)

In light of this metaphor, the Arrow–Debreu equilibrium is an indispensable starting point for economic theorizing. As we climb the mountain of understanding the world, we discover new connections between the Arrow–Debreu starting point and its rich environment, identified by Keynes and others who draw our attention to actual features of real economies. In mastering these Keynesian obstacles, we broaden our understanding. In this broader terrain, the Arrow–Debreu starting point continues to exist, but naturally *appears* smaller. If we connect this to what he claimed earlier, its small size is merely an appearance. This starting point 'is asked to illuminate' changes in real economic circumstances and it is so constructed that 'it is possible to pinpoint with great accuracy where a change is required' (Hahn 1973(a): 3). It suggests that, in economic theorizing, the Arrow–Debreu equilibrium is used to illuminate different domains, and it is adjusted in different ways depending on the domain in question.

In this way, it could be argued that for Hahn the Arrow–Debreu equilibrium theory remains an indispensable part of the core of the correct economic understanding of the real world. Depending which aspect of the real economy we wish to understand, we *adapt* this core to it 'by relaxing some of the usual assumptions' of that theory (Hahn 1991(b): 71).[16] This brings us to the final topic in our analysis of Hahn's thesis that theoretical economics is a partial but indispensable grammar of argumentation in that 'it provides clear limits to understanding' (Hahn 1993(b): 164).

Understanding and its limits

As we already noted, according to Hahn, neoclassical economics is vastly superior to preceding economic theories. As currently the best theory, it imposes contingent constraints on our economic understanding. We say contingent constraints, because they could change in the future when a better theory to the present one emerges. After all 'neo-classical economic theory is not theology' (Hahn 2005(a): 12), in that there is no *a priori* ruling out a change in theory. These contingent constraints range from limitations on the correct questions and possible answers to values like coherence, clarity and distinctiveness, to the correct techniques to be used, and to substantive beliefs or commitments.[17]

In connection with the limitations on the questions to be asked, Hahn is emphatic that some of the central questions posed by classical theorists should be dropped. For instance Ricardo and others sought to answer that question 'what is the standard value?' but, as Hahn points out, in neoclassical theory 'there is no such thing' (Hahn 2005(b): 18). Hahn, however, appears to go further; it is not simply that within neoclassical theory there is no such thing, rather it is that there is no such thing full stop. Thus he accuses Sraffa of 'not coming clean on that' in any of his monthly dinners with Hahn. As methodologists, we would suggest that one should not confuse what a theory says exists or does not exist, with what actually exists. Of course, this distinction, which clearly holds for the physical sciences, is nuanced in a discipline like economics, where beliefs, even false ones, are acknowledged by Hahn as factors in the real world. If enough economists and economic agents act on Hahn's assertion, then, as a Wittgensteinian would point out, perhaps it is the case that a real economic form of life in which the standard of value was believed in and acted upon simply ceased to exist. Be that as it may, there is no doubt that neoclassical economics, like the current best theory in any discipline, puts contingent limits on the proper questions to be asked. Moreover, it also constrains the range of possible answers. As we have already discussed, neoclassical economics furnishes economists with a sophisticated language, the resources of which are used to answer the questions posed. As Hahn remarks 'one can go on and on to demonstrate how theory generates the questions and provides the language for attempted answers' (Hahn 1985: 9).

We now move onto the role of values in constraining our understanding. Among the values admired by Hahn is the value of clarity, especially that of a clear definition. The logical advantages of clear definitions have been celebrated since the time of Plato. Thus, we see Socrates looking for precise definitions of terms like justice. In the case of neoclassical theory, for instance, the term 'rationality' is clearly defined via specific axioms and assumptions that are, in turn, clearly and explicitly stated. However, according to many Wittgensteinians, the absence of a clear definition is not a symptom of the inadequacy of our ordinary language. On the contrary, it can represent *the mental sophistication* of the agent/speaker. Thus, for instance, Simon's approach to rationality does not share, to the same extent, Hahn's Socratic value of the necessity for clear definitions. The same would appear to apply to Sen, at least as Hahn understands him. The rational agent in neoclassical economics 'does not have the split personality attributed to her by Sen, and does not act in various roles but has an overriding ordering of actions in a wide domain' (Hahn 2005(a): 7). The issue of course is whether or not Simon's or Sen's notions of a rational agent aid our understanding of the real world – an issue that we will address more fully in subsequent chapters. Here, we are simply noting that commitments to values like clear Socratic definitions can constrain our economic understanding.

We now turn to how the techniques of neoclassical economics also constrain our understanding. In this connection, we briefly address the role of mathematics in neoclassical theory. As we already noted, Hahn demands a very high standard of mathematical sophistication. The theoretician has to know sophisticated traditional mathematics including the intricacies of Cantorian set theory. 'To be a good theoretician you have to be good at mathematics' (Hahn 2005(b): 14). For the moment, let us assume that sophisticated mathematical ability is necessary for theorizing. The question, as we shall see in later chapters, is whether or not the mathematical resources of Cantorian set theory are legitimate when it comes to proving the existence of equilibrium. Certainly, in the domain of what is called intuitionist mathematics, these resources are not legitimate techniques. As we will see in Chapter 8, the understanding of a theoretical economy in the mathematical domain of Cantorian set theory is very different to the understanding furnished in the domain of intuitionist mathematics. Thus, the use of Cantorian mathematical techniques constrain our understanding of a theoretical economy in surprising ways.

Finally, we turn to the limitations imposed by substantive beliefs or commitments. We have already briefly noted some of the limitations imposed by Hahn's commitment to rationality. Hahn sums up his commitment to equilibrium as follows:

> it embodies two insights: we cannot rely on benevolence etc. to produce spontaneous order in a decentralized economy if for no other reason than that no benevolent agent would know what to do. The second insight is that decentralized order is nonetheless possible, but is only contingently so. That is, the abstract conditions may not be met. The ever deeper study of the limits of both these insights has been immensely fruitful.
>
> (Hahn 2005(a): 12)

With this study under way, Hahn has 'some confidence' in the view 'that we require an equilibrium notion to make precise the limits of economics' (Hahn 1973(a): 38). In this connection, however, one must be careful. Hahn's commitment to equilibrium does not mean that theoretical economists are limited to studying an economy which is in equilibrium *at all times*. Such a limitation would remove 'a vast range of economic phenomena' from enquiry and 'thereby from the realm of understanding. One would have a theory which closes rather than opens doors' (Hahn 1985: 14). Alternatively, 'economic theory thus narrowly constructed makes many important discussions impossible' (Hahn 1984: 4). But the reason for not opting for limiting economic analysis to nothing but equilibrium is more fundamental. While Arrow–Debreu equilibrium is proven to exist, it is not unique. The multiplicity of equilibria means the necessity to construct 'a theory of the economy out of equilibrium' (Hahn 1984: 4).

So far, we have merely noted some of the contingent limitations which result from claiming that neoclassical theory is, at present, the best available. It would appear, however, that Hahn goes further. Neoclassical theory, as we already noted, is also a grammar of argumentation which, while incomplete, is indispensable to economic analysis and thereby to economic understanding. According to Hahn, 'we need its grammar even *to begin to think about the economic world*' (Hahn 1996: 194, italics added). Neoclassical theory, in this sense, is imposing limitations in a *grammatical*, *not* in a merely *contingent*, way. If we assume that neoclassical economics, as specified by Hahn, is not simply an accidental, contingent, grammar – and the fact that it is 'needed' even to begin to think about the economic world implies that it is necessary – it is very close to some kind of Kantian limiting concept, in that it is specifying conditions of the possibility of economics as an objective discipline. Hahn's three commitments and his mode of theorizing, rather than simply being an intriguing methodological account of general equilibrium theorizing, is, by virtue of its grammatical nature, also prescriptive. The grammar requires them.

For those who have little empathy with Kantian conditions of the possibility of economic understanding, one could restate Hahn's thesis by saying that the three commitments combined with the mode of theorizing outlined in this chapter constitute a grammatical, rather than a contingent, benchmark for theoretical economists. The benchmark is not an arbitrary baseline and neither is it contingently imposed on the grounds that neoclassical theory is the best currently available. The grammar of the situation imposes it.

The plausibility of Hahn's thesis may be seen as follows. Theoretical economists aim at understanding the complex, messy reality of the whole economic world, rather than, say, a national economy.[18] In face of this highly complex network of relationships, one can either say it is too complex to understand at all or else fallibly, but courageously, face the challenge by attempting to understand it. In particular, rather than dogmatically asserting that we require a benevolent hand or dogmatically insisting that an invisible hand can produce some kind of spontaneous order, the proper first step is to prove one or other of these claims. Arrow–Debreu kind of theorizing proved that, under certain conditions, decentralized order was possible, and that we cannot rely on benevolence to produce decentralized order. Without this grammatical starting point, we would be unreasonably arbitrary in our attempts at understanding the very complex order of the real economic world. With this secure, non-arbitrary starting point, how is one to proceed? If we do not theorize *à la* Hahn, by, for instance, relaxing its assumptions and by taking Keynesian and other realistic factors into account, how else can we enhance this understanding which is guaranteed in a quasi-Cartesian fashion as a secure (but not the Cartesian indubitable) starting point? Of course, Hahnian theorizing

> leaves out much of interest and importance and there are many phenomena it cannot account for adequately but that is not so by devilish design but by *the limitations of our capacity to form a unified and coherent account of the whole world.* For the recognition of this limitation we should praise rather than condemn theorists.
>
> (Hahn 1985: 19, italics added)

In short, adherence to Hahn's grammatical benchmark demonstrates the limitations of our capacity to understand the whole economic world and, in view of the complexity of that world, one can't see any other grammar which would accomplish the aim of understanding that world. In Chapter 7, we will investigate how Kaldor challenges this thesis and Hahn's response to that challenge.

A philosophical architecture for Hahn's defence

In our opinion, Hahn's defence of economic theorizing, especially his grammatical defence of general equilibrium theory, has an admirable philosophical architecture to it. Arrow–Debreu equilibrium theory, as the crown of neoclassical economics, was, and is, not infrequently viewed as a major contribution to economics as an empirical science. Also, for numerous economists and methodologists, scientific explanation or understanding is inextricably linked to successful predictive capacity. In this connection, however, according to Hahn, the Arrow–Debreu theory is singularly unsuccessful. Thus, Hahn has no option but to sever the inextricable link between economic understanding and scientific prediction. To sever this connection, he has recourse to Moore's naturalistic fallacy. This is the first philosophical cornerstone in Hahn's defence.

Having thus severed economic understanding from its assumed connection to scientific understanding – an action which, in the eyes of card-carrying positivists, could be moving economic understanding into the realms of meaningless metaphysics – Hahn is obliged to furnish economists with a coherent account of economic understanding. Numerous philosophers might wish to locate Hahn's concept of understanding in the hermeneutical tradition. Hermeneutical philosophers insist that the so-called human sciences are not predictive *à la* physics. Rather, the human sciences serve the human interest of understanding human actions and their social settings. As we already noted, nineteenth and early twentieth-century hermeneutics connect understanding to the private mental states of agents, thereby making the concept of understanding inherently subjective. Hahn, however, requires an objective notion of understanding. The next cornerstone in Hahn's defence of economic understanding is to ignore hermeneutics and to build his concept of economic understanding on the foundations of the Frege–Wittgenstein linguistic turn. With this turn, the concept of understanding is freed from its alleged connection to private mental states and is shown to be objective. We have already elaborated on this cornerstone. What we wish to focus on here is Hahn's thesis that, in the context of the linguistic turn, economic theory is an indispensable grammar of argumentation.

This brings us to his third philosophical cornerstone, namely a *Cartesian determination to avoid misunderstanding*. This Cartesian dimension is evident in Hahn's quest for a solid starting point in accomplishing the aim of understanding the complex, messy nature of our whole, world-wide economy. This solid starting point is supplied by the objective, indubitable proof of the existence of equilibrium as characterized clearly and distinctly by Debreu. This indubitable proof is the objective guarantor of the existence of 'spontaneous' or, more precisely, de-centralized, economic order. With this solid starting point, Hahn's method of climbing the mountain of understanding, i.e. his grammar of argumentation, ensures there is no scope for misunderstanding within economic theorizing. This grammar of argumentation is unambiguous and clear. This, of course, does not guarantee that the theory will not be misunderstood. In Hahn's grammar of argumentation, if and when the theory is misunderstood, the sources of misunderstanding are external to the theoretical developments of general equilibrium. Whatever misgivings or objections one might have to Hahn's defence, one cannot but admire the sheer elegance of this architecture.

5 The core of neoclassical economics?

> He (Hahn) may want to deny that there is such a core, but the denial would not be consistent with his practice or with the dominant current practice of economists.
>
> (Hausman 1996: 211)

Introduction

In the last two chapters we attempted to present, in a sympathetic fashion, Hahn's methodology. In this and the following chapters we will continue with this expository work. Another layer, however, will be added, namely the task of methodological critique or evaluation. Our first step in the accomplishment of the two-fold aim of both appreciation and critique of Hahn's methodology, is to compare and contrast Hahn's approach with that of Hausman. There are numerous reasons for this choice. First, Hahn has explicitly engaged Hausman's methodology. Second, Hausman's methodology, like that of Hahn, is centrally focused on theoretical orthodox microeconomic theory in conjunction with general equilibrium theory. Third, as Hausman himself admits, his methodology has been read 'as an apology' for orthodox equilibrium economics[1] (Hausman 1997: 395). Finally, Hausman's methodology has also been read as 'the best philosophical account of traditional microeconomics written thus far' (Mäki 1996: 35). It should be highly instructive and informative to compare and contrast Hahn's defence of orthodox economic theorizing which, if not the best available from an eminent practising economist, is certainly challenging and intriguing – with a sophisticated methodological analysis of the same economic practice by a proficient philosopher, who explicitly acknowledges an 'intellectual debt' to Hahn (Hausman 1992(a): 9).

Hausman's portrait of fundamental economic theory

As Mäki points out, Hausman's methodological corpus is very extensive. It ranges over issues in the metamethodology of economics, to a critical analysis of J.S. Mill's economic methodology, to his analysis of the structure and strategy of economic theory as displayed in both orthodox microeconomic theory and general equilibrium theory, to his specification and evaluation of the method of theory appraisal used in orthodox economics.[2] Since our primary focus is to clarify and evaluate Hahn's methodology, our portrait[3] of Hausman's methodological contribution will naturally be incomplete.

Before outlining Hausman's portrait of what he calls 'fundamental theory,' we will use his convention of calling both theoretical orthodox microeconomic theory and general equilibrium theory 'equilibrium economics.' Clearly, equilibrium economics refers to a vast domain, ranging from neoclassical textbooks, to pioneering research and analysis by well known neoclassical economists, to research by less well known economists published in mainstream journals and other research outlets. In old fashioned terminology, both Hahn and Hausman are largely in agreement on the subject matter of economics. In developing his economic methodology, however, Hausman does not accept this subject matter as we find it. He *reconstructs* it by specifying what he calls 'the theoretical heart of equilibrium economics' (Hausman 1997: 396). This theoretical heart is 'basic' or 'fundamental:' it constitutes the fundamentals of mainstream theorizing (Hausman 1992(a): 53, 55). He calls this theoretical heart 'equilibrium theory or the basic equilibrium model' (Hausman 1992(a): 53). He is insistent that one must distinguish this heart from the whole body of equilibrium economics. The total corpus of equilibrium economics 'is the articulation, elaboration and application of equilibrium theory' (Hausman 1992(a): 272). In particular, 'partial equilibrium theories consist of equilibrium theory plus simplifications with a focus on one or two markets. General Equilibrium theories… consist of equilibrium theory plus similar simplifications and a focus on the interdependencies in whole economies' (Hausman 1997: 398).

Hausman, by his reconstruction, is making a number of claims about the structure of equilibrium economics. First, equilibrium economics has a heart which is basic or fundamental. Second, equilibrium economics is more than this basic heart. Third, and, as Mäki points out, controversially[4] (Mäki 1996: 13), general equilibrium theory is not fundamental: it 'is a particular application of the fundamental theory' (Hausman 1992(a): 55), or 'general equilibrium theories are augmentations of equilibrium theory' (Hausman 1992(a): 54). Two questions immediately arise: what is this theoretical heart, and in what sense is it basic/fundamental? The heart consists of 'seven laws: those of the theory of consumer choice, those of the theory of the firm and the assertions that markets "clear" or come quickly to equilibrium' (Hausman 1992(a): 51). Hausman notes that these laws would be ten rather than seven if we were to elaborate on the law that the consumer is rational. The heart is comprised of the following laws.

Theory of the consumer

- The consumer's preferences are complete (a consumer can compare all options).
- The consumer's preferences are transitive.
- The consumer's preferences are continuous. (This is required by mathematical tractability.)

- The consumer is a utility maximizer (he or she does what he or she most prefers).
- The consumer's preferences are bundles of commodities consumed by her or him, with no interdependence between the preferences of different individuals, and with the consumer preferring larger commodity bundles to smaller ones.
- For all consumers and all commodities x and y, the consumer is willing to exchange more of y for a unit of x as the amount of y the consumer has increases relative to the amount of x she or he has (diminishing marginal rates of substitution).

Theory of the Firm

- The law of diminishing returns, i.e. the increase in output from an increase in the quantity of input R, other inputs remaining constant, is a decreasing function of the quantity of R used.
- The law of constant returns to scale: if in the neighbourhood of the equilibrium point all the inputs into production are increased or decreased in some ratio, output will increase or decrease in that ratio.
- The law of profit maximization, i.e. firms attempt to maximize net returns or profits.

Equilibrium

- Markets 'clear' or come quickly to equilibrium.

These ten theses constitute equilibrium theory, which is the theoretical heart of equilibrium economics.[5] This is the basic, fundamental model or theory which is applied/augmented in both partial and general equilibrium theorizing. Let us now address our second question, namely in what sense is this theory basic? Negatively, this heart is neither a Lakatosian hard core nor a Kuhnian paradigm.[6] In Hausman's eyes, a Lakatosian hard core is too rigid: it does not allow for any major changes within its core. Equilibrium economics, however, is not that rigid: it can allow for the rejection of some of the ten theses, but if a piece of research 'denies most of them,' it 'is not equilibrium economics' (Hausman 1997: 396). All equilibrium economists must have recourse to a subset of the postulates of equilibrium economics in engaging in their research, and if any piece of research either explicitly or by implication rejects or denies most of these postulates (i.e. more than five or six) then that research falls outside the pale of equilibrium economics. There is thus no ambiguity about Hausman's specification of 'fundamental neoclassical theory' and the manner in which it is fundamental.[7] His substantive thesis is that equilibrium economics has the theoretical heart of equilibrium theory. As we will see, Hahn challenges this substantive claim.

The blessing and the curse of equilibrium economics

On a number of occasions Hausman sums up the unique methodological status of equilibrium economics by the claim that it is both blessed and cursed. It is 'blessed with behavioural postulates that are plausible, powerful and convenient and cursed with the inability to learn much from experience' (Hausman 1992(a): 226). Later, he sums up as follows: 'Economists… are blessed with the knowledge that there is a great deal of truth to equilibrium theory, and they are cursed with sufficient difficulties in testing that they are rarely in any position to change their initial assessment' (Hausman 1992(a): 276). When these two claims are conjoined together, it is not difficult to see how Hausman has been read as a defender of the status quo, and thereby of equilibrium economics.

Indeed, the case for reading Hausman's analysis as a defence of the status quo is strengthened by his additional blessing, namely his justification of equilibrium economists' theory of confirmation. He reads his own work as a defence of 'equilibrium theorists from criticisms that they accept an unjustifiable theory of confirmation' (Hausman 1997: 396). This, in turn, is linked to his distinction between unacceptable and acceptable dogmatism.[8] Equilibrium economists' method of theory assessment is such that 'it is not unacceptably dogmatic to refuse to find disconfirmation of economic "laws" in typical failures of their market predictions' (Hausman 1992(a): 207). Rather, the unacceptable dogmatism of equilibrium economists results from their commitment to economics as a separate science, i.e. as one that investigates 'a domain in which a small number of causal factors dominate' (Hausman 1992(a): 225), and as one that 'encompasses all the major causes' (Hausman 1992(a): 217). In Hausman's opinion, once equilibrium economists abandon their unjustifiable commitment to economics as a separate science, this opens the door to more extensive empirical investigation. This empirical investigation would imply the expansion of the use of laboratory experiments, refining the techniques of field reports, improving statistical techniques for the analysis of data and so on. Those who read Hausman as defending orthodox economics, however, would in all probability point out that, in view of the blessings of equilibrium economics, especially its acceptable dogmatism, this additional empirical range of investigations will leave basic equilibrium theory standing as a permanent inner sanctum in the developing edifice of equilibrium economics.[9]

Clearly, we need to analyse in some detail Hausman's account of the blessing and the curse of equilibrium economics. The blessing is twofold. First, there is a great deal of truth to basic equilibrium theory with its plausible, powerful and convenient axioms. This great deal of truth is the principal source of confidence in the implications of equilibrium economics. Second, when equilibrium economists abandon their commitment to economics as a separate science, their method of theory assessment is justifiable. On the other hand, economists are cursed with 'bad' market data which leads to their 'inability to learn much from experience' (Hausman 1992(a): 226). Economic phenomena are complex, and, given the absence of controlled experiments, economic data is poor in that it is inconclusive as a means of testing. The lack of telling data, however, does not signal a cautionary role towards the basic theory in Hausman's eyes. He argues that the commitment to basic equilibrium theory is merely 'apparent dogmatism' on the grounds that there is a great deal of truth to fundamental equilibrium theory, coupled with the claim that 'the weakness of empirical control exerted by economic data provides for a *legitimately large role* for pragmatic factors' (Hausman 1992(a): 237, italics added).

Let us now turn to the first blessing, namely the thesis that 'there is a great deal of truth to equilibrium theory.' This thesis plays a key role in Hausman's economic methodology. As Mäki points out, he uses it to defend the conclusion 'that economists are justified in being reluctant to reject the basic tenets of equilibrium theory when faced with negative evidence' (Mäki 1996: 23).[10] In this connection, the perceptive reader may wish to distinguish between a Hausman_1 and a Hausman_2. Hausman_1 subscribes to the strong thesis, i.e. there is a *great* deal of truth to fundamental equilibrium theory, a thesis repeated more than once (Hausman 1992(a): 210, 276). Hausman_2 subscribes to a much weaker thesis, namely there is *some* truth to basic equilibrium theory. Thus, Hausman_2 draws our attention to 'the good reasons economists have to find some truth in equilibrium theory' (Hausman 1992(a): 277). Our analysis focuses on Hausman_1. In our opinion, Hausman_2 is too weak. Almost every theory that merits inclusion in the history of science, in general, and the history of economic thought, in particular, has some truth to it. This 'some truth,' however, is not sufficient to engender reluctance to reject basic tenets when faced with negative evidence. To legitimate his reluctance to abandon basic equilibrium theory, Hausman requires the blessing that there is a great deal of truth to it.

The impact of this blessing becomes more evident when we contrast Hausman's position with standard Popperian methodology of the physical sciences. In this Popperian methodology, axioms are bold conjectures. Confidence in one's axioms is solely derived from the successful empirical testing of the consequences of these conjectural axioms. This Popperian methodology, however, gives a misleading account of basic equilibrium economics. Neoclassical economists' confidence in the laws of basic equilibrium theory is derived from the fact that these laws are blessed with a great deal of truth, which is known independently of the testing of their consequences. Without this blessing the neoclassical economist's reluctance to abandon basic equilibrium theory could collapse into an illegitimate dogmatism. In short, the laws of basic equilibrium theory have a great deal of truth.[11] In this connection, Hausman contrasts these laws with the laws of physics. He tells us that the laws of basic equilibrium theory 'do not have the same status as fundamental natural laws. They are inexact...' (Hausman 1992(a): 52).[12] Hausman's analysis of inexactness helps to spell out in what sense these generalizations are blessed with a great deal of truth. Take, for instance, the axiom that firms aim to increase profits. This is not a simple universal truth. Rather, it is an inexact law, and, once we grasp what this inexactness is, we understand how this axiom has a great deal of truth to it.[13]

First, Hausman is clear that 'inexactness' in his interpretation does not mean that the laws are true within some margin of error. To claim basic economic laws are subject to a margin of error is merely another way of saying that they are inexact: there is no additional clarification.[14] In Hausman's view, basic economic laws are inexact in that they are qualified with vague *ceteris paribus* clauses.

Economic laws, when, as it were, unpacked, are not simple universal claims; they are always qualified claims, and the qualification takes the rubric of *ceteris paribus*. Moreover, this qualification is vague, in that the list of factors covered by a *ceteris paribus* clause is open-ended and context dependent.[15] Hausman readily admits that, because the *ceteris paribus* clauses, which are the source of the inexactness of basic economic laws, are vague or imprecise, they are problematic. This vagueness, however, does not mean that their use results in nonsense or empty verbiage. Hausman adopts a strategy similar to that adopted in Chapter 3, when we encountered a similar problem with Hahn. He shows the concept is viable by indicating clear counter instances or abuses, such as *ceteris paribus* we are all immortal or *ceteris paribus* all dogs have six legs, and clear exemplars such as Coulomb's Law which says *ceteris paribus* 'any two bodies with like changes q_1 and q_2 separated by distance r will repel one another with a force proportional to $\frac{q_1q_2'}{r_2}$ (Hausman 1992(a): 135 footnote 13). Moreover, Hausman, in true philosophical spirit, goes on to discuss the meaning or truth conditions of laws qualified by these vague *ceteris paribus* clauses.

In this connection, he points out that economic laws are qualified with *ceteris paribus* clauses in two different ways. For instance, in partial equilibrium theories, the demand for coffee depends on the price of coffee, the price of other goods (substitutes or complements), income and tastes. In this case, we say *ceteris paribus* the demand for coffee is a function of the price of coffee only. This is the first sense of *ceteris paribus* clauses as used by economists. In this sense, the constituents of the *ceteris paribus* clause are clearly identified by the theory and are discussed separately. These *ceteris paribus* clauses are not open-ended with their constituents varying from context to context. But this is the case with the second sense of *ceteris paribus* clauses used by economists, and it is in this second sense the basic laws of equilibrium theory are qualified by *ceteris paribus* clauses. These basic laws 'are true only under various not fully specified conditions' (Hausman 1992(a): 134). When we say '*ceteris paribus* consumers' preferences are transitive' we are using *ceteris paribus* in a vaguer way than that used in saying '*ceteris paribus* the demand for coffee is a function of its price.' In the case of the transitivity of preferences, the factors excluded by the *ceteris paribus* are not fixed, i.e. they may vary from context to context.

For instance, the *prima facie* logical form of the basic law '*ceteris paribus* people's preferences are transitive' is '*ceteris paribus* every F is G.' This cannot be conveyed by 'every F is G.' Rather, '*ceteris paribus* every F is G' really has the following logical form: there exists a set C (picked out by the *ceteris paribus* clause in a specific context) such that everything which is both C and F is G. Thus, for instance, '*ceteris paribus* all preferences are transitive' has the surface appearance of a qualified generalization. However, when properly analysed, it is the logical conjunction of a number of unqualified, complex universal propositions. 'Thus *ceteris paribus* all preferences are transitive' sums up a number of exact laws, each of which is derived from everything which is both C and F is G. The condition C is identified in the appropriate context. The crucial point is that each such generalization in 'Every C and F is G' is a universal, law-like truth. In this way, the so-called inexactness of the generalizations of basic equilibrium theory in no way adversely effects the law-likeness of these specific and exact universal propositions. Hausman's notion of inexactness, contrary to Hahn's suggestion, is itself very exact.

The battle for the heart of equilibrium economics

In opening his critique of Hausman's methodology, Hahn repeats his longstanding reservations vis-à-vis methodology by pointing out that he 'is by no means favourably disposed to methodology for economists,' and adds in brackets 'its results seem to have been pretty disastrous' (Hahn 1996: 183). In particular, while acknowledging that Hausman's contribution is interesting and instructive, he maintains 'not all is well, largely because Hausman is a philosopher first and an economist a poor second' (Hahn 1996: 183). This is not a rhetorical *argumentum ad hominem* on the part of Hahn. It is central to his negative critique of Hausman. According to Hahn, almost all of the economics in Hausman's analysis, with the exception of a chapter on Overlapping Generations, 'is simple textbook economics' (Hahn 1996: 185). For Hahn, Hausman the philosopher has recourse to an 'elementary undergraduate vision' of economics and misses out on 'the rich and indeed sophisticated body of theory we now have' (Hahn 1996: 183).[16] Not surprising, Hausman's methodology is in no way adequate to the extensive work at the frontiers of economic research.

Indeed Hausman, in his response to Hahn, expressly takes up this crucial issue. He replies as follows.

> What Professor Hahn took to be simplistic text-book economics was a focus on the theoretical core of economics. He may want to deny that there is such a core, but the denial would not be consistent with his practice or with the dominant current practice of economists.
>
> (Hausman 1996: 211)

In Hausman's eyes, the conflict between himself and Hahn is a tug of war for the heart of equilibrium economics. In our opinion, he is correct on this. However, as we will see later, he is wrong in suggesting that Hahn's rejection of Hausman's core is inconsistent with Hahn's own practice. Hahn has a very sophisticated economic methodology worked out, which is novel and challenging but which does not at all fit into Hausman's portrait outlined above.

In order to appreciate and, in part, evaluate this not insignificant disagreement between Hausman's and Hahn's approach to textbook economics, let us briefly look at Thomas Kuhn's classic account of the role of textbooks in the physical sciences in his *Essential Tension*, published in 1977. Kuhn's classic account displays a perceptive appreciation of both the advantages and disadvantages of these textbooks.[17] In the first place, textbooks are completely distinct from the historical classics. For instance, very few physics textbooks include Einstein's original paper on the special theory of relativity. Rather than presenting the historical classics, these textbooks 'are the unique repository of the finished achievements' of successful physicists (Kuhn 1977: 180). Hausman is suggesting, *prima facie*, that the same holds for mainstream economics. Its textbooks give 'the unique repository' of the achievements of researchers in that it accurately conveys the core or heart of equilibrium economics.

In Kuhn's analysis, however, there is also a considerable downside to textbooks. Indeed, he argues that 'the textbook mode of presentation must inevitably be misleading' (Kuhn 1977: 181). While education in the physical sciences is centred around textbooks, and this educational policy has paid off, this education is 'a dogmatic initiation in a pre-established tradition that the student is not equipped to evaluate' (Kuhn 1977: 229). Moreover, and this is Hahn's point vis-à-vis economic theorizing, textbooks frequently fail to convey 'the sorts of problems that the professional may be asked to solve and the variety of techniques available for their solution' (Kuhn 1977: 229). Indeed, innovative research can include the creation of novel techniques for the solution to these problems. In short, while textbooks are an indispensable pedagogical tool, those who continue with research produce 'most consequential sorts of innovation' (Kuhn 1977: 230), and much of this 'is found in the journal literature,' not in textbooks' (Kuhn 1977: 179).

Thus, textbooks can and do go out of date, and not just out of fashion, in that new ones are required in order to incorporate these innovations. In physics, however, these incorporations are *not* simple additions to the pre-existing textbooks: they are not added to the existing corpus of the textbook in the way new recipes are added to an already successful cookery book. 'To assimilate them the scientist must usually rearrange the intellectual and manipulative equipment he has previously relied on, discarding some elements of his prior belief and practice while finding new significances in and new relationships between many others' (Kuhn 1977: 266, 267). Clearly, the theoretical heart of physics is not conveyed by excellent textbooks. Research requires that the textbook heart of physics undergoes radical transplants from time to time. Hausman, however, privileges the heart of equilibrium economics, in that it has a great deal of truth to it and it is properly conveyed in the best textbooks. Moreover, in Hausman's methodology, research innovations are incorporated into equilibrium economics as 'extensions' or 'particular applications' of the core theory. Thus, equilibrium research does not affect the core in the above Kuhnian fashion.

Hahn, by contrast, is much closer to the Kuhnian end of the spectrum than Hausman. Thus, for Hahn, Hausman's identification of the heart of equilibrium economics, and consequently his account of mainstream theoretical research as mere augmentation of his privileged core, does not adequately represent orthodox economic theorizing. The core is not privileged *à la* Hausman, and the reason Hausman erroneously believes so is his philosophical reading of textbooks combined with his failure to properly appreciate the manner in which much of theoretical research in mainstream economics has altered his so-called core. Thus, Hausman fails to grasp the full implications of Hahn's critique in claiming that 'Hahn finds methodological work of value only when it… addresses *specific* questions at the frontiers of economic research' (Hausman 1996: 208, italics in original). Any suggestion that Hahn and Hausman's positions could be reconciled by insisting that Hahn gives an accurate account of specific methodological questions at the frontiers of economic research while Hausman gives an accurate account of the core would utterly misrepresent Hahn's methodological rejection of Hausman's portrait of basic or fundamental equilibrium theory. Hausman's core is too static and fails to accommodate the changes that are necessitated by ongoing research.

In particular, in claiming that markets 'clear' or come quickly to equilibrium is an axiom or fundamental law of the heart of mainstream economics, Hausman unduly privileges the notion of equilibrium conveyed by elementary textbooks. This textbook notion of equilibrium, though useful for pedagogical purposes, is inadequate for much of neoclassical research. In this context, Hahn, quite correctly, points out that 'Hausman does not notice that economists have many equilibrium concepts' (Hahn 1996: 188). Theoretical research has forced economists to *rethink* the notion of equilibrium which still reigns in elementary textbooks. As we have already, seen many of the usages of equilibrium in theoretical research are a long way from its use in elementary textbooks. Hausman's methodology fails to appreciate their significance for his privileging of the textbook axiom in the fundamental core of equilibrium theory. Hahn is equally critical of many of the other elements in Hausman's core. He is almost dumbfounded when he reads Hausman's claim that the law of constant returns to scale is integral to his core.

> Lastly, to my surprise, Hausman thinks that increasing returns must be ignored (or ruled out). Even Professor Lucas does not do that, although he cannot bring himself to allow increasing returns internal to the firm. But the whole concept of the firm depends on some increasing returns, if nothing else, in the form of set-up costs.
>
> (Hahn 1996: 191)

In a similar vein, Hahn also objects to Hausman's specification of the fundamental core of rationality. He sums up Hausman's position as follows: 'an agent is rational if it has a monotone utility function defined on commodity space and this is maximized subject to budget constraint' (Hahn 1996: 186). Hahn, however, maintains that for 'many purposes of neo-classical economics this is an unnecessary postulate' (Hahn 1996: 186). In this connection, Hahn draws our attention to the work of Sonneschein (1972), Debreu (1974) and Mantel (1971).

In addition to these and other specific issues, Hahn maintains that 'there are deeper difficulties with the concept of rationality which, to my disappointment, are not discussed in the (Hausman's) book' (Hahn 1996: 187). His disappointment is due to the fact that he expects philosophers to address these. For instance, 'As Simon noted long ago our current practice requires us to deny rationality to a chess player who cannot foresee all possible moves, which suggests that rationality is not a suitable idealized concept for a "science"' (Hahn 1996: 187). Indeed, given Hausman's 'splendid chapter on preference reversal,' Hahn was hoping that Hausman would discuss what philosophers have to say about rationality and then address two issues: '(a) the problem for a "science" of using terms whose common denotation is different from its role in the theory, and (b) whether the narrow definition which he discusses is likely to lead to the most acceptable idealization' (Hahn 1996: 187). In connection with (b), Hahn refers to the notion of rationality used by a 'school of macroeconomists' who postulate 'the infinitely lived agent' (Hahn 1996: 188). For Hahn, 'the urgent question' concerns whether or not this notion of rationality is 'a usable idealization?' (Hahn 1996: 188). For Hahn, 'a "science" exact or inexact' would choose 'a less ambiguous' and 'less implausible' notion (ibid.: 188).

As we already noted, Hausman responds to this Hahnian critique. He makes three distinct points. First, he unequivocally accepts the results of Sonneschein, Debreu and Mantel and turns this around to buttress his own emphasis on the unjustifiable inertia of economists in failing to respond to this research. The blame for this lies in their commitment to economics as a separate science, a notion that Hahn failed to appreciate in his reading of Hausman. Thus, he argues:

> But what has actually happened during the decades since Sonneschein, Debreu and Mantel proved their theorems, vindicates the claim that economists are committed to regarding economics as a separate science. The fact that axioms concerning individual rationality and individual demand remain ubiquitous in economic modelling – even when they have been shown to be dispensable – reflects this commitment.
>
> (Hausman 1996: 211)

For Hahn, however, Hausman's explanation is beside the point. Given that Hausman is conceding the 'dispensability' of his axioms of individual rationality and individual demand, then surely these axioms do not constitute the fundamental heart of mainstream economics. Hausman, by implication is conceding that Hahn's critique of his core is correct. We will address the issue of separateness in the next section.

The second point, which Hausman makes in his own defence, is that, while Hahn may wish to deny that there is such a core to mainstream economics, 'that denial would not be consistent with his own practice' (Hausman 1996; 211). The only thing we can say about this defence is that it is factually false: there is simply no way in which Hahn's research in the late eighties and early nineties is consistent with Hausman's core. This is clearly evident in Hahn's Introduction to the collection of essays on *The Economics of Missing Markets, Information, and Games* published in 1989. According to Hahn, these research papers were presented in the 'conviction that it was urgent to move beyond the Walrasian paradigm *without abandoning the commitment to lucid and rigorous theorizing in which Arrow and Debreu have so memorably pointed the way*' (Hahn 1989:

1, italics added). This clearly sums up Hahn's unequivocal commitment to a specific mode of theorizing outlined in Chapter 2. Unfortunately, Hausman did not pay sufficient attention to Hahn's own methodological writings. Hahn goes on to point out that the Walrasian paradigm is not useless but is seriously incomplete. The papers in this volume address many of the questions that were 'not allowed' by the manner of construction of Walrasian theory, as well as addressing 'purely "internal" problems with the theory' (Hahn 1989: 2). Far from requiring Hausman's core, that core would be the kiss of death to many of Hahn's own research projects.

Hausman's final point is that the denial of his core would be inconsistent with the 'dominant current practice of economists' (Hausman 1996: 211). This, *prima facie*, is a more promising line of defence for Hausman and is consistent with his commitment to the thesis that the methodology of economics is an empirical science (Hausman 1992(a): 211). Methodology modelled on an empirical science will take the corpus of economics as it is and will be loathe to engage in being prescriptive. In Hahn's view, however, such an attitude is too simplistic. For instance, this would imply too much tolerance for the notion of rationality used by those macro-economists working with 'the infinitely lived agent.' Hahn uses his methodology to undermine such moves: they constitute bad economics. Thus, Hahn is much more prescriptive than Hausman in his methodological reflections. Hausman's methodology is descriptive in the sense that it is a methodological account of the current practice of neoclassical economists, whereas Hahn's is an *apologia* for a specific mode of theorizing, which is much more prescriptive.

This is a substantive divide between Hahn and Hausman. For Hausman, the business of methodology is not to reform current practice: It largely leaves economics and its practices as they are found. For Hahn, however, 'there is a lot of "hot air" in technical garb' within neoclassical economics' (Hahn 1996: 185, footnote 2). He uses his methodology to expose this. In this connection, it should be noted that this substantive divide is not unique to economics. As, for instance, Benacerraf and Putnam point out, the same holds in the philosophy of mathematics. On the one hand, eminent scholars, 'predominantly mathematicians,' refuse to take 'existing mathematics and mathematical activity as sacrosanct and immune from criticism; according to them, there are justifiable and unjustifiable methods in mathematics' (Benacerraf and Putnam 1983: 2). On the other hand, eminent philosophers of mathematics 'do not want to *promulgate* certain mathematical methods as *acceptable*: they want to *describe* the *accepted* ones. Mathematics is something given and to be accounted for, explained and accurately described' (Benacerraf and Putnam, 1983: 3, italics added). If we replace the term 'mathematics' by 'economics,' it is evident that Hahn is at home in the first group, while Hausman is at home in the second. Of course, we are not claiming that Hausman's account is purely descriptive with no prescriptive element, and that Hahn's is purely prescriptive, with no descriptive component. Both are descriptive and prescriptive, but Hahn has a much more extensive prescriptive dimension to his methodology than Hausman.

Separateness and privileging the core

In the previous section, we have seen how Hahn's methodological position differs from Hausman's. We have also seen how Hausman views neoclassical economics as being both blessed and cursed. Hahn is in agreement with Hausman about the curse. In Chapter 2 we addressed Hahn's detailed account of the pragmatics of prediction and on how these preclude using predictions as straightforward empirical tests. Thus, Hahn would be in total agreement with Hausman's claim that 'the weakness of empirical control exerted by economic data provides for a legitimately large role for pragmatic factors' (Hausman 1992(a): 237). Vis-à-vis the blessing, Hausman oscillates between some truth and a great deal of truth. Hahn, via his distinction between axioms and assumptions discussed in Chapter 4, is much more forensic about the blessing than Hausman. For instance, when economists use the notion of rationality, their use may be read as an explication of the truism that economic agents are persons combined with assumptions that are introduced on grounds ranging from casual empiricism to tractability–simplicity considerations. In so far as one emphasizes the truism that economic agents are persons one is well grounded in reality, but as one emphasizes the assumptions one is moving further and further from reality. Whether this constitutes a good or a great deal of truth, Hahn is silent. His silence is, we speculate, because such claims, i.e. a good or a great deal of truth, are too vague. He would push us back to the analysis into axioms and assumptions.

Nonetheless, one must admit, whether or not one agrees with Hausman, he is very clear on the theoretical core of neoclassical economics, which leads to the question: for Hahn, is there a core and, if there is, what is it? Hausman is not sure: he remarks that Hahn 'may want to deny that there is such a core' (Hausman 1996: 211). Certainly, Hahn rejects any reading of neoclassical theory which insists that it is an empirical science with a fundamental core of scientific laws. This includes Hausman's reading of these as *ceteris paribus* laws. Moreover, Hausman is correct in claiming that Hahn puts the emphasis on the activity of theorizing at the frontiers of economic research. However, there is much more to Hahn's methodology than what is suggested by Hausman. Hahn certainly rejects Hausman's reading of the theoretical core of neoclassical economics, but this should not be interpreted as implying that there is no core. For Hahn, there is a core, but the core is not set in the stone chosen by Hausman.

As we have seen in the Introduction to his *Equilibrium and Macroeconomics* in 1985, Hahn outlines the specific sense in which he accepts being labelled a neoclassical economist. In this connection, he identifies three "commitments" (Hahn 1984: 2). We repeat these here.

1 I am a reductionist in that I attempt to locate explanations in the actions of individual agents.
2 In theorizing about the agent I look for some axioms of rationality.

> 3 I hold that some notion of equilibrium is required and that the study of equilibrium states is useful.
>
> (Hahn 1984: 1–2).

As we saw, each commitment in turn is explained. In particular, his commitments to rationality and equilibrium are elaborated in light of his activity of theorizing at the frontiers of economic research. Thus, the manner and results of how he, in Hausman's terminology, 'addresses specific questions at the frontiers of economic research' form learning–feedback loops, which result in the theory-laden elaboration of both rationality and equilibrium. Moreover, the key elements of understanding and the grammar of argumentation buttress his conception of the activity of theorizing. Finally, he emphasizes what we may call his methodological commitment to a qualified fallibilism.

> The most strongly held of my views I have left to the last of these general reflections. It is that neither is there a single best way for understanding in economics nor is it possible to hold any conclusions other than purely logical deductions with certainty.
>
> (Hahn 1984: 7)

Indeed, 'on the final truths of economics I am completely agnostic' (Hahn 1984: 18). Clearly, if the notion of core is taken to mean a set of final, basic truths, Hahn is rejecting such a notion. But that does not imply that neoclassical economics has neither indispensable commitments nor a grammar of argumentation. These constitute the core of neoclassical economics. Unlike Hausman's core, these cannot be stated in *ceteris paribus*, law-like, universal propositions.

This brings us to Hausman's distinction between the legitimate versus the illegitimate dogmatism of neoclassical economists. As we have already seen, according to Hausman, neoclassical economics demonstrated its illegitimate dogmatism in its failure to take on board the research of Sonnenschein, Debreu and Mantel. This shows that neoclassical economists have a commitment, not identified by Hahn, namely 'they are committed to regarding economics as a separate science' (Hausman 1996: 211). Hausman borrows the term 'separate science' from John Stuart Mill. He correctly notes that the terminology appears to have 'confused Professor Hahn' (Hausman 1996: 209) since Hahn had stated that 'while Hausman must have had some special purpose in mind when he used the adjective (separate), it is unlikely to be an important matter' (Hahn 1996: 184). There is no doubt that Hahn fails to appreciate the significance of the thesis that economics is a separate science in Hausman's methodology. Contrary to Hahn, Hausman maintains that this thesis 'is absolutely central to the understanding of contemporary economics' (Hausman 1996: 209).

The commitment to economics as a separate science was, according to Hausman, clearly identified by J.S. Mill. The same or analogous commitment is, in Hausman's view, evident in neoclassical economics. In this connection, Mill 'suggests that the domain of political economy is defined by the causal factors with which economists are mainly considered' (Hausman 1996: 210). For Mill, the central causal factor was the pursuit of wealth. Neoclassical economics similarly defines economics 'in terms of a small set of causal factors (rational pursuit of material self-interest, diminishing returns, etc.)' (ibid.: 210). Moreover, the separateness thesis also postulates that this small set of causes explains the whole of the domain of economics. Economic theory spans the entire domain of economics. 'At a certain level of approximation, it is complete' (ibid.: 210). As well as this, 'the fundamental causal factors are already known' and thus 'a single theory incorporating these established truths captures (inexactly) the whole subject' (ibid.: 210). Finally, neoclassical economists deductively explore the implications of their set of known causes, in particular circumstances. Psychologists and sociologists may be able to help economists with the smaller disturbing causes 'that lead to ubiquitous imprecision and occasional refutation, but they have nothing to contribute to economics as a separate science' (ibid.: 210).

Hausman is clearly correct in maintaining that this neoclassical commitment to economics as a separate science 'raises disturbing normative questions,' and *prima facie* neoclassical economists are guilty of hubris 'in assuming that they already know all the important causes' (Hausman 1996: 211). Hausman is claiming that this commitment is either explicitly or implicitly integral to the mindset of most neoclassical economists.[18] It is evident in the manner in which, for instance, neoclassical economists on the whole, despite the results of Sonnenschein, Debreu and Mantel, continue their economic modelling without taking these results on board. Once again, we see that Hausman is attempting to take economics as it is and, in the spirit of an empirical scientist, describes and explains the actual situation on the ground. Hahn, however, is describing what is happening at the frontiers of research, and from that position is prescribing what should be the case. The infamous 'is-ought' issue raised by Hume centuries ago still continues in economic methodology!

Indeed, we are tempted to go further. If we take the notion of separateness as a Wittgensteinian family resemblance one, Hahn, it could be argued, also subscribes to the commitment of the separateness of neoclassical economics. Clearly, if we follow Hausman in connecting economic causes to economic laws, Hahn will refuse to go down the road of economic laws. For Hahn, any economic assertion with the logical form of all C and F are G – the logical form of an economic law according to Hausman – is at best asserting a contingent empirical regularity which holds only in very limited circumstances. These regularities are a long way from the laws of physics. Thus, Hahn objects to Hausman's definition of separateness in terms of a set of causal, i.e. law-like, factors. However, for Hahn, neoclassical economics is separate in its choice of starting point and in its grammar of argumentation. We have already seen how the Arrow–Debreu proof is the indispensable starting point in our quest for understanding. The domain of neoclassical economics is not closed or limited *à la* Hausman, in terms of specific empirical laws and their consequences. It is, nonetheless, limited by virtue of Hahn's grammar of argumentation. In so far as Hahn's methodology is driven by his commitment to an indispensable grammar of argumentation, rather than by the claim that neoclassical economics is at the moment the best theory available, there are grammatical limits to economic understanding. Within those grammatical limitations, economics is, in Hausman's phrase, complete. The grammar of argumentation imposes more than a contingent 'must' in the economist's quest for understanding. Grammatically, we must adhere to Hahn's methodology if we wish to attain the correct understanding of the economic world.

To conclude, we mentioned above Hahn's commitment to a qualified fallibilism. Is there not a paradox here? On the one hand, Hahn is a fallibilist – he portrays his position as being very open and non-dogmatic – and, on the other, he emphasizes economics as an indispensable grammatical activity. In our view, this paradox can be resolved by noting that Hahn is a fallibilist vis-à-vis the final truths of economics, but the grammar of understanding the economic world is not similarly open. Hence we said he espoused a qualified fallibilism. The truths of economics when finally discovered or as they are known at present are contingent, but our grammar of understanding the economic world is prescriptive. In Hausman's terminology, Hahn's 'dogmatism' is grammatical. The issue of hubris, i.e. this is the unique, correct way to understand the economic world required by the grammar, we leave to Chapter 8.

6 Economics and axiomatization

A theory will typically have a logical structure derived from axioms.

(Hahn 1985: 5)

Introduction

The focus of this chapter is on Hahn's approach to the axiomatization of economics. This choice of topic may appear surprising. It suggests or presupposes that Hahn's axiomatic approach to economics has unique characteristics clearly distinguishing it from other approaches. Hahn himself, however, does not explicitly make any such claim. Indeed, he appears to suggest the opposite. Thus, when asked whether or not he is 'a representative of the deductivist tradition in economics?' Hahn replied 'I never understood that properly. Using deduction… I do not see how else to work. This is how humans behave.[1] They use logic' (Hahn 2005(b): 17). It is not unreasonable to construe Hahn's position as follows. Economists, just like physicists or others engaged in the quest for objectivity, use deduction, and the consensus among logicians is that a deductive system is an axiomatic one. Economists in opting for axiomatization are not unique. Thus, Hahn totally disagrees with Kaldor, Kornai and other economists who find 'axiomatic-logico deductive theory anathema' by subscribing to the very general thesis that 'any coherent general propositions are decomposable into this form' (Hahn 1985: 5).

Obviously, Hahn subscribes to the thesis that economic theory can be presented in axiomatic form. The aim of this chapter is not to dispute that obvious truth. Rather, we focus on how distinguished logicians and mathematicians such as Frege and Hilbert differed in their understandings of axiomatic systems. In particular, for the purposes of economic methodology, we distinguish three distinct approaches to axiomatic systems, which we name the Fregian approach, the implicit definition approach and the Hilbert–Bourbaki formalist approach. Our central thesis is threefold. First, there are significant methodological differences between Hahn, Hausman and Debreu with respect to their axiomatic approaches. Second, these differences result from the fact that Hahn's approach to the axiomatization of economics is, in the main, Fregian, whereas Hausman, by and large, adopts the implicit definition approach, and Debreu, on the whole, opts for Hilbert–Bourbaki formalism. Third, Hahn correctly identifies the meaning of existence which Debreu rigorously provided in his *Theory of Value* (1959), and thereby exposes how various economists sympathetic to Debreu's work have misunderstood Debreu's proof.

Hahn's Fregian approach

Euclid's *Elements*, over the centuries, was seen as the paradigmatic example of an axiomatic, or strictly deductive, system. A small number of basic propositions are stated at the outset. These are divided into axioms and postulates. The axioms were taken to be self-evidently true, e.g. any two quantities equal to a third are equal to each other. The postulates, for instance 'the Parallel Postulate,' which states that, given a point outside a straight line, one and only one line can be drawn through the given point parallel to the given line, while obviously not self-evidently true, was assumed to be true. In addition to the axioms and postulates, Euclid introduced explicit definitions. New terms are never introduced without being explicitly defined by recourse to the basic notions of the system (which in turn were claimed to be grounded in the human intuition of space). Armed with axioms, postulates and definitions, the geometer deduces new propositions from the axioms and postulates by strictly logical means. In other words, the geometer applies, in a finite number of steps, logical rules of inference to the basic propositions, and thereby arrives at the theorems of the system. The theorems thus derived may be empirically true, but no appeal to experience is made in establishing, i.e. in proving, them. The theorems are necessarily implied by the axioms and postulates. The necessity here is logical necessity. In this way, Euclid's *Elements* was seen as the paradigm of a deductive system.

Over the centuries and, in particular, during the course of the nineteenth century, mathematicians attempted to distinguish more sharply pure mathematics from applied mathematics. With more attention being focused on pure mathematics, the quest for strict logical rigour became more exacting. Thus mathematicians began to see logical imperfections in Euclid's *Elements* as a paradigm of a deductive system in pure mathematics. For instance, the construction of non-Euclidean geometries, suggested that, within pure mathematics, the issue of the internal consistency of the system was the central concern. The issue of the self-evidence or empirical truth of the axioms or postulates was not of concern to the pure mathematician. In this vein of thought, the distinction between axioms and postulates has no significance within a purely deductive system. The terms 'axiom' and 'postulate' may be used interchangeably to indicate the basic or logical starting point of a deductive system.

This brings us to a key issue in the philosophy of mathematics, which was vigorously debated at the turn of the twentieth century, namely what role do axioms play in a deductive system? This debate was initiated by the publication in 1899 of Hilbert's Festschrift *On the Foundations of Geometry*. The aim of this Festschrift was to prove, using the most stringent requirements of logic, the consistency (and independence) of the axioms of Euclidean geometry as stated by Hilbert in that work. These axioms were interpreted in two distinct ways: (1) implicit definitions and (2) strict formalism.[2] In (1) the axioms are not, as such, propositions, i.e. sentences that are either true or false. Remember that, for some, Euclid's axioms, as distinct from the postulates, were taken to be self-evidently true. Clearly, if axioms are not propositions at all, then any reading of them as either self-evidently or empirically true is ruled out. Rather, the axiomatic system, consisting of its axioms and its logical consequences, is a very complex definition, called an implicit definition. On the surface, an axiomatic system does not look like a definition. Indeed, it clearly is not an explicit definition, as any explicit definition is limited to the introduction of a new term within a system. Nonetheless, an axiomatic system is another kind of definition, called an implicit definition: it is defining a complex predicate, and the axioms are defining characteristics of the complex predicate.[3]

According to some logicians, Hilbert himself espoused this approach in his Festschrift.[4] Frege, who is considered to be the father of contemporary logic, rejected the proposed implicit definition interpretation as being logically confused. Frege saw logical merit in the traditional view, where axioms and definitions play totally different roles. For Frege, definitions are arbitrary stipulations. A definition 'is only a means for collecting a manifold content into a brief word or sign, thereby making it easier for us to handle' (Frege 1971(b): 24). Its logical use is 'to settle the reference of a word or sign' (Frege 1971(b): 25). That is not the logical role of an axiom. The axioms of geometry are propositions which are true or false, and not attempts to settle the reference of a word or sign. Frege has a range of technical objections to the notion of implicit definition.[5] It would take us too far away from our main concern to address the merits or otherwise of his objections here. Our main concern is twofold. First, leading figures of contemporary logic and contemporary mathematics, such as Frege and Hilbert, have radically different views on the role of axioms in deductive systems such as with Euclidean geometry. Second, Hahn in his approach to the axiomatization of economics is on the Fregian, rather than the implicit definition side of this divide.

According to Hahn, one of his 'first reasons for praising theory, at least in its modern mode, is that it comes clean on both its axioms and assumptions' (Hahn 1985: 5). As we have already seen in Chapter 4, the axioms 'constitute claims about the world' (Hahn 1985: 5), i.e. they are propositions that are true or false. Indeed, while he does not use the notion of self-evidently true, the axioms are such 'as to make further argument unnecessary' (Hahn 1985: 5). In this context, they are basic in a twofold sense. First, the axioms are the basic starting point for economic theory, and, second, they are basic truths about the world in the sense that any further argument about them, given present consensus, is unnecessary. In short, the axioms are making claims about the real world and thus are not defining complex concepts or complex predicates. It is via its axioms that theoretical economics is a deductive system making claims about the real economic world. Theoretical economics is not occupying some remote abstract logical space which, as such, has no connection whatsoever to the real economic world.

Moreover, in the spirit of Euclid, when Hahn looks at the basic assertions of neoclassical theory, he distinguishes between axioms and assumptions. Like Euclid's postulates, as distinct from Euclidean axioms, Hahn's assumptions, though basic to economics as a deductive system, have not the same truth status as the axioms. In particular, those assumptions based on 'casual empiricism' are clearly propositional in nature. Indeed, they are taken as correct in so far as they are 'not implausible in the light of experience' (Hahn 1985: 11). Finally, assumptions introduced on pragmatic grounds of, for instance, simplicity–tractability considerations are also propositions, known not to be strictly true. Like the axioms, the assumptions do not simply exist in some purely logico-mathematical space of abstract concepts which are not propositions, i.e. sentences that are true or false. In short, for Hahn, his axioms and assumptions are propositional in nature: they are sentences that are true or false, they are not implicit definitions.

The Hahn–Hausman altercation revisited

In the previous chapter, we engaged the Hahn–Hausman altercation, without any reference as to how they view the axiomatization of economics. In his piece 'What are General Equilibrium Theories?' Hausman claims that

> My views are closest to those expressed by Kenneth Arrow and Frank Hahn. They largely deny that general equilibrium theories say anything about the real world, but they insist, rather unclearly, that they remain a serious and valuable part of economics.
>
> (Hausman 1992(b): 170)

In light of the previous chapter, we cannot concur with Hausman. There is no lack of clarity to Hahn's thesis that general equilibrium theory is a privileged starting point in the objective understanding of the real economic world. In particular, via it's axiom of rationality, it has some truth content. Moreover, it is valuable in that it, for the first time, delivered a rigorous proof of the existence of equilibrium. If our thesis is correct, how did Hausman get it wrong? Clearly, just as economic theoreticians are not, as Hahn says, 'slouches,' neither are philosophers of Hausman's ability and standing. The reason lies in Hausman's philosophical commitment to the implicit definition reading of the axioms and assumptions of general equilibrium theory. This commitment is explicitly articulated in his piece 'On the Conceptual Structure of Neoclassical Economics – A Philosopher's View' (Hausman 1992(b): 25–32).

According to Hausman 'the models that economists employ should be regarded as complex predicates or as definitions of such complex predicates or concepts' (Hausman 1992(b): 25). He is quite emphatic on this point. He continues, 'a model is of the same logical kind as a predicate, such as "is triangular," or as a definition of what it is to be triangular.' In logic the proposition 'Japan is not a perfectly competitive economy' is read as the negation of the elementary proposition 'Japan is a perfectly competitive economy.' This elementary proposition is logically speaking either true or false. Indeed, a logician totally ignorant of economics still knows it is either true or false, but does not know which truth value holds. The crucial point, however, is that this elementary proposition is logically analysed into the proper name 'Japan' and *the complex predicate* 'is a perfectly competitive economy.' While the elementary proposition is true or false, the complex predicate on its own is neither true nor false. Thus, Hausman claims that 'a model of a perfectly competitive economy, for example, *does nothing more than define* the theoretical term "a perfectly competitive economy"' (Hausman 1992(b): 25, italics added).

In this philosophical view, a model is a definition of a complex predicate. The next question Hausman addresses is how is such a model constructed? According to Hausman, 'one constructs or presents a model typically by listing a number of "assumptions." *These assumptions should be regarded as clauses in a definition*' (Hausman 1992(b): 25 italics added). In our terminology, these assumptions are defining characteristics of the complex predicate in question. In this connection, Hausman gives another example. Economists in studying consumer choice often begin with a simplified situation of two commodities and their prices, where the consumer spends all of his or her income on the two commodities. 'The various assumptions made in this bit of analysis can be regarded as defining a new concept – call it "a simple consumption system"' (Hausman 1992(b): 25). Given that an economic model has an axiomatic structure, its axioms are the basic assumptions of the model. But these axiomatic assumptions make no claims whatsoever about the economic world. Rather, they are defining clauses of a new complex predicate or concept. In the frequently used terminology of logicians and mathematicians, the postulates of the axiomatic system implicitly define a new complex predicate. As we saw in the last section, Hahn is not reading neoclassical theory through the philosophical lens of the identification of an axiomatic system with a definition of a complex predicate. Given Hausman's philosophical commitment to the identification of an axiomatic system with an implicit definition of a complex predicate, he misreads Hahn's theoretical work 'as purely conceptual or mathematical. One is only exploring and developing a complicated concept or definition' (Hausman 1992(b): 270). Hahn, however, is doing no such thing. Arising from his Fregian reading of axioms as propositions grounded in reality, which should not be confused with a definition, Hahn is exploring and developing a partial, but objective, understanding of the real economic world.

This difference is also evident in Hausman's view of the realism of assumptions debate in economic methodology discussed in Chapter 3. According to Hausman in so far as economists are working with a model, i.e. an implicit definition, 'one can reject any question about the realism of assumptions one makes. But remember the reason is that one is saying *nothing* about the world' (Hausman 1992(b): 26). On the contrary, for Hahn, the realism of assumptions requirement cannot be so dismissed. The moral is clear. Hahn is not reading neoclassical theory through the lens of the identification of an axiomatic system with a definition of a complex predicate, where one would be saying nothing about the world.

Of course, as we have already emphasized in the last chapter, for Hausman neoclassical economics is a science. However, in his view there is a clear-cut division of labour in that science. On the one side, theoreticians, like Hahn, are engaged in the abstract process of implicitly defining complex predicates. This activity, as such 'is of little interest to empirical scientists' (Hausman 1992(b): 26). On the other side, the empirical becomes central when one hypothesizes or asserts that these complex concepts are true of aspects of the real economic world. On this side of the division of labour, economics is an empirical science. Moreover, in contrast with physics, 'this is precisely where things become uncomfortable' (Hausman 1992(b): 27). These clearly defined terms 'will never apply to economic reality very simply or clearly' (Hausman 1992(b): 27). However, with the appropriate choice of complex concepts thus defined, empirical economists can make assertions about the world which 'if not strictly true... may be reasonable approximations' (Hausman 1992(b): 27). We have already discussed in the last chapter the choice made by Hausman and Hahn's response to it. In this section, our objective is to show how Hausman and Hahn have divergent views of the role of axioms or principles in neoclassical economics. For Hahn, the axioms of neoclassical economics give him a foothold in the real economic world, whereas for Hausman, Hahn is merely defining very complex predicates.

To conclude, the critical reader will notice that we are sitting on the fence in the sense of merely noting the existence of divergent views on the role of axioms in a deductive system. We have avoided the crucial philosophical question, namely which is the correct view? A Hausmanite might want to argue that, while we are historically correct, Frege lost the battle with Hilbert. Most logicians today do not read the axioms of a purely deductive system *à la* Frege. The latter claim is probably true. However, one should not forget that, for Hahn, theoretical economics is not simply a piece of pure mathematics. Its aim is to furnish us with an objective understanding of the actual economic world. Like Frege's perception of Euclidean geometry, at the end of the nineteenth century, neoclassical economics in axiomatic garb had its feet in two worlds – the real world and the world of logical rigour. Be that as it may, one may conclude that in the end Hilbert won out. But it was not the Hilbert of implicit definitions. Rather, it was Hilbert the strict formalist. And Debreu, unlike Hahn, uses this strictly formalist view of an axiomatic system in the methodological explanation of his work.

Fregian formal, and Hilbert formalist, systems

In the previous sections the focus was on geometry as the paradigm of a deductive system. By the first decade of the twentieth century, pure mathematicians and logicians had also axiomatized arithmetic and logic. By way of illustrating the shift from a Fregian formal system to a Hilbert formalist one, we will focus on propositional logic. Traditionally, since the time of Aristotle, logic was concerned with the validity of inferences. Moreover, we know, since Aristotle, an inference is valid by virtue of its form, not its content. For instance, the inference 'if the cat is on the mat then the mouse is at play and the mouse is not at play therefore the cat is not on the mat' has the logical form if p then q, and not q, therefore not p. The form is obtained by introducing variables 'p,' 'q,' 'r,' etc. In this context 'p,' 'q,' 'r,' etc. are propositional variables. Logicians also introduced other symbols for the so-called logical constants 'and,' 'or,' 'not' and 'if – then.' These were replaced respectively by '&,' 'v,' '~,' and '→.' Finally, by spelling out the truth conditions for complex propositions, a technique was developed to determine the validity, or otherwise, of an infinite number of inferences using the logical constants 'and,' 'or,' 'not' and 'if – then.'

Frege was the first logician to emphasize that, if one wanted to attain the highest standards of rigour for propositional logic, one would need to construct an ideal language, with no ambiguity and everything explicitly stated. In light of this Fregian ideal, logicians reconstructed propositional logic along the following lines.[6] A finite list of primitive, undefined symbols is specified. These include the symbols listed in the previous paragraph. Rules of syntax are explicitly stated. These rules unambiguously determine the well-formed formulae (the wffs) of the language. New symbols may be introduced by explicit definition. Any new symbol is reducible to the primitive ones. The bivalence principle is stated: every elementary proposition has two and only two truth values, i.e. is either true or false. The truth-table method for ascertaining the validity, or otherwise, of any inference, represented by its wff, is specified.

Propositional logic in this rigorous form can now be axiomatized. A very limited set of wffs, called axioms, are selected. Next, a finite set of transformation rules (sometimes called rules of inference) are explicitly stated. These rules are mechanically applied to the axioms in a finite number of steps. The final line is called a theorem. The transformation rules can also be applied to a combination of these theorems and axioms to prove other theorems. Any axiom or theorem is called a thesis. Among the other tasks awaiting to be done are proofs of the consistency and completeness of the axiomatic system. The system is inconsistent if for any wff, α, both α and $\sim\alpha$ are theses. The system is complete means that if any wff not derivable as a theorem is added to the axioms, the system would no longer be consistent.

Such axiomatized systems are, in Frege's sense, formal deductive ones. The form is conveyed by the symbols. For Frege, if a letter used as a symbol does not designate anything or does not have the purpose of designating anything then it is not a logical symbol at all. For instance a Fregian logician is trained to read the symbol 'p' as a propositional variable. Its logical role is to enable logicians to attain the appropriate level of generality or abstractness in the *semantical* domain of propositions. Deductive systems attain a very high level of generality or abstractness by using symbols. However, even at the most abstract level possible, such symbols retain their semantical roots. Frege uses a slightly different metaphor to convey this relationship. A formal deductive system is similar 'to a creeper twining around' its original, semantical non-formal support, 'loosing all hold once its support and source of sustenance are removed' (Frege 1971(b): 137).

Hilbert's purely formalist approach to a formal deductive system rejects this Fregian approach as being based on confusion. Frege was wrong in claiming that a symbol in a formal deductive system has the logical purpose of designating something. As Nagel and Newman express it, a Hilbertian purely formalist approach to a formal deductive system entails 'the complete formalization' of the system. 'This involves draining the expressions occurring within the system of all meaning: they are to be regarded as empty signs' (Nagel and Newman 2005: 19). A formal deductive system is completely independent of any semantical element. A formal deductive system is a purely syntactical calculus, with semantics playing no role whatsoever. The Fregians simply got this wrong. Frege's analogy must be inverted. A purely syntactical calculus is the rooted trunk of the tree of a formal deductive system. It stands on its own and it is the logical source and sustenance of the creeper of semantics wound round it. Thus, a formal deductive system has a twofold structure: (1) It is a purely syntactical machine for constructing wffs, i.e. strings of meaningless signs; (2) A purely syntactical calculus for deriving purely syntactical theorems by mechanically applying purely syntactical transformation rules to an arbitrarily chosen set of wffs, called axioms or theorems, already derived. No meaning or no interpretation whatsoever is attached to its symbols.[7]

We will follow the Hilbertain convention of calling such a deductive system mathematics. Hilbert draws a sharp distinction between mathematics and meta-mathematics. Precisely because Fregians do not recognize this distinction, their conception of a deductive system is confused. Mathematics is a system of meaningless symbols. For instance, the symbol 'p' in mathematics has no meaning or interpretation. Meta-mathematics, however, consists in meaningful statements about mathematics, the symbols occurring in its calculus, their arrangement and so on. For instance, the statement 'p' is a variable, does not belong to mathematics; it does not occur within the system as 'p' does. That statement belongs to meta-mathematics. For Hilbert, two very interesting meta-mathematical statements are 'the system is consistent' and 'the system is complete.' These never occur in the mathematical calculus. They are statements about the system. In light of this distinction, part of the Hilbert programme was to construct a meta-mathematical, absolute proof of the consistency of deductive systems which would be finitist. Finitist means that no reference must be made to an infinite number of operations with wffs or to an infinite number of structural properties of wffs. For instance, logicians succeeded in constructing such a proof for Frege's propositional logic. The aim was to do the same for other systems such as arithmetic. Moreover, it should be noted that such a conception of a formal deductive system is at variance with the implicit definition reading used in the previous section. The implicit definition reading mislocates a formal system within semantics, which is an elementary confusion similar to that of the Fregians.

Before addressing the relevance of Hilbert's formalist reading of a deductive or axiomatic system to Debreu and Hahn, we need to emphasize one final issue that is crucial for them. Much of theoretical research, ranging from theoretical physics to theoretical economics, would be impossible without mathematics. In this sense, there is much more to mathematics than pure mathematics. To grasp the correct understanding of the use or application of pure mathematics in these concrete domains we need to address, in general terms, the issue of applied mathematics in this Hilbertian formalist setting. In general, applied mathematics consists in giving an interpretation to the purely syntactical symbols of the system. This process of interpretation is also called constructing or finding a model of the system. In the process of interpretation, different semantical meanings may be given to the empty symbols of the axiomatic system. For instance, the symbol 'p' within the calculus can be interpreted as a propositional variable and the string 'p & q' will then be interpreted as the form of a conjunctive proposition, 'p and q.' Alternatively 'p' could be interpreted as a set in classical set theory. Then the same string 'p & q' would be interpreted as the intersection of the two sets p and q. The same syntactical string is given different interpretations.

In particular, once a formal proof is given in the calculus of pure mathematics, semantical interpretation can range over an extensive variety of domains, from classical set theory through various idealizations of real world situations to actual or empirical real world theories, hypotheses or descriptions. The spectrum of semantical interpretation for applied mathematics is vast. Clearly, it would be a mistake to assume that, when an interpretation of a syntactical theorem is correctly specified, the interpretation is either a description of, or a law-like truth about, the real world. Such an assumption is based on an utter misunderstanding of the process of interpretation. Interpretations are not necessarily empirical. Rather, the term 'interpretations' merely signals a legitimate move from the domain of the syntactical into the domain of the semantical.

Debreu, Hahn and Hilbertian formalism

Since the publication of his *Theory of Value* in 1959, Debreu has drawn our attention to the fact that this kind of Hilbertian, purely formalist approach is the logical framework for his research. In his *Theory of Value*, he unequivocally espouses this formalist approach on the grounds of rigour.

> Allegiance to rigor dictates the axiomatic form of the analysis where the theory, in the strict sense, is *logically entirely disconnected from its interpretations*. In order to bring out fully *this disconnectedness* all the definitions, all the hypotheses and the main results of the theory, in the strict sense, are distinguished by italics; moreover the transition from informal discussion of interpretations to the formal construction of the theory is often marked by one of the expressions 'in the language of the theory,' 'for the sake of the theory,' 'formally.'
>
> (Debreu 1959: x, italics added)

Writing twenty one years later the same theme is clearly expressed. In his 'Theoretical Models: Mathematical Form and Economic Content' he gives a brief 'schema' of an economic theory and adds:

> According to this schema an axiomatized theory has a mathematical form that is *completely separated from its economic content. If one removes the economic interpretation* of the primitive concepts... its bare mathematical structure must still stand... The divorce of form and content immediately yields a new theory when a novel interpretation of a primitive concept is discussed.
>
> (Debreu 1986: 1265)

In this passage, the Hilbertian strictly formalist usage of key terms like 'primitive concept,' 'axioms,' 'interpretation of primitive concepts,' 'separation of form and content' is clearly evident. Indeed, according to Debreu, this approach 'contributed powerfully to the rapid expansion of mathematical economics after World War II' (Debreu 1986: 1265).

As we have already seen, for Hahn, axioms are propositional in nature. He is using a very different conception of an axiomatic system to that of Debreu. Hahn's use of an axiomatic system is, as we have already seen when discussing Hausman's implicit definition approach, much more traditional, whereas Debreu's is appealing to the more contemporary, purely formalist approach. Moreover, this purely formalist approach places Debreu's *Theory of Value* in a historico-economic vacuum: this major landmark in twentieth-century economic theory is, logically speaking, a piece of pure syntactical mathematics, which merely happens to have an economic interpretation. It could, as Debreu explicitly claims, be given some other interpretation with nothing whatsoever to do with economics. Mathematically its relationship to economics is incidental. However, as Ingrao and Israel point out, 'Debreu's *Theory of Value* is consciously *inspired* by a group of well-defined economic themes and its explicit reference to "the tradition of the Lausanne school" is proof of this' (Ingrao and Israel 1990: 284, italics added). The purely formalist approach, however, is utterly silent on this historico-economic inspiration; indeed, it simply adds on the economic dimension at the end of a piece of mathematics as a possible interpretation. In reality, however, the economic dimension is there from the very beginning and is not just added on at the end as a possible semantical interpretation.

Hahn also explicitly acknowledges the historico-economic trajectory of Debreu's *Theory of Value*, through Walras to its origins in Adam Smith. Indeed, he elaborates on that trajectory in his piece 'General Equilibrium for Intellectual Historians.' In our opinion, one can easily respond to this historico-economic lacuna in the purely formalist approach, by adopting a strategy suggested by Frege in his discussion of Hilbert's Festschrift 'On the Foundations of Geometry.' As we already noted, Hilbert's Festschrift was given two distinct readings: the implicit definitional reading discussed earlier and the purely formalist one used in this section. Frege identified the historico-geometric presupposition in the purely formalist reading of Hilbert's Festschrift. Frege acknowledges this presupposition by drawing a sharp distinction between the definitions and axioms of a deductive mathematical system and a third kind of proposition.

Propositions of this third kind are 'the explanatory propositions which, however, I should not like to consider as belonging to mathematics itself but instead should be relegated to the preamble or propaedeutic' (Frege 1971(b): 8). In their propaedeutics, mathematicians work by 'hints' based on 'co-operative understanding' (ibid.: 8). These propaedeutic sentences, however, cannot be used in proofs 'for they lack the requisite precision.' Rather, they inspire or guide the choice of the primitive terms or axioms. Thus, as a piece of pure geometry, Hilbert's axiomatic system is purely formal, in that its proofs depend solely on its formal axioms and its formal rules of inference. However, it is geometric because of its geometric propaedeutic. Similarly, the Walrasian programmes serve as a Fregian propaedeutic in Debreu's *Theory of Value*. Thus, Debreu admits that 'although an axiomatic theory may flaunt the separation of its mathematical form and its economic content in print, their interaction is sometimes close in the discovery and elaboration phases' (Debreu 1986: 1266). In this modified Hilbertian account, economic theorizing has three phases. First, propaedeutic work inspires or guides the choice of axioms. Second, this work is transformed into a purely formalist deductive system. Third, the system is given an economic interpretation.[8] In this context, Debreu delivers his existence theorem. In short, in proving the existence of equilibrium, Debreu has recourse to what was perceived as the highest possible standards of proof that are specified in a Hilbertian, purely formal system.

We are now in a position to explain the difference between Hahn's and Debreu's approaches to deductive systems and their use in economic theorizing. Our explanation is based on Solow's insight that 'problems must dictate methods not vice versa' (Solow 1954: 374). Debreu's problematic is to construct, in the most rigorous possible way, a proof of the existence of general equilibrium. To accomplish this he has recourse to Hilbert's purely formalist account of a proof. This furnishes him with the appropriate rigorous method, which entails the three steps outlined in the previous paragraph. Hahn, on the other hand, is faced with a different problematic. He is building on, and eventually reconstructing, Debreu's *economic interpretation*. He knows that the Arrow–Debreu general equilibrium is not unique. He also knows that the conditions under which Debreu proved the existence of equilibrium are very far from the conditions that obtain in the real economic world. An integral part of his research programme in theoretical economics is to relax some of the usual assumptions of the theory and thereby enhance the economic understanding of the real world. Hahn is thus working deep inside the domain of semantics and, in that domain the Hilbertian, purely syntactical approach is not the most appropriate method. The Fregian approach is more appropriate in the domain of semantics, and it is also more appropriate to Hahn's specific task of gaining objective understanding of the real economic world, given his grammar of argumentation. Clearly, this does not imply that Hahn would object to Debreu's choice of Hilbertian formalism as the most appropriate method given Debreu's problematic. As Hahn remarks 'if we did not have Arrow–Debreu theory it would be priority number one to construct it' (Hahn 1985: 13–14) and this would include the use of a Hilbert-type rigorous proof.

We now turn to two final points which, in our opinion, are crucial for the methodological understanding of Hahn's appeal to Debreu's *Theory of Value*. The first is the very wide spectrum of possible interpretations that can be given to a Hilbertian purely formalist system. As we have already seen in the previous section, a wide spectrum of domains of possible interpretations exist. The methodological question is the following: in what domain should one place Debreu's economic interpretation of his rigorous formal proof? In Hahn's view, numerous economists misunderstood Debreu's proof by interpreting it as a description, either factual or law-like, of the actual economic world. For Hahn, Debreu, when properly interpreted, is not describing the world, but 'there are influential economists who take a version of the theory as descriptive' (Hahn 1985: 14), and they are mistaken. Indeed, he is very emphatic on this point:

> Neo-classical theory in general and G.E. in particular has been given more empirical weight than it can, or *was designed to support*. This is almost entirely due to American economists… I believe that one could spin a very convincing theory of why it is that so many Americans regard G.E. and Neo-classical theory as Science in the same way as one regards the laws of gravity. But this is not the place. Suffice it to say that they have *misunderstood* what the project is about.
>
> (Hahn 2005(a): 10, italics added)

Given that Debreu's *Theory of Value* is an existence proof using the resources of a Hilbertian formalist deductive system, it cannot be interpreted as a description of how economic order is brought about. Rather, 'when a G.E. theorist (a good G.E. theorist) shows how indeed there might be order, he is not claiming that there is order' (Hahn 2005(a): 11). Given what it was designed to do, i.e. prove the existence of general equilibrium, and the nature of the proof, its domain of interpretation is not the actual economic world but an idealized economic situation, idealized by a very restrictive set of conditions which preclude the theory being either an empirical or law-like description of the actual economic world. For Hahn, economists who interpret Debreu's *Theory of Value* as a major contribution to an economic science directly applicable to the actual economic world are *mistaken*. They utterly fail to properly understand what was actually accomplished by Debreu.

Once again, we see Hahn's prescriptive methodology at work. Hahn is not, *à la* Hausman, either describing or explaining in a scientific manner what orthodox economists are doing in their modelling and other research. As we have already noted, according to Hahn, orthodox modelling on the assumption that Debreu's theory is a scientific description or is directly applicable to the real world is just bad economics. It is based on an utter misunderstanding of the phenomenal achievement of Debreu. This achievement was to rigorously prove – and thereby 'put beyond doubt' – that 'in suitable circumstances order was indeed possible' (Hahn 2005(a): 6). As he said 20 years earlier:

> No ambiguity of what it is that is being done is possible. We are concerned with the existence of a particular state of the economy in which the best choice of individuals are mutually compatible when these choices are entirely determined by preferences, technology, endowments and market prices. *There is nothing here to tell us that any given economy will be in that state or that it tends to that state.* The theory is what it is and not something else.
>
> (Hahn 1985: 12, italics added)

This brings us to our final point, namely how to interpret the word 'exists.' Hahn correctly identifies what the word 'existence' means when applied to the interpretation of an existence proof in a Hilbertian formalist system. According to Hahn, Debreu's work

> establishes the astonishing claim that it is logically possible to describe an economy in which millions of agents, looking no further than their own interests and responding to the sparse information system of prices only, can still attain a coherent economic disposition of resources. Having made that clear, let me nonetheless emphasize the phrase 'logically possible'. Nothing whatever has been said of whether it is possible to describe any actual economy in these terms.
>
> (Hahn 1982(a): 114)

Existence as established by Debreu's proof does not mean empirical existence i.e. existence in the real economic world. What the theory delivers is existence in the sense of logically possible or, negatively put, freedom from contradiction. This, and no more, was the 'major intellectual achievement' of Debreu which constitutes 'the crown of neo-classical' economics (Hahn 2005(a): 8). Unfortunately, 'people, including G.E. theorists, got hold of the wrong end of the stick. That wrong end is simply the belief that it provides a fully fashioned description of actual economies' (Hahn 2005(a): 7). We would add that they got the wrong end of the stick because they did not pay sufficient attention to the correct meaning of the term 'existence' when used in the interpretation of a Hilbertian formalist existence proof. Hahn correctly identifies this meaning.

In the course of this chapter we have clarified Hahn's specific understanding of the axiomatization of economics. Contrary to Hausman's analysis, economic axioms are not defining characteristics of complex predicates, which, as such, are not a part of our empirical knowledge. Moreover, unlike Debreu, Hahn's axioms are not purely syntactical strings of meaningless symbols which mathematically have no connection to any world, physical or economic. For Hahn, economic axioms, as distinct from assumptions, are mathematically rigorous explications of common sense truths. Moreover, in his analysis of the objective meaning of Debreu's existence proof, Hahn correctly recognizes that Debreu's method of proof entails that the proven existence has one and only one meaning, namely logical possibility. This logical possibility does not mean that the proven equilibrium is a description of some actual situation. In the following chapter we will, among other issues, elaborate on the presuppositions of Debreu's existence proof.[9] In particular, we discuss Kaldor's claim that, given the nature of Debreu's proof, it is impossible to give it an economic interpretation.

7 Kaldor and Hahn on equilibrium economics

> I fear that in tilting at the windmill of some old-fashioned textbook Professor Kaldor has missed the dragon.
>
> (Hahn 1973(a): 32)

> Kaldor of course was criticizing very heavily people like me and so on for building castles in the air, or that we were making science fiction. There is something true in it, but at least we built something.
>
> (Hahn 2005(b): 17)

Introduction

In Chapter 3 we briefly discussed Hahn's dismissal of the methodological thesis that neoclassical economics is in crisis. In that connection, we distinguished between the diagnosis of crisis made by eminent economists, such as Kaldor, on the one hand, and the same diagnosis made by professional methodologists who view economics through the lens of some preferred methodology adopted from the physical sciences, on the other. We felt that, while Hahn's dismissal of the claims of crisis had merit in the case of methodologists who failed to address what was happening at the frontiers of neoclassical research, one should keep an open mind on the merits of that claim made by expert economists of the calibre of Kaldor.

The central target of Kaldor's uncompromising negative assessment was, what he termed, 'equilibrium economics,' especially the general equilibrium variant of this mode of theorizing, as articulated in the work of Debreu. His criticism of this approach to economic theory and theorizing was relentless and unflinching. According to Kaldor, equilibrium economics is 'barren and irrelevant as an apparatus of thought to deal with the manner of operations of economic forces,' and it 'has become a major obstacle to the development of economics as a science' (Kaldor 1972: 1237). In Kaldor's opinion, real progress in economics requires 'a major act of demolition' (Kaldor 1972: 1240). What for Hahn is 'the crown' of neoclassical economics is for Kaldor 'thoroughly misleading and pretty useless – in terms of the theory's declared objective of explaining how economic processes work in a decentralized market economy' (Kaldor 1972: 1240).

When Kaldor heard that Hahn proposed to address the notion of equilibrium in his inaugural lecture at Cambridge, Kaldor, according to Hahn, urged him to take notice of his own piece 'The Irrelevance of Equilibrium Economics' published in the *Economic Journal* in 1972. Hahn welcomed Kaldor's suggestion, and hence he made numerous references to Kaldor's piece in his inaugural lecture in 1973. This is the background to this chapter. In the next section, we give a summary account of Kaldor's critique. However, this summary account is not limited to his 1972 piece in the *Economic Journal*. This is followed by an analysis of Hahn's defence of equilibrium economics in response to Kaldor. Finally, by focusing on the notions of mathematical existence and contrasting it with economic existence, we introduce a novel defence of Kaldor's negative methodological thesis that 'equilibrium theory has reached the stage where the pure theorist has successfully (though perhaps inadvertently) demonstrated that the main implications of this theory *cannot possibly hold in reality*' (Kaldor 1972: 1240, italics added).

Kaldor's non-monist critique of equilibrium economics

Kaldor was unquestionably one of the pivotal post-war figures in the Cambridge critique of orthodox theory, but he pioneered an altogether broader attack on orthodoxy than many of his Cambridge colleagues. This arose from his strongly held view that there was not 'a single, overwhelming objection to orthodox economic theory: there are a number of different points that are distinct though interrelated' (Kaldor 1975: 347–8). He sometimes referred to his Cambridge colleagues as 'monists' for maintaining that exposing the logical inconsistencies of marginal productivity theory was 'alone sufficient to pull the rug from under the neoclassical value theory' (Kaldor 1975: 348). Kaldor felt strongly that this 'monist' approach was badly flawed and that marginal productivity theory was not the most significant domain of orthodoxy to contest. Other aspects of orthodox economics, he believed, were 'in some ways... even more misleading than the application of marginal productivity to the division between wages and profits, which has been the main subject of discussion' (Kaldor 1975: 348).

In contrast to his Cambridge colleagues, Kaldor's non-monist critique extended to a number of key areas, all of which pointed to the emergence of his penetrating and substantive critique of equilibrium economics. The critique of these areas were elaborated in the course of Kaldor's major post-war methodological writings, but were most systematically delineated in his Okun Lectures. There, Kaldor identified three major issues, which he analysed in some detail. The first referred to how markets work and why their *modus operandi* precluded a pure price system of market clearing; second, he addressed the issue of how prices are formed and how competition operates in the context of 'the quasi-competitiveness or quasi-monopolistic markets that embrace a very large part of a modern industrial economy' (Kaldor 1985: 12); and, finally, Kaldor presented 'an outline of an alternative approach to orthodox equilibrium theory' (ibid.: 12), which examined how to reincorporate the powerful influences of increasing returns into economic theory.

In formulating his 'alternative approach,' centred on increasing returns to scale, Kaldor developed some of his most fundamental objections to equilibrium economics. The notion of equilibrium Kaldor had in mind was that 'of the general economic equilibrium originally formulated by Walras,' but which had been developed 'with increasing elegance, exactness, and logical precision by the mathematical economists of our own generation,' most notably Gerard Debreu (Kaldor 1972: 1237). Thirlwall (1987) has identified three main strands to Kaldor's critique of equilibrium economics. The first was Kaldor's objection to the use made of axiomatic assumptions in equilibrium economics. For Kaldor, unlike any scientific theory, 'where the basic assumptions are chosen on the basis of direct observation of the phenomena,' the basic assumptions of economic theory 'are either of a kind that are unverifiable' – such as, consumers 'maximize' their utility or producers 'maximize' their profits – or 'are directly contradicted by observation.' The latter included the following extended list: 'perfect competition, perfect divisibility, linear-homogenous and continuously differentiable production functions, wholly impersonal market relations, exclusive role of prices in information flows and perfect knowledge of all relevant prices by all agents and perfect foresight' (Kaldor 1972: 1238). The use of such assumptions, which were not just 'abstract' but 'contrary to experience,' was inconsistent with good science and rendered economics vacuous as an empirical science.

Second, Kaldor argued that the primacy accorded to the principle of substitutability within the framework of the allocative function of markets, was at the expense of the principle of complementarity within the dynamic process of accumulation. For Kaldor, complementarity was paramount, not just between factors of production, but between whole sectors of the economy, as his work on the relation between agriculture, manufacturing and services demonstrated. The overarching emphasis on substitutability and trade-offs in equilibrium economics led to a neglect of the crucial role of complementarities in economic development, Kaldor argued. Allied to this concern was Kaldor's hostility to the emphasis on static allocation of a given set of resources in equilibrium economics. For him, the central economic problem was to understand the highly dynamic processes of accumulation and development (Kaldor 1996).

Finally, Kaldor rejected the basic assumption of constant returns which dominated theorizing in equilibrium economics. More particularly, he abhorred the fact that 'the general equilibrium school (as distinct from Marshall) has always fully recognized the *absence* of increasing returns as one of the basic "axioms" of the system.' As a result, 'the existence of increasing returns and its consequences for the whole framework of economic theory have been completely neglected' (Kaldor, 1972: 1241, 1242). Kaldor was strongly influenced by Allyn Young, one of his teachers at the London School of Economics in the 1920s. In a now classic paper, Young (1928) drew on insights from Adam Smith to re-establish the importance of increasing returns for economic progress. Kaldor believed that Young's paper was 'many years ahead of its time,' but that economists had 'ceased to take any notice of it long before they were able to grasp its full revolutionary implications' (Kaldor, 1972: 1243). Kaldor was also familiar with Sraffa's (1926) contribution to this issue. Kaldor became committed to the view that, contrary to the position in equilibrium economics, increasing returns were central to understanding production processes at the level of the firm, and this, in turn, explained his view of the manufacturing sector as the primary 'engine of growth' in the development of capitalist economies. In light of this critique, as summarized above, Kaldor forged a marriage of the 'Smith–Young doctrine on increasing returns with the Keynesian doctrine of effective demand' (Kaldor, 1972: 1250) within the framework of a theory of cumulative causation for the analysis of economic change in decentralized market economies.

However, Kaldor's critique of equilibrium economics was not limited to the above issues. His conception of 'economics as a science' was also fundamental to his critique of equilibrium economics. For Kaldor, science was 'a body of theorems based on assumptions that are empirically derived, and which embody hypotheses that are capable of verification both in regard to the assumptions and predictions' (Kaldor, 1972: 1237). Starting from this view of science, he subjected equilibrium economics to a stringent methodological critique, the prevailing theme of which was the fundamental empirical inadequacy of equilibrium theory and its incapacity to engage the complexities of advanced market economies in a meaningful way.

Although this position represented a fundamental rejection of the methodological basis of equilibrium economics, Kaldor did not provide a systematically formulated, much less a complete, alternative methodology for economics. Instead, what we find scattered among his economic writings are a number of important methodological suggestions. According to Kaldor, any attempt to construct a scientific theory must begin with a summary of the known facts in the domain under investigation. In the case of economics, since the initial summary is normally presented in a statistical framework, the economic theorist starts with a 'stylized' compendium of the facts. These 'stylized facts' are statistical, but not universal, generalizations that describe empirical regularities. Economists then proceed to construct their economic theory on what Kaldor calls the 'as if' method. Although Kaldor does not spell out the full details of this method, we can reconstruct his position as follows. First, the economist 'abstracts' or develops higher-level hypotheses consistent with the stylized facts and then proceeds to construct an economic theory. Second, the economist attempts to express the constructed theory in a systematic way. Finally, the theory is inductively tested, i.e. its predictions are tested empirically by observation of the economic world. In this connection, as Lawson (1989) has pointed out, Kaldor argued that the process of inductive testing was altogether more important than the process of axiomatization.

We now turn to Kaldor's specific critique of Debreu. As Kaldor (1972: 1237) pointed out, Debreu's *Theory of Value* (1959) gives us an 'elegant, exact and logically precise' account of general equilibrium. Methodologically, Debreu's work has two distinctive, though interrelated, characteristics. First, Debreu ingeniously exploited the powerful mathematical resources of Cantorian set theory. His approach marks a major shift in the process of the mathematization of economics in the course of the twentieth-century. In the first phase, initiated by Walras and others, the mathematical resources of Cantorian set theory were not exploited. However, in the second phase, which occurred in the second half of the century and is exemplified in the work of Debreu, Cantorian set theory becomes indispensable in proving the existence of general equilibrium (Weintraub, 2002). Second, the strictly formalist character of Debreu's axiomatic approach is explicitly noted by Kaldor; 'In the strict sense, as Debreu says, the theory is "*logically entirely disconnected from its interpretation*"' (Kaldor, 1972: 1237, italics added). According to Debreu, theoretical economics must attain the highest standards of logico-mathematical rigour, as spelled out in the Hilbert axiomatic programme which is, as we saw in the last chapter, purely formalist.

Moreover, Kaldor claims that Debreu's theory 'is not *intended* to describe reality' (Kaldor, 1972: 1238). If we pause, we may ask the question: if Debreu's theory is primarily logical and not empirical, and if it is not even intended to describe reality, what makes it a piece of theoretical economics? Surely, theoretical economics, understood as an empirical (as distinct from empiricist) science, ought to make claims about actual economies, either at the descriptive or explanatory level? Again, Kaldor draws the obvious conclusion. General equilibrium is neither a description nor an explanation of actual economies, as these terms are understood by empirical scientists. Rather, it is:

> a set of theorems that are *logically* deducible from precisely formulated assumptions; and the purpose of the exercise is to find the minimum 'basic assumptions' necessary for establishing the existence of an 'equilibrium' set of prices (and output/input matrixes) that is (a) unique, (b) stable, (c) satisfies the conditions of Pareto optimality.
>
> (Kaldor, 1972: 1237)

In other words, Debreu's *Theory of Value*, seen as a work aimed at attaining the highest standards of logico-mathematical rigour and precision, is a purely formal uninterpreted system, having no connection whatsoever to any branch of reality in general or real economic processes in particular. However, it is economic in that its *choice* of axioms *prior to* the logical exploitation of these axioms is informed by *the desire to prove, when interpreted, the existence* of an equilibrium set of prices that is (a) unique, (b) stable, (c) satisfies the conditions of Pareto optimality. In this fashion, according to Kaldor, Debreu's *Theory of Value* became for numerous economists 'the necessary conceptual *framework*... for any attempt at explaining how a "decentralized" system works' (Kaldor 1972: 1238).

In total opposition to this latter thesis, Kaldor maintains that general equilibrium theory amounts to a set of:

> propositions which the *pure* mathematical economist has shown to be valid only on assumptions that are manifestly unreal – that is to say, directly contrary to experience and not just 'abstract.' In fact, equilibrium theory has reached the stage where the pure theorist has successfully (though perhaps inadvertently) demonstrated that the main implications of this theory cannot possibly hold in reality, but has not yet managed to pass his message down the line to the textbook writer and to the classroom.
>
> (Kaldor, 1972: 1240)

Unfortunately, Kaldor did not spell out the methodological reasons for this latter uncompromising claim. In a subsequent section we will address this lacuna. In the meantime, we hope we have given the reader some appreciation of what informed Kaldor's non-monist critique. Overall, there are three dimensions to it. First, equilibrium economics either ignores or inadequately explains numerous prevalent facts or tendencies in real economies. Second, Kaldor assumes that all of economics is an empirical science, and, on this assumption, equilibrium economics is both descriptively and explanatorily inadequate. Finally, because of the manner in which general equilibrium theorists use very sophisticated, non-constructive mathematics in proving the existence of equilibrium, their proof is such that the mathematically proven equilibrium 'cannot possibly hold in reality' (Kaldor 1972: 1240).

Debreu's achievement: contested interpretations?

According to Hahn, Kaldor's critique of general equilibrium is based on 'perennial misunderstandings' (Hahn 1973(a): 8). In the first place, Kaldor misunderstands Debreu's achievement because of his basic assumption that 'Debreu was looking for the minimum basic assumptions for establishing the existence of an equilibrium set of prices which is (a) unique (b) stable' (Hahn 1973(a): 8). Second, Hahn addresses Kaldor's objection based on the reality of increasing returns and on Debreu's failure to address these. Finally, in dismissing Debreu's rigorous research on the grounds that it makes no contribution to economics understood as an inductive, empirical science, Kaldor fails to appreciate (1) its economic significance and (2) the legacy of its grammar of argumentation.

Debreu's *Theory of Value* is correctly seen as an outstanding, indeed epoch-making, contribution in the history of twentieth century economic thought, especially in the neoclassical paradigm. The monograph itself is short, precise, technical and a logically impeccable piece of monumental research. As we have already seen, despite his call for 'a major act of demolition,' Kaldor, like Hahn, praises Debreu's work for its 'elegance, exactness and logical precision' (Kaldor 1972: 1237). Hahn notes that some may find it 'odd... that so clear a writer as Debreu should be misread' (Hahn 1973(a): 8). Whatever about misreading, *prima facie* it may be odd or surprising that such a precise and technical piece of research should be subjected to a number of conflicting interpretations. However, when we look at other similar pieces of epoch-making but technical research, such as Gödel's incompleteness theorems in pure mathematics, they share the same fate as Debreu, i.e. lack of consensus on the correct interpretation of the significance of the technical results for their respective disciplines. The source of this plurality of understandings lies in the fact that the research is technically impeccable but its significance is judged to be epoch-making or monumental for the discipline or the paradigm as a whole. However, the judgement of epoch-making is not a technical issue: the argument that a piece of technical research is monumental goes beyond the bounds of what can be established by the technical apparatus. The judgment is based on the commitments – epistemological, ontological and methodological – of the claimants. It is more akin to an argument in favour of the correct moral which should be drawn from some truth than to a logico-mathematical proof. In our present state of knowledge, there is no known calculus or algorithm for conclusively deciding such issues.

In the case of Debreu's research, as with Gödel's, theoreticians with varying epistemological, ontological and methodological commitments will privilege their own understandings and attempt to show that those of their opponents are misunderstandings. In particular, this is true of Hahn and Kaldor. As methodologists, our primary task is, in Hahn's phrase, to expose their respective 'grammars of argumentation.' Moreover, if and when we favour some position, we explain in a Socratic spirit – especially the spirit of later Socrates when all contributors to the dialogue make genuine contributions – the grounds for our decisions.

As a first step in accomplishing this task, we outline a sample of the various ways in which Debreu's *Theory of Value* was claimed to be monumental. According to Hahn, Debreu's research[1] was 'a natural development' of 'the vision' of a decentralized economy emphasized by Adam Smith (Hahn 2005(a): 7). This vision inspired 'the project of General Equilibrium theorists from Walras onwards' (Hahn 2005(a): 6). This project was finally accomplished by Arrow and Debreu. They 'put the matter beyond doubt – in suitable circumstances order was indeed possible' (Hahn 2005(a): 6). We will see later that Kaldor, while acknowledging that in suitable circumstances order is shown to be possible, thinks the matter is far from being beyond doubt – the kind of mathematics used by Debreu in proving the existence of equilibrium is such that it *cannot* be given an economic interpretation.

Like Hahn, Kaldor places Debreu's achievement in the context of the Walrasian programme. In particular, '*the purpose* of the exercise is to find the minimum "basic assumptions" necessary for establishing the existence of an "equilibrium" set of prices that is (a) unique, (b) stable, (c) satisfies the conditions of Pareto optimality' (Kaldor 1972: 1237, italics added). However, according to Hahn, this is a misunderstanding of Debreu's achievement. Also, for Kaldor there is 'the deep underlying belief common to all economists of the so-called "neo-classical" school, that general equilibrium theory is *the one and only* starting point for any logically consistent *explanation* of the behaviour of decentralized economic systems' (Kaldor 1972: 1238, italics added). Kaldor's aim is to show that this belief does not stand up to critical scrutiny. Finally, according to Hahn, various neoclassical economists have 'got hold of the wrong end of the stick' and thus 'have misunderstood what the project is about' (Hahn 2005(a): 10). In this connection, he singles out 'American general equilibrium theorists' who read the theory as a well-corroborated scientific theory or, in Hahn's concise expression, 'Science in the way one regards the law of gravity' (Hahn 2005(a): 8). These economists are the target of both Hahn and Kaldor. According to Hahn, they misrepresent the achievement of Debreu, whereas according to Kaldor, equilibrium economics, when taken as an empirical science, is falsified by the evidence.

Hahn on Debreu's achievement: the grammar of argumentation vindicated

According to Hahn 'the Arrow–Debreu theory has been widely misunderstood and misused' (Hahn 1985: 13). Clearly, the misunderstanding is not confined to its opponents. As we have emphasized, according to Hahn, neoclassical theory is not an empirical science with a primary interest in predicting. Hence, if the term 'explanation' is taken in its normal methodological sense, Debreu's *Theory of Value* is not attempting to explain actual economies. In particular, it is not a science that has successfully discovered the laws of motion of a capitalist economy. The range of interpretations of Debreu's achievement based on the assumption that it is a successful empirical science by various orthodox economists is a gross misunderstanding. On the contrary, the proper context into which Debreu's achievement is to be placed is in Hahn's, rather Platonic, domain of objective understanding.[2] In this context,

> it is a major intellectual achievement… It establishes the astonishing claim that it is *logically possible* to describe an economy in which millions of agents, looking no further than their own interests and responding to the sparse information system of prices only, can still attain a coherent economic disposition of resources.
>
> (Hahn 1982(a): 114, italics added)

Prior to Debreu's achievement, the metaphor of the invisible hand was just that: a metaphor. Indeed, it was an implausible metaphor. As Hahn says, without Debreu's proof, 'there is no reason why, at arbitrary prices, trades should balance so that the amount of anything offered for sale is equal to what is demanded for purchase' (ibid.: 114). We could say that Debreu utterly recasts the metaphor of the invisible hand in a rigorous non-metaphorical way and, by exploiting mathematical resources, unknown, for instance, to Walras, 'puts the matter beyond doubt' (Hahn 2005(a): 6) by proving the existence of equilibrium as defined by the theory.

Hahn is at pains to clarify what exactly is established by Debreu. In the first place, he focuses on the notion of existence presupposed by Debreu. He correctly points that the notion of existence used simply means what is logically possible or, in other words, freedom from contradiction. This is the notion of mathematical existence propounded by Hilbertian formalists, discussed in the last chapter. Thus, Hahn is very accurate when he says what has been accomplished by the proof is that 'there might be order.' It 'is not claiming that there is order' (Hahn 2005(a): 11) in the actual economic world. It is logically possible that an equilibrium, as defined by Debreu, could exist. However, 'nothing whatever has been said of whether it is possible to describe an actual economy in these terms' (Hahn 1982(a): 114). In short, Debreu's *Theory of Value* 'does not describe the world' (Hahn 1973(a): 14). Neither does it explain the world in the sense of explanation used in the physical sciences. Rather, 'it is a solid starting point for the quest for understanding it' (Hahn 1973(a): 14). As we noted in Chapter 4, the 'solidity' of the starting point rests in the fact that the existence proof is absolutely impeccable.

Having correctly clarified the notion of existence in Debreu's *Theory of Value*, Hahn proceeds to address the concept of equilibrium. Our thesis is that, for Hahn, the concept of equilibrium in Debreu's achievement is an explication, in the Quinean sense explained in Chapter 4, of a pre-theoretical notion of equilibrium. Moreover, Debreu's explication is merely a solid starting point in the process of further explication which culminates in a different notion of equilibrium. In short, as we saw in Chapter 4, according to Hahn, there are multiple concepts of equilibrium that are distinct from the concept of multiple equilibria, i.e. the denial of the uniqueness of a given equilibrium concept.

According to Hahn, the Arrow–Debreu equilibrium 'is motivated by a very weak causal proposition' (Hahn 1973(a): 7). In the terminology of Quine, this weak causal proposition is given a very specific clear and distinct explication by Debreu. The weak causal claim is 'that any process purporting to describe an actual economy could terminate, if it terminates at all, only in an equilibrium' (Hahn 1973(a): 10). In Debreu's explication of this pre-theoretical concept, an equilibrium is

> a triple; a non-negative price vector, a vector of demand and a vector of supply, such that (a) the demand vector is the vector sum of household action at these prices, (b) the supply vector is the vector sum of firms' actions at these prices and (c) for no good does demand exceed supply.
>
> (Hahn 1973(a): 7)

In this explication goods are distinguishable by their location in space and in time, and by the physical state of the world. Also, a price is defined for each good. Each household chooses an action (which defines a point in the space of all goods), subject to its budget constraint, such that the choice is preferable to any other action available, and firms choose an action (represented by a point in the space of all goods) such that no other technologically feasible action is more profitable. Hahn is at pains to point out that Debreu's explication should not be confused with the very weak causal claim. They are not equivalent in meaning. One is pre-theoretical, the other is a very precise, theory-laden concept. Neither is Debreu's explication a real definition of the notion of equilibrium in the pre-theoretical weak causal claim, i.e. it is not specifying necessary and sufficient conditions. Thus, Hahn claims that Debreu's equilibrium construction 'must relinquish the claim of providing necessary descriptions of terminal states of economic processes' (Hahn 1973(a): 16). Indeed, 'it does not describe properties of all potential terminating points of any actual process' (Hahn 1973(a): 16). Debreu's equilibrium 'is not sequential in an *essential* way' (Hahn 1973(a): 16, italics in original).

For some critics this is a major defect, demonstrating that the concept of equilibrium as characterized by Debreu is theoretically useless. Hahn emphatically rejects this conclusion; Debreu's *Theory of Value* is a monumental achievement, despite the fact that its concept of equilibrium is not sequential in an essential way. It has both a negative and a positive contribution. Negatively, for instance, it exposes 'many false and harmful views on the role of prices' (Hahn 1973(a): 41). This negative role is 'almost sufficient justification' for Debreu's explication, since 'practical men and ill-trained theorists everywhere in the world do not understand what they are claiming to be the case when they claim a beneficent and coherent role for the invisible hand' (Hahn 1973(a): 14). Positively, it provides a solid starting point for theoretical researchers in their search for an explication of equilibrium that will be 'sequential in an essential way' (Hahn 1973(a): 16). As Hahn points out, among other things, this requires 'that information processes and costs, transactions and transaction costs and also expectations and uncertainty be explicitly and essentially included in the equilibrium notion. That is what the Arrow–Debreu construction does not do' (ibid.: 16). Content wise, Hahn finds Debreu's explication deficient and he proposes the following explication (Hahn calls it a definition[3]); 'an economy is in equilibrium when it generates messages which do not cause agents to change the theories which they hold or the policies which they pursue' (Hahn 1973(a): 25).

Clearly, economic theoreticians in the future need not start with Debreu's explication: they may be better advised to start with Hahn's explication. Hahn appears to be aware of this. He sums up his position vis-à-vis the content of Debreu's explication as follows. 'I attach the greatest importance to the continuity of intellectual enterprises and would consider it a sure signal of bad scholarship and reasoning if I had kicked away all the ladders which we have' (Hahn 1973(a): 41). We assume that Hahn is alluding to Wittgenstein's *Tractatus* with his refusal to kick away the ladder supplied by Debreu in reaching a more sequential explication of equilibrium.[4] At *Tractatus* 6.54 Wittgenstein concludes:

> My propositions serve as elucidations in the following way: anyone who understands me eventually recognizes them as nonsensical when he uses them as steps – to climb up beyond them. (He must, so to speak, throw away the ladder after he has climbed up it).
>
> He must transcend these propositions and then he will see the world aright.
>
> (Wittgenstein 1963: 151)

Content wise, we must transcend Debreu's explication of equilibrium and then we will understand the economic world aright. The continuity of the intellectual enterprise, however, constrains us, as scholarly historians of economic thought, to acknowledge Debreu.

However, if in the final analysis – from a theoretical as distinct from a scholarly historical point of view – Debreu's explication of equilibrium is dispensable, what is not dispensable is its grammar of argumentation. In skeletal form, this grammar is the following. The theoretician's starting point is a pre-theoretical notion of equilibrium. This pre-theoretical notion is given a rigorous mathematical explication. Then the theoretician demonstrates, i.e. proves, the existence of this explication. This explication can be recast in the form of axioms and assumptions. Thus, the theoretician can 'pinpoint difficulties precisely' (Hahn 1973(a): 12). Also, the grammar of argumentation requires that the theoretician 'be precise about the difficulties' (ibid.: 12). Of course, at the initial stage of constructing the appropriate explication, one may 'not be at all clear of what the precise formulation should be' (Hahn 1973(a): 26). However, it is 'important not to relax precision just when it is most required' (Hahn 1973(a): 15). In this phase, the so-called outcome is not a finished or closed theory, rather it is 'work in its infancy' (Hahn 1973(a): 17). Like all work in its infancy, it is not difficult to find objections. The search for the final explication is an ongoing challenge. Nonetheless in this grammar of argumentation, with its focus on proving the existence of any suggested well-argued explication, 'the whole subject is plainly on a promising track' (Hahn 1973(a): 18).

To conclude, one may be tempted to sum up Hahn's evaluation of the legacy of Debreu by asserting that Debreu's achievement lies more in its grammar of argumentation rather than in his deficient explication of equilibrium. We would prefer the following summary. For the first time in the history of the neoclassical tradition, an indispensable grammar of argumentation is *displayed in action* in Debreu's research. Moreover, this grammar of argumentation is learned in and through its practice; the skeleton outlined above, as it were, is given flesh and comes to life in its usage. This grammar of argumentation is integrated into 'the habit of thought which G.E. has instilled' (Hahn 2005(a): 8).

Hahn's Platonism or Kaldor's Aristotelianism?

As already emphasized, Hahn and Kaldor are at the opposite ends of the spectrum in their evaluations of the legacy of Debreu's *Theory of Value*. We have seen that, according to Hahn, it is the crown of neoclassical economics. If it were not already constructed, it would be among economists' top priorities to invent it. In particular, it is a secure starting point in the quest for an objective, rigorous understanding of a decentralized economy. The security of the starting point is guaranteed by its emphasis on proving the existence of an equilibrium and on its grammar of argumentation. However, Hahn insists that numerous economists in the neoclassical tradition 'have misunderstood what the project is about' (Hahn 2005(a): 10). Many of these fail to appreciate its grammar of argumentation on the one hand and its existence claim on the other. They read the achievement as a chapter of empirical science. In Hahn's estimation, these give general equilibrium 'more empirical weight than it can, or was designed to, support' (Hahn 2005(a): 9). Kaldor, however, is not among these: he clearly appreciated that Debreu's *Theory of Value* was not a contribution to empirical science, *à la* Newton. As we noted in an earlier section in this chapter, Kaldor emphasized the purely formalist nature of Debreu's work and insisted that it was not intended to describe or explain, *à la* physics, economic reality.

In this connection, one point of difference between Kaldor and Hahn is worth noting. In his non-monist, methodological attack on Debreu, Kaldor emphasizes what he calls 'the purpose of the exercise' (Kaldor 1972: 1237). Hahn interprets this to be referring to what Debreu had in mind, and he correctly points out that Debreu's *Theory of Value* is solely focused on the existence of equilibrium and, contrary to Kaldor's assumption, is not concerned with either uniqueness or stability. As Hahn insists 'Debreu did not concern himself with these' (Hahn 1973(a): 8) in his *Theory of Value*. However, what Hahn fails to acknowledge is that Kaldor is taking the theme 'the purpose of the exercise' in a much broader sense. He located this purpose in the context of those neoclassical economists – not small in number – committed to the reality of the invisible hand. These, as Ingrao and Israel point out, identified existence, uniqueness and stability as 'the *invariant paradigmatic nucleus*' or 'core' (Ingrao and Israel 1990: 3) of the invisible hand. In this broad context, Debreu's *Theory of Value* was seen as a major contribution to this core. Thus, in different senses, both Hahn and Kaldor are correct: Hahn is correct vis-à-vis Debreu's *Theory of Value*, whereas Kaldor is correct vis-à-vis its significance for those committed to the invariant paradigmatic nucleus. Moreover, it should be clear that Hahn himself rejects this invariant nucleus.

We now turn to Kaldor's non-monist critique. Like Hahn, he draws our attention to a variety of notions of equilibrium displayed in economics. Kaldor correctly notes that 'the word "equilibrium" in economics is used, of course, in all kinds of contexts – in Keynesian economics for example, or in the theory of the balance of payments, and so on' (Kaldor 1972: 1237). He is quite explicit that his target is the notion of perfect competition equilibrium as developed by Debreu. As we already noted, according to Kaldor, increasing returns are a telling objection to that notion. In this connection, Hahn concurs with Kaldor; 'thus while it is the case that I agree with Professor Kaldor that increasing returns are a telling objection to the perfect competition equilibrium notions I have so far discussed, it seems to me important not to let this observation be an occasion for the slackening of our intellectual muscles' (Hahn 1973(a): 12).

Here is a clear case of the classic divide noted by Thomas Kuhn, namely the polarization of the economic community. On the one side we have Hahn, 'the conservative,' committed to the ability of the resources of general equilibrium theorists to meet various challenges. On the other hand we have Kaldor, the 'revolutionary' calling for a major act of demolition. In relation to increasing returns to scale, Hahn points out that equilibrium theorists have addressed this challenge.

In particular he draws our attention to the work of Ross Starr (1967) who proved that, if increasing returns to scale are small relative to the scale of the economy, an Arrow–Debreu equilibrium is an approximate equilibrium for such an economy. As Hahn acknowledges, and indeed has sympathy for, a Kaldorian could retort that the increasing returns may not be small enough for such an approximation. If one concedes this, Hahn will still continue 'to flex his intellectual muscles' and proceed to construct a more appropriate notion of equilibrium. Methodologically, without going into the specific details, this toing and froing between these two outstanding economists may be read as symptomatic of a close-to-crisis stage of the discipline.

Finally, vis-à-vis the issue of increasing returns, Hahn makes the point 'that the rather uncontroversial view that increasing returns cause difficulties for perfect competition seems to me to bear no logical relationship to the claim that therefore equilibrium notions are not required or they are sterile' (Hahn 1973(a): 14). However, as we noted at the beginning of this section, Kaldor makes no such sweeping claim: his target is what Hahn calls Arrow–Debreu equilibrium, not the concept of equilibrium per se. Kaldor's critique, as we have repeated time and again, is non-monist, i.e. it is based on a constellation of arguments, the weight of which, taken in totality, justifies the claim that if economics as a science is to progress, the conceptual framework of general equilibrium must be demolished. Clearly, increasing returns is a key component in this constellation. Another component is the failure of equilibrium theorists to successfully relax their unreal assumptions. 'The process of removing the "scaffolding" as the saying goes – in other words of *relaxing* the unreal basic assumptions – has not yet started' (Kaldor 1972: 1239, italics). Taken literally, this is not true. As Hahn correctly notes, there is a large literature on removing the scaffolding. However, it is clear from the context that what Kaldor is claiming is that the process has not *successfully* started. This is clear from his scaffolding metaphor when he immediately adds: 'Indeed, the scaffolding gets thicker and more impenetrable with every successive reformulation of the theory, with growing uncertainty as to whether there is a solid building underneath' (Kaldor 1972: 1239). According to Ingrao and Israel, Debreu's decision not to address the issues of stability and uniqueness in his *Theory of Value* can, in light of subsequent developments, 'be said to show great foresight'[5] (Ingrao and Israel 1990: 313). In view of these same developments, especially what has been called the Sonnenschein–Mantel–Debreu (SMD) theorem, Kaldor's remark about the thickening of the scaffolding displayed great foresight. Kaldor would almost certainly concur with Kirman that 'the full force of the SMD result is often not appreciated. Without stability and uniqueness the intrinsic interest of economic analysis based on the general equilibrium is extremely limited' (Kirman 2006: 257). Hahn, however, would not agree. The SMD result and other developments call for further flexing of one's intellectual muscles. What Kaldor sees as telling objections, Hahn sees as further challenges. Whatever the merits or otherwise of their respective positions, the SMD result is a telling objection to those neoclassical economists committed to the invariant paradigmatic nucleus of the invisible hand.

In our opinion, neither Hahn nor Kaldor possess a telling, knockout argument in favour of their respective stances. A central critical question is how one is to decide on the merits of their respective cases. The Kaldorians see Hahn's flexing his intellectual muscles as being akin to pre-Copernicans adding epicycle upon epicycle to their creaking system of Ptolemaic astronomy. The Hahnians reject this analogy. They have successfully relaxed some of the basic unreal assumptions and their grammar of argumentation will enable them to meet new challenges.

This brings us to what, in our opinion, is a crucial difference between Hahn's view of economic theory and Kaldor's view. To emphasize and sum up these conflicting but basic methodological stances, we call Hahn's position Platonic and name Kaldor's position Aristotelian. Of course, these terms are not to be taken in strict scholarly senses. Just as, for instance, in the philosophy of mathematics Frege's overall position is called Platonism, we are calling Hahn's position Platonic. Like Plato, Hahn subscribes to two quite separate worlds: the world of objective understanding on the one hand and the real socio-economic world on the other. Equilibrium economics, with its grammar of argumentation, is located in the domain of objective understanding, which, *à la* Plato, neither describes nor explains, but nonetheless illuminates our approach to the real economic world. Like Plato, Hahn analyses the real world from the perspective of the world of understanding, where the observable economic world is but a shadow of the Platonic one.

Just as Aristotle rejected Plato, Kaldor rejects Hahn. Kaldor shares the Aristotelian epistemic commitment to the primacy of the empirical. Given this epistemic commitment, Kaldor insists that economics must be an inductive empirical science. Like any empirical scientist, the economist starts with the facts and empirical regularities and then constructs explanations. These explanations are brought before the bar of experience and, if found wanting, the economist is rationally compelled to construct alternative explanations. For instance, according to Hahn, 'it is absolutely correct to maintain that every feature of an actual economy which Keynes regarded as important is missing in Debreu' (Hahn 1973(a): 34). This, according to a Kaldorian, amounts to the admission that Debreu's theory is descriptively inadequate. Hahn, however, does not share this Aristotelian commitment to the primacy of the empirical. In practising economics he says 'I have found... that the more descriptive you are the less you can do' (Hahn 2005(b): 17). In his Platonic world of understanding, Kaldor's inductive method is not the key. Rather, in the world of objective understanding, a Debreu-like grammar of argumentation is what is required. For instance, in the case of the Keynesian features noted in the previous paragraph, the grammar of argumentation takes these on board, leading the economist to a better understanding. This better understanding, however, is not an empirical science. Once again, we clearly see the to-and-fro between Hahn and Kaldor.

The perceptive reader, however, will note that in the above toing and froing we did not address the actual proof of the existence of equilibrium in Debreu's *Theory of Value*. Kaldor's objections discussed above do not touch the actual proof. In the next section we address this issue. Indeed, we will suggest that Kaldorians have legitimate grounds for questioning the economic interpretation of Debreu's formal, uninterpreted, proof. In this connection, economic methodologists will have to familiarize themselves with the philosophy of mathematics in which the notions of existence and its proof have been put under the spotlight. Thus, while there is some plausibility to Hahn's thesis that the philosophy of the physical sciences is irrelevant to the methodology of general equilibrium, the same cannot be said of the philosophy of mathematics. We will see in the next section that a Debreu-type existence proof, using the powerful resources of Cantorian set theory, can be challenged in the domain of the foundations of mathematics.

Existence in mathematics and in economics: a Kaldorian challenge

In this section we suggest that the Achilles' heel of Debreu's *Theory of Value* lies in his use of the powerful resources of Cantorian set theory to prove the existence of general equilibrium. To this end, we focus on a distinctive characteristic of Cantorian set theory: namely actual, as distinct from potential, infinity. In this context, we focus on different notions of mathematical existence and on acceptable methods of proving existence claims discussed in the foundations of arithmetic. In light of these distinctions, we show how some specific methods of existence proofs, legitimate in the domain of Cantorian set theory, fail to legitimise existence claims in either the physical or the socio-economic world. We then apply this result to Debreu's proof. To achieve this, we start with the foundations of arithmetic. One may feel, *prima facie*, there is no connection between issues in the foundations of arithmetic and issues in economic methodology. This *prima facie* appearance, however, is misleading, particularly when we realize that central methodological issues in the foundations of arithmetic are focused on Cantorian set theory and, as Weintraub (2002) correctly points out, it is precisely the powerful resources of this theory that are used by Debreu in his proof of the existence of general equilibrium.

In one sense, the philosophical debate, or perhaps more accurately, the philosophical battle, in the foundations of arithmetic has its origins in Cantor's highly original contribution to set theory in the 1870s. Prior to Cantor's challenging contribution, sets were assumed to be either finite, e.g. the set of apostles, or potentially infinite, e.g. the set of natural numbers 1, 2, 3 ... n, ... and so on. The only kind of infinite set relevant to mathematics was a potentially infinite one. A potentially infinite set is one to which we can systematically add new members *ad infinitum*. It is open-ended, or never complete. The hegemony of potential infinity was challenged by Cantor; there is much more to mathematical infinity than potential infinity. This may be seen from the following examples. The infinite set of even numbers can be put in one-to-one correspondence with the infinite set of natural numbers. There are, as it were, as many even numbers as there are natural numbers. However, the infinite set of real numbers (which includes numbers like $\sqrt{2}$) cannot be put in one-to-one correspondence with the natural numbers. The infinite set of real numbers is, as it were, 'bigger' than the infinite set of natural numbers. Hence, contrary to the traditional view, there is for Cantor a variety of infinities in mathematics, and these infinities, contrary to potential infinity, are complete. To mark this crucial difference, numerous philosophers of mathematics follow Hilbert in calling Cantorian infinity actual infinity, the contrast being with the traditional notion of potential infinity. As Dummett puts it, 'it is integral to Cantorian mathematics to treat infinite structures as if they could be completed and then surveyed in their totality' (Dummett 2000: 41). For those committed to potential infinity, this 'destroys the whole essence of infinity, which lies in the conception of a structure which is always in growth, precisely because the process of construction is never completed' (ibid.: 41).

This ingenious Cantorian contribution to pure mathematics appears to be irrelevant to economic methodology. However, let us not jump too hastily to conclusions. In Cantorian set theory a number of theorems can be provided *which are not provable* in non-Cantorian set theory. The mathematical resources available in Cantorian set theory are, as it were, more powerful than those available in pure mathematics limited to the domain of the potentially infinite. Moreover, as argued by Velupillai, some of these specific Cantorian-based theorems are indispensable to Debreu's proof of the existence of equilibrium (Velupillai, 2000).[6] In principle, there is nothing *mathematically* wrong with that. On the contrary, as we already noted, a major part of Debreu's originality resided in his ability to exploit the novel and powerful resources of Cantorian set theory in formulating his mathematical proof. *The crucial methodological question is whether or not such a mathematical proof can be given an economic interpretation?* This methodological problem emerges with the discovery of skeletons in the closet of Cantorian set theory.

The first hint of these skeletons arose at the beginning of the twentieth century after Frege, in Germany, and Russell, in Britain, began their foundational studies in arithmetic. They used Cantorian set theory as an indispensable cornerstone in their foundational studies. In these studies, Cantorian set theory gave rise to a range of paradoxes. These paradoxes had a profound influence on future developments, both in philosophy and in mathematics. Indeed, it is not an exaggeration to say that the mathematical and philosophical communities divided on how best to respond to these paradoxes. For our methodological purposes, we focus on the divide between Poincaré, who wished to prune pure mathematics of its Cantorian excesses, and those, like Hilbert, who cherished the growth of Cantorian actual infinity.

The French mathematician, Henri Poincaré, was regarded as the most outstanding European mathematician at the turn of the twentieth-century. He is probably best known among economic methodologists and historians of economic thought as the mathematician to whom Walras turned for support for his programme of the mathematization of economics. Poincaré insisted that the source of the paradoxes lay in the specifics of Cantorian set theory. To avoid the paradoxes he suggested, what we have called, the Poincaré finitist programme in the foundations of mathematics (Boylan and O'Gorman 2007). This programme culminated in the 1930s in the birth of what is today called constructive mathematics – which basically is mathematics without actual Cantorian infinities.[7] In the terminology of Benacerraf and Putnam, Poincaré's approach to the practice of pure mathematics is informed by his own 'epistemology of mathematics' (Benacerraf and Putnam 1983: 2). A basic cornerstone of Poincaré's epistemology is that pure mathematics is the outcome of mathematical activity on the part of finite human beings. In particular, the pure mathematician is more a constructor than a discoverer. Mathematicians construct their logico-mathematical edifices, and what is crucially important is that the rigorous conceptual resources used in these constructions are both linguistically based and finite. Rigorous mathematics is the output of finitely bounded, rational, linguistic agents. Thus, Poincaré objects to Cantorian mathematics because he refuses 'to argue on the hypothesis of some infinitely talkative divinity capable of thinking an infinite number of words in a finite length of time' (Poincaré 1963: 67). Contrary to Cantorian mathematics, constructive mathematics in the Poincaré programme is limited to the domain of the finite and potentially infinite, thereby excluding Cantor's actual infinity. In particular, and crucially for economic methodology, in the Poincaré programme of constructive mathematics, some of the theorems of Cantor's set theory used by Debreu in proving the existence of equilibrium are not theorems at all. Their method of proof violates the Poincaré principle that any legitimate mathematical proof must be capable of being carried out in a finite number of steps. We will return to this point later.

Other philosophers and mathematicians argued that a Poincaré-type solution was too draconian. These wished to retain Cantorian set theory. Among them were Platonists and Hilbertian formalists. For Platonists, Cantorian actual infinity subsists in a real, Platonistic world. This Platonistic world consists of real objects, which, unlike objects in the empirical world, neither initiate nor undergo change. Thus, for Platonists, mathematical existence transcends empirical existence in general and socio-historical existence in particular. Existence in this Platonistic world is independent of spatio-temporal existence.

As we already noted, Hilbert proposed a strict formalist reading of pure mathematics. In this strictly formalist setting, Hilbert proposed an ingenious, non-Platonistic way of retaining Cantorian set theory. He divided pure mathematics into a finitist part (*à la* Poincaré) and an idealized, infinite part (*à la* Cantor). The idealized infinite part is not open to interpretation; only the finite part may be interpreted. However, the idealized infinite part is heuristically indispensable as an instrument for deriving finitist results otherwise unobtainable. In this reading of Hilbert's ingenious solution, Cantorian actual infinity is a non-empirical, non-finite, heuristic fiction, justified by its enormous mathematical power and utility. Crucially for Hilbert, such idealized fictions cannot be arbitrarily introduced into mathematics; the extended system of Cantorian infinity combined with the finite must be proven to be consistent. In this way, one could say that Hilbertian formalism equates Cantorian mathematical existence with freedom from contradiction.[8] Clearly, in these Cantorian settings Debreu's proof is a genuine one.

In short, in the context of the Poincaré programme, Debreu's proof is invalid as a piece of mathematics, whereas in a Cantorian framework it is a valid proof! The moral is clear: the process of the mathematization of economics via Cantorian set theory requires closer methodological scrutiny. In particular, we are now in a position to address the crucial methodological question noted above, namely whether or not Debreu's proof can be given an economic interpretation? Debreu's *Theory of Value* is said to prove the existence of a set of signals, market prices, in a Walrasian exchange economy, leading economic agents to make decisions that are mutually compatible. This, as we have already seen, is the economic interpretation of Debreu's mathematical proof given by Hahn. Our thesis, which we call the P–K thesis (Poincaré–Kaldor), is that there is no justification for this *economic interpretation* of Debreu's ingenious piece of Cantorian pure mathematics.

Debreu's proof does *not* support this economic interpretation. Debreu's so-called economic equilibrium exists either in the domain of Cantorian actual infinity, which transcends any process limited to socio-historical time, or in Hilbert's abstract space, which cannot be given a finite interpretation. More precisely, since the method of the proof of existence is inherently non-constructive, i.e. cannot be carried out in a finite number of steps taken one at a time, Debreu's equilibrium cannot be given either a finite or a potentially infinite interpretation.[9] Debreu's equilibrium point is merely shown to exist in a non-temporal, actual infinite Platonic or purely idealized Hilbertian domain, which cannot in any finite effective way be realized in the socio-historical world in which economic agents operate.

There are a number of aspects to the P–K thesis that should be noted. First, there is no obligation on economic methodologists to take the Poincaré side in the philosophico-mathematical debate in the foundations of mathematics. The P–K thesis assumes that, even though Platonists and the Hilbert 'school' fail in different ways to defend Cantor's paradise of actual infinity, Cantorian set theory is an authentic part of pure mathematics. In other words, in the spirit of Debreu's own distinction between a rigorous proof in pure mathematics and its economic interpretation discussed in the last chapter, the P–K thesis accepts that, as a piece of pure mathematics, without an economic interpretation, Debreu's proof is valid. What is crucial to the defence of the P–K thesis hinges on what is proven to exist by Debreu's proof. Mathematically, Debreu's proof establishes existence in the Cantorian domain of actual infinity which transcends the domains of the strictly finite and potentially infinite. This claim is justified by the fact that, as Velupillai for instance demonstrated, the method of proof is endemically non-constructive, i.e. cannot be carried out in a potentially infinite setting by a finite number of steps, however large, taken one step at a time (Velupillai, 2002).[10] Debreu's equilibrium solution, though valid in pure mathematics, cannot in any empirically meaningful way be interpreted as 'obtaining' in our historically situated, socio-economic world where real time matters.

In short, the legitimacy of Debreu's proof is in the realm of Cantor's paradise, which in principle is not realizable in our socio-economic world where decisions have to be arrived at in finite time settings and signals must be transmitted under similar real time constraints. Thus, one may argue that Kaldor's uncompromising claim is fully vindicated; the existence of general equilibrium, as articulated by Debreu, 'is shown to be valid only on assumptions that are manifestly unreal' (Kaldor, 1972: 1240). The P–K thesis shows how this economic unreality is endemic to Debreu's mathematical proof. The so-called equilibrium point, by virtue of the Cantorian non-constructive manner in which it is demonstrated to exist by Debreu, exists only in a non-temporal, idealized realm, which is completely cut off from the economic world of finitely bounded economic agents, with limited capacities, where real time impinges on decisions taken and signals given.

The P–K thesis is very specific; it is concerned with the Debreu explication of general equilibrium and, in particular, its existence proof. It is not concerned with either uniqueness or stability conditions. It presupposes, *à la* Weintraub, an appreciation of the second phase in the mathematization of economics, namely the recourse to Cantorian set theory in proving the existence of general equilibrium. Moreover, it also presupposes, *à la* Debreu, the distinction between a rigorous piece of pure mathematics and its subsequent economic interpretation. The P–K thesis is based on the fact that there are real time constraints on existence claims in economic theory that do not apply in pure Cantorian mathematics. A non-constructive existence proof in the domain of Cantor's actual infinity places what is proven to exist outside the real time constraints of existence in the economic sphere. Debreu's mathematical existence in Cantor's non-temporal paradise cannot be given an empirical interpretation in economic theory in which real historical time constraints are operational. Cantor's paradise contains mathematical truths that are empirical fictions, and among these mathematically true, empirical fictions is Debreu's equilibrium solution. In this fashion, we suggest that Kaldor is fully justified in claiming that 'in fact equilibrium theory has reached the stage where the pure theorist has successfully (though perhaps inadvertently) demonstrated that the main implications of the theory *cannot possibly* hold in reality' (Kaldor 1972: 1240, italics added). Debreu's non-constructive proof 'inadvertently,' but endemically, necessitates that what is demonstrated to exist cannot be an equilibrium set of prices which could subsist in real historical time.

In light of the range of issues raised by Kaldor's non-monist critique and our reconstruction of the to-and-fro between Hahn and Kaldor, Hahn's early summary of his response to Kaldor's critique, namely that 'in tilting at the windmill of some old-fashioned textbook Professor Kaldor has missed the dragon' (Hahn 1973(a): 320), is in our opinion a piece of grossly exaggerated rhetoric. His revised summary, 28 years later, is more accurate, i.e. Kaldor criticized equilibrium theorists, like Hahn, 'for building castles in the air or that we were making science fiction. There is something true in it but at least we built something' (Hahn 2005(b): 17). If some version of the P–K thesis is a correct methodological insight, we can say that the building is in Cantor's paradise and not in the real economic world.

However, as we already maintained, there is no knock-out punch in the intriguing match between Hahn and Kaldor. Certainly, the P–K thesis, although landing an unanticipated, perhaps staggering, blow, does not force the referee to award the fight to Kaldor. In the next round, Hahn can still flex his intellectual muscles by drawing on developments in computable general equilibrium.[11] Eventually, one is faced by Hahn's question of 'when to say: "enough is enough", we need a new theory' (Hahn 1996: 191). In this connection, methodologists have not got some formal algorithm at their disposal, to which all and sundry can and should appeal, to arrive at a unique rational answer to Hahn's question. Experience from science suggests that the decision to retain the old or to begin the search for a novel theory rests with economists themselves. Eminent economists on both sides of the divide behave like legal counsellors in a court of law by exposing the strengths of their own positions and the weaknesses of their opponents. Methodologists contribute by exposing the ontological, epistemological and, where necessary, the ideological commitments implicit in the cases of both sides. In this way the decision rests primarily with economists, with methodologists playing a secondary, but indispensable, role in this process.[12]

8 Economics, mathematics and rationality

A new grammar of argumentation?

> I am pretty certain that the following prediction will prove to be correct: theorizing of the 'pure' sort will become less enjoyable and less and less possible.... The reason for its demise are all 'internal' to pure theory itself. By this I mean that there will be an increasing realization by theorists that rather radical changes in questions and methods are required, if they are to deliver, not practical, but theoretically useful results.
>
> (Hahn 1991(a): 47)

Introduction

The Economic Journal in 1991 published the views of eminent economists on how they perceived the future of economics. Among these, Hahn's 'The Next Hundred Years' is interesting, not least in the context of the Hahnian question posed in the last chapter, namely when should economists judge that their theory needs replacement? Hahn's forecast is that economic theory as practised and defended by him will 'wither.' Its 'demise' will not be due to 'the scorn of practical men and women' (Hahn 1991(a): 47). Rather, pure economic theory, being a thriving research programme, internally raises novel challenging questions. Hahn's claim is that 'it is becoming ever more clear that almost none of them can be answered by the old procedures. Instead of theorems we shall need simulations, instead of simple transparent axioms there looms the likelihood of psychological, sociological and historical postulates' (Hahn 1991(a): 47). Thus, Hahn sees more and more emphasis on computer simulation with less emphasis on axioms, proofs and theorems. Moreover, the study of history and path dependency at a more empirical level will not be integrated into existing theory. Rather, affinities to biology with the emphasis on evolutionary algorithms for computers will become more prevalent. Also, more empirical attention will be placed on firms, their transaction costs and increasing returns 'which resist incorporation into traditional modes of analysis' (Hahn 1991(a): 49). Indeed, according to Hahn, 'one could go on and on in this vein for a long time' (Hahn 1991(a): 50). In keeping with his commitment to clear and distinct ideas, his hope is that future economists will resist the temptation of 'grand and woolly theories... and patiently wait for a new dawn such as shone on those of us who came to economic theory after the last war' (Hahn 1991(a): 50).

Despite this prediction and hope, Hahn is not conceding that Kaldor was correct in maintaining that general equilibrium theory was barren and irrelevant. Rather, he expressly defends pure theory from the charge of 'being scholastic and so by implication bound to be irrelevant to the world' (Hahn 1991(a): 47). Once again, at the core of his defence we find the theme of understanding. Pure theory has given us objective understanding of 'how decentralized choices interact and perhaps get coordinated' (Hahn 1991(a): 49). He sums up as follows: 'My point has not been that twentieth-century theory sheds no light, nor indeed that its methods will not continue to provide some illumination. But it is my prediction that the latter will increasingly be found to be too faint in the search for answers to questions which have quite naturally arisen from twentieth-century theoretical developments' (Hahn 1991(a): 50).

Clearly, Hahn is well aware of the winds of change across the terrain of traditional theory and theorizing. Although his methodology gives us a richer appreciation of the contribution of equilibrium theorizing to twentieth century economics, for many he is very realistic in recognizing the ever diminishing role of equilibrium theorizing, particularly in the research agendas of younger economists. His advice appears to encourage these to adopt the Aristotelian approach outlined in the last chapter, or at least to avoid woolly theories while patiently waiting for a new Platonic approach meeting the rigour, precision and unification attained in general equilibrium.

Indeed, Hahn not only expects the demise of pure theory to which he was an outstanding contributor and to which he so innovatively and consistently defended, he also sees the withering occurring before his eyes. He castigates a number of his fellow theorists who, in 'attempting to stem the tide,' have

> abandoned attempts to understand the central question of our subject, namely: how do decentralized choices interact and perhaps get coordinated, in favour of a theory according to which an economy is to be understood as the outcome of the maximization of a representative agent's utility over an infinite future?... it is clear that this sort of thing heralds the decadence of endeavour just as clearly as Trajan's column heralded the decadence of Rome. It is the last twitch and gasp of a dying method.
>
> (Hahn 1991(a): 49)

In view of this demise, impending or actual, one can legitimately ask, does it entail the demise of Hahn's commitments to rationality, equilibrium and methodological individualism? How will these commitments fare in the context of 'the radical changes in questions and methods' (Hahn 1991(a): 47) anticipated by Hahn? In this chapter we address this issue by venturing into the deep 'Wittgensteinian waters' (Hahn 1985: 3) to which Hahn alludes. In this connection, we simultaneously take up Hahn's explicit challenge to philosophers. When discussing Hausman's methodology, Hahn expresses his disappointment that Hausman, as a philosopher, did not address 'the deep difficulties with the economic concept of rationality,' and adds that 'it would have been nice if he devoted a chapter to what philosophers have to say on the subject' (Hahn 1996: 187).

In response to Hahn's challenge, we navigate these deep Wittgensteinian waters by recourse to Dummett's later Wittgensteinian approach to mathematics. In this connection, we make three methodological claims. First, this later Wittgensteinian approach exposes some of 'the deep difficulties' with the mathematical model of rationality which was so creatively exploited by Debreu, Hahn and numerous other neoclassical economists. Second, it buttresses the P–K thesis, outlined in the previous chapter. Third, it furnishes theoretical economists, working at the frontiers of research, with *a different kind of mathematics* to that exploited in neoclassical economics, recourse to which could enable them to *construct a novel mathematical theory of rationality* compatible with Simon's insight of bounded rationality. In other words, if one wishes to mathematically model economic rationality, a new kind of mathematics is required and Dummett's later Wittgensteinian approach identifies such a mathematics for economic theorists.

Hahn, Simon and the mathematization of economics

In Chapter 4 we saw how Hahn rejects Simon's satisficer approach to economic rationality. He suggested that, when evaluated as a grammar of argumentation, Simon's approach is vastly inferior to neoclassical theory. Neoclassical theory, as a grammar of argumentation, is inextricably linked to very sophisticated mathematical procedures, whereas Simon's satisficer hypothesis lacks this mathematical sophistication. Hahn is quite correct in drawing our attention to the intimate, indispensable relationship between neoclassical theorizing by Arrow–Debreu and major developments in what philosophers of mathematics call realist mathematics. The role of these developments is also signalled by Weintraub (Weintraub 2002). Weintraub emphasizes a major shift in the process of the formalization or mathematization of economics from that initiated by Walras and others at the turn of the twentieth century to that accomplished by Arrow, Debreu and others in the 1950s. Walras exploited the resources of differential calculus, whereas Debreu exploited the resources of the modern axiomatic approach coupled to the resources of set theory, pioneered by Cantor, i.e. realist mathematics. Arrow–Debreu economic theorizing uses the powerful resources of this realist mathematics. Hahn, the theoretician, clearly recognizes that these realist mathematical resources are indispensable to neoclassical theorizing and that Simon's satisficer approach lacks this sophisticated mathematical grammar. Indeed, he suggests that it lacks any comparable mathematical grammar.

In our opinion Hahn is correct in two elements of this threefold claim. First, he is absolutely justified in pointing out that Arrow–Debreu theorizing is inextricably bound to the powerful resources of realist mathematics – the dominant mathematics of the twentieth century. Second, he is correct in assuming that these resources are not operable in Simon's satisficer approach. However, the suggestion that no comparable mathematics is available to those committed to

Simon's satisficer approach to match the powerful resources of realistic mathematics is not correct. Dummett's later Wittgensteinian philosophy of mathematics exposes the ontological–epistemological difficulties of realist mathematics, while simultaneously legitimating a novel, anti-realist mathematics. This Wittgensteinian, anti-realist mathematics opens up an extensive range of novel mathematical techniques and resources. These anti-realist, mathematical resources offer the theoretical economist a novel way of theorizing economic rationality under the rubric of Simon's bounded rationality. Of course as anticipated by Hahn in the opening section of this chapter, 'a radical change in questions and methods' (Hahn 1991(a): 47) will accompany this novel, challenging way of theorizing economic rationality.

We saw in Chapter 3 that, for Hahn, theoretical economics is mathematical – as a grammar of argumentation there is no non-mathematical theory available to match its success. In this chapter the mathematization of economics is not at issue. Rather, the methodological issue is: which kind of mathematics, realist or anti-realist, is more appropriate for theoretical economics? Hahn does not appear to be aware that such a choice is available to those theorizing at the frontiers of economic research. Our thesis is that Dummett's later Wittgensteinian approach to the philosophy of mathematics may be adapted to justify the choice of anti-realist rather than realist mathematics in the economic theorizing of rationality. Moreover, this non-realist mathematical theorizing of rationality is compatible with Simon's thesis of bounded rationality. In the following sections we argue for this thesis.

Realist and anti-realist mathematics – key themes

In this section we give a brief survey of some of the methodological themes in the realist/anti-realist debate in the philosophy of mathematics. In the next section we will show how these are relevant to Hahn's challenge to philosophers. The confrontation between realists and anti-realists in European philosophy after Kant became focused on the *metaphysical* theme of *idealism*. Realists about a specific class of entities claimed that the entities in the specific class exist and that their existence is independent of the human mind and its capacities. On the other hand, idealists, when not denying existence, claimed the entities in the specific class are mind dependent. Mathematics, especially arithmetic, became a central battleground in this metaphysical debate. In the case of arithmetic, realists insist that numbers exist. They are real objects. Moreover, these numbers exist independently of the human mind and its capacities. One version of this realism was clearly articulated by Frege. For Frege, the idea 'the positive square root of nine' and the idea 'eighteen divided by six' are *distinct mental* entities, which do *not* exist independently of the human mind.[1] However, these distinct ideas *refer* to the *same object* that *does exist independently of the human mind*, namely the number three. Philosophers of mathematics characterize Frege'e realism vis-à-vis numbers as Platonism. Numbers are real objects, but not like material objects. Material objects can initiate change or undergo change, whereas mathematical objects lack these characteristics. Numbers, however, are not mental entities – they are neither images nor ideas. They, as it were, subsist in a Platonic third world, different from the psychological, mental world on the one hand and the physico-spatial world on the other.

In the first half of the twentieth century, anti-realist *idealism* vis-à-vis arithmetic was associated with Brouwer.[2] His anti-realist mathematics is known as *intuitionism*. Influenced by Poincaré's[3] response to the paradoxes that emerged in the realist programme, Brouwer returned to Kant's *idealist* philosophy. For Brouwer, arithmetical truths are grounded in the *a priori* intuition of time. Ontologically, the natural number sequence is a construct of the human mind arising from the mind's intuition of the passage of time. Indeed, as noted by van Dalen, arithmetic for Brouwer is basically 'an essentially languageless activity of the mind having its origins in the perception of a move of time' (van Dalen 1981: 4).

For the purposes of economic methodology, we focus on three characteristics of Brouwer's intuitionist mathematics. The first characteristic is what is known as intuitionist, as distinct from realist, logic. In traditional Aristotelian logic and in the contemporary logic of Frege and Russell – both of which are realist – the principles of double negation and of the excluded middle are necessary truths, i.e. hold in all possible cases. These principles are, however, not necessary truths in intuitionist logic. For instance, according to the principle of double negation, the proposition 'it is not the case that the sun is not shining' is logically equivalent to the proposition 'the sun is shining.' Thus, the proposition 'the sun is shining' necessarily implies 'it is not the case that the sun is not shining' and *vice versa*. In intuitionist logic, however, the principle of double negation is not a necessary truth, i.e. it does not hold in all possible cases. In intuitionist mathematics, if one proves proposition p then, as in realist logic, that necessarily implies that the negation of p will not be proved. However, if one proves that we will never have a proof of the negation of p, contrary to realist logic, that does not necessarily imply that we can prove p. In simple terms, in intuitionist mathematics saying 'p is true,' where p is a mathematical proposition, amounts to saying 'we can prove p' and 'p is false' amounts to 'we cannot prove p.' By contrast, in realist mathematics, 'p is true' holds independently of our capacity to give a proof of it. In other words, in intuitionist mathematics, mathematical truth is inextricably linked to proof, whereas in realist mathematics mathematical truth is independent of proof.

Second, in any finite domain in which we can inspect the individual elements, there is no difference between realists and intuitionists. The difference occurs when we move, as we do in number theory, into the realm of the infinite. As Dummett puts it:

> In the case of a statement involving quantification over a finite, surveyable, domain our knowledge of what it is for the statement to be true consists in our knowledge of how we might, at least in principle, set about to determine whether or not it is true: but in that of a statement involving quantification

> over an infinite domain we have no such capacity, and hence to conceive of the statement as possessing a determinate, objective truth-value independently of our being able to prove or disprove it is to make *a fallacious assimilation of the infinite to the finite case* . . .
>
> (Dummett 2000: 4, italics added)

As we saw in the last chapter, the theme of mathematical infinity is one on which there is no consensus among mathematicians. Realist mathematicians are ontologically committed to Cantorian actual infinity, whereas intuitionist mathematicians, under the influence of Poincaré, reject actual infinity used by Cantor and others in set theory. Like Poincaré they limit mathematical infinity to potential infinity. As we have already discussed this major difference between actual and potential infinity when developing the P–K thesis, we move on to the third substantial difference between realists and intuitionists.

The third area of conflict concerns the notion of mathematical proof, a theme briefly alluded to in the P–K thesis. Both realists and intuitionists agree that a mathematical proof must conform to the canons of logic. However, as we have already seen, they do not agree on the specific canons of logic – realists favour their realist logic, whereas intuitionists favour their anti-realist logic. Moreover, both realists and intuitionists agree with the common sense notion that a proof must be algorithmic, in the sense of being an effective mechanical procedure that can be carried out in a finite number of steps. The proof is mechanical in the sense that it is rule governed, where all the rules are explicit, and each rule is applied one step at a time. However, intuitionists, following Poincaré, insist that a proof must be constructive. Non-constructive proofs used by realists are, according to intuitionist mathematicians, not acceptable as mathematical proofs. Poincaré summed up the constructive attitude as follows:

> A theorem must be capable of proof, but since we ourselves are finite, we can only deal with finite objects. Thus even though the notion of infinity plays a role in the statement of a theorem, *there must be no reference to it in the proof: otherwise the proof is impossible.*
>
> (Poincaré 1963: 66, italics added)

Realist non-constructive proofs appear *prima facie* to comply with the common sense notion of a proof shared by realists and intuitionists. However, if a non-constructive theorem is used as one step in a proof, when this non-constructive theorem is unpacked, it contains an infinite number of steps. Hence the Poincaré requirement noted above: namely, even though the notion of infinity may legitimately be used in the statement of a theorem, 'there must be no reference to it in the proof' (Poincaré 1963: 66). In short, a proof that has a non-constructive theorem as one step fails to meet the exacting requirement that a mathematical proof must consist of a finite number of steps.

This commitment to constructive proof was clearly illustrated by Poincaré. According to realist mathematicians, Zermelo's non-constructive theorem proves 'that space is capable of being transformed into a well-ordered set' (Poincaré 1963: 67). The imagined dialogue between the anti-realist and the realist goes as follows:

'You (the realist) say that you can transform space into a well-ordered set. Well! Transform it.'

'It would take too long,' replies the realist.

'Then at least show us that someone with enough time and patience could execute the transformation.'

'No, we cannot, because the number of operations to be performed is infinite' replies the realist.

Poincaré terminates the dialogue with the conclusion 'the theorem is devoid of (pragmatic) meaning or false or at least not proved' (Poincaré 1963: 67).[4]

With the emphasis on constructive proof, mathematicians developed an extensive range of mathematical techniques and methods in their efforts to rigorously characterize in strict mathematical terms the common sense notion of an effective, mechanical, rule-governed procedure. These novel, constructive mathematical approaches included Turing machines, Church's lambda calculus and recursion theory. This novel, highly original plethora of constructive approaches gave rise to the famous Church–Turing thesis. Various formulations of this thesis may be found in the literature. The following is Velupillai's summary:

> Many different, independent attempts were made in the formative years of recursive function theory to formalize the intuitive notion of effectively calculable or computable function, number, object, etc. Thus, there was Turing's device of a machine... there was the Gödel–Herbrand notion of general recursiveness coming down from Dedekind, Peano and others who used mathematical induction and iteration to build up the number system; there was Church's attempt... leading to the λ-calculus; and so on. Church's thesis is a statement encapsulating the phenomenological fact – or, as Emil Post called it, a natural law – that all of these independent attempts ultimately yielded one and the same class of functions, numbers and objects as effectively calculable or computable.
>
> (Velupillai 2000: 1)

In other words these various systems proposed as rigorous formulations of the common sense, informal notion of effective mechanical procedure are equivalent. For instance, 'given a definition of a partial recursive function Æ, we will produce a Turing machine which calculates that function; and given a Turing machine which calculates a function Æ, we will produce a partial recursive definition of Æ' (Epstein and Carnielli 2000: 144).

It should be noted that the Church–Turing thesis is not a mathematical theorem that can be proved or disproved in an exact mathematical sense. This is so because it states the identity of two notions, only one of which is mathematically defined. Moreover, much has been written for and against various interpretations of the Church–Turing thesis. Whatever position one adopts, there appears to be consensus on one thing, namely that the thesis is not part of mathematics. Nonetheless, the mathematics of Turing machines and recursion theory stand, even if one has reservations about the thesis.

The mathematical outcome of these and other related developments is that anti-realist inspired, constructive mathematics has a variety of forms. Historically, the first to emerge was Brouwer's intuitionism. Another version is the Russian school of Markov. This version 'develops Turing's ideas based on the acceptance of Church's thesis' (Epstein and Carnielli 2000: 249). Another version comes from Bishop who sees Brouwer's intuitionism as too idealistic and too infinitist, although recursive analysis is too formal and limited. Our concern here, however, is not with the 'internal' debate about constructive mathematics per se. There is a voluminous literature on the technical development of constructive mathematics – useful guides are provided by Bridges and Richman (1987) and Bridges and Vîta (2006). The thesis is that these novel constructive developments supply theoretical economists with a more appropriate and more acceptable, rigorous grammar of argumentation than that used by Hahn in their quest for a richer understanding of rational economic agents and their actions. In the following section we elaborate on this thesis.

Constructive mathematics and economic theorizing: towards a new grammar of argumentation?

As we saw in the last section, Brouwer's intuitionist mathematics was inextricably linked to post-Kantian idealism. For numerous philosophers in the broad church of Analytic Philosophy, post-Kantian idealism was highly questionable. Frege's anti-psychologism and the later-Wittgensteinian critique of the private mind exposed fundamental difficulties in that idealism. Indeed, for many other philosophers influenced by logical positivism, the metaphysical debate between realists and anti-realists was completely meaningless. For others the debate was rather pointless in that it resisted scrutiny by systematic philosophico-linguistic analysis. A crucial dimension of Dummett's originality lies in his efforts to explore the classical metaphysical confrontation between realists and anti-realists in the context of the linguistic turn in philosophy effected by, in particular, Frege and the later Wittgenstein. Thus, Dummett rejects the logical positivist thesis that metaphysics is an utterly meaningless project. There are genuine, indeed crucial, philosophical issues in the metaphysical confrontation between realists and idealists which may be fruitfully addressed in the philosophy of language. Under the influence of Frege, Dummett, contrary to the later Wittgenstein, is optimistic about our philosophical capacity to construct a *systematic* and *comprehensive* theory of meaning compatible with Frege–Wittgensteinian anti-psychologism. This comprehensive theory of meaning, moreover, must be worked out in the light of the later-Wittgensteinian central thesis that the meanings of words and sentences are inextricably linked to their usage. According to the later Wittgenstein, 'for a large class of cases – though not for all – in which we employ the word "meaning" it can be defined thus: the meaning of a word is its use in the language' (Wittgenstein 2000: 20e). Of course these usages are located in Wittgensteinian language games. 'I shall also call the whole consisting of language and the actions into which it is woven the "language-game" ' (Wittgenstein 2000: 5e). By developing a comprehensive theory of meaning appropriate to this Wittgensteinian language–action symbiotic union, Dummett's intention is to show how 'we can abandon realism without falling into subjective idealism' (Dummett 1978: 19).[5] In particular, while being fully aware of how central idealism was to Brouwer, for Dummett 'it (idealism) is by no means essential to the acceptance of an intuitionist conception of arithmetic' (Dummett 2000: 22). Dummett liberates intuitionist mathematics from its post-Kantian idealist moorings by showing how intuitionist mathematics is justified in the context of his neo-Wittgensteinian theory of meaning, while simultaneously showing that realist mathematics is incompatible with that theory.

In Dummett's approach, contrary to the strict formalism of a Hilbert-type mathematician – a view already discussed in relation to both Debreu and Hausman – the sentences of mathematics are genuinely meaningful. He asks us to view these meaningful sentences through the lenses of three distinct theories of meaning: the intuitionist theory, the strict finitist theory and the realist theory. 'The intuitionist holds that the expressions of our mathematical language must be given meaning by reference to operations which we can *in principle* carry out' (Dummett 2000: 43, italics added). For Dummett this is consistent with the later Wittgensteinian position that any meaningful sentence must be capable of usage by human beings whose linguistic–cognitive capacities are finite. The strict finitist holds that the sentences of mathematics 'must be given meaning by reference to operations which we can *in practice* carry out' (Dummett 2000: 43, italics added). The strict finitist position is also compatible with the later Wittgensteinian position. However, it is open to, what we call, the Poincaré objection. This objection goes as follows: for the strict finitist, the number of humanly possible, mathematical operations is some enormously huge, finite number: call it F. According to Poincaré, the pure mathematician can legitimately conceive of a mathematical operation containing F + 1 steps. Hence, one opts for the intuitionist notion of operations that we, in principle, can carry out, rather than the strict finitist approach. Finally, the realist holds that mathematical sentences 'can be given meaning by reference to operations which we *cannot even in principle carry out*, so long as we can conceive them as being carried out by beings with powers which transcend our own' (Dummett 2000: 43, italics added). In connection with Dummett's reference to 'beings with powers which transcend our own,' it is worth noting that, according to Brian McGuinness, Dummett in an unpublished paper argued that realism is only defensible on a theistic basis (McGuinness 1994: 229). This theistic theme is also suggested by the later Wittgenstein. He remarks that realist set theory 'seems to have been designed for *a god who knows what we cannot know*' (Wittgenstein 2000: 127e). In Poincaré's phrase, the realist assumes 'some infinitely talkative divinity capable of thinking of an infinite number of words in a finite length of time' (Poincaré 1963: 67).[6] Be that as it may, this realist theory of meaning is utterly contrary to the later

Wittgensteinian insight that our linguistic–cognitive capacities are finite in principle.

In connection with Hahn's defence of his realist grammar of argumentation,[7] it is crucial to note that we are *not* insisting that the theoretical economist must adopt Dummett's theory of meaning. The issue of which theory of meaning, if any, is the most appropriate to all possible human usages of our vast store of linguistic–cognitive capacities we happily leave to philosophers. Our question is rooted in economic methodology, namely do our finite, linguistic–cognitive capacities impose any restrictions on the mathematics to be used in modelling rational economic decisions and actions, including their social outcomes? In our opinion the answer is yes. In line with the computational and linguistic boundedness of our cognitive capacities emphasized by, among others, Poincaré, the later Wittgenstein and Simon, we maintain that a Dummett-like condition is a reasonable constraint to impose on the terms of theoretical economics used in the mathematical modelling of economic decisions and actions. This Dummett-like condition prescribes that the theoretical terms used in modelling economic rationality obtain their *economic meaning*[8] by reference to operations that a human being could either in principle or in practice carry out. This condition guarantees that rational economic decisions and actions as characterized in the model are, in principle, realizable in real historical time, and this is facilitated by constructive mathematics.

In light of this Dummett-like condition, theoretical economists from Debreu to Hahn theorize economic rationality and equilibrium in such ways that their models are *humanly impossible* to realize in real historical time. As we already pointed out in the previous chapter, Debreu's non-constructive existence proof demonstrates a logical possibility holding in an actual Cantorian infinite sequence. However, non-constructive logical possibility precludes economic possibility, whereas constructive logical possibility in principle includes economic possibility.[9] On the one hand, our Dummett-like constraint demonstrates that the theoretical terms of economics conveyed by non-constructive realist mathematical theorems or techniques presuppose operations that are not realizable in real historical time. On the other hand, if one were to mathematically model economic situations, by exploiting the vast resources of intuitionist–constructive mathematics, one is logically guaranteed that the resulting mathematical models are *in principle* realizable in real socio-historical time.

Of course, as Hahn clearly saw, when theoretical economists change their grammar of argumentation 'a radical change in questions and methods' will be required 'to deliver, not practical, but theoretically useful results' (Hahn 1991(a): 47). This is certainly true in the case of economists adopting a grammar of argumentation which is mathematically rooted in intuitionist–constructive mathematics. In this connection, we point in the direction of Velupillai's constructive mathematical research agenda in theoretical economics, which he is carrying out under the rubric of 'economics needs to be algorithmetic' (Velupillai 2010: 1). His research programme 'has been evolving, very gradually towards a mathematical economics that is formalized exclusively in terms of strict *Brouwerian*

Constructive Mathematics' (Velupillai 2010: 245, italics in original). The radical change in questions and methods to those of orthodox theorizing is clearly evident in Velupillai's work. For Velupillai, rational economic agents are Turing machine problem solvers 'with their "rich" repertoire of incompletenesses, uncomputabilities, and undecidabilities operating in equally "exotic" recursively represented metric and other spaces' (Velupillai 2000: 151). In investigating economic problems the theoretician gives 'them recursion-theoretic interpretations and content and draws the ensuing economic implications' (Velupillai 2000: 3). We are not suggesting that our Dummett-like defence of a mathematical economics exclusively formalized in terms of intuitionist–constructive mathematics is abstracted from Velupillai's intriguing research agenda. Velupillai, over the years, has supplied his own defence. Rather, we are suggesting that his theoretical research displays in a very clear way what Hahn called 'the radical change in questions and methods' required if and when one adopts a different grammar of argumentation.

To conclude, in this chapter we attempted to imaginatively respond to Hahn's challenge for philosophers to address 'the deep difficulties with the economic concept of rationality' (Hahn 1996: 187). By using Dummett to navigate through 'the deep Wittgensteinian waters in which, however, I do not propose to splash or drown' (Hahn 1985: 3), we exposed one major source of these difficulties, namely the use of non-constructive, realist mathematics in the neoclassical modelling of rationality and in its proof of equilibrium. Nonetheless, we feel that Hahn does not have to drown in these Wittgensteinian waters of intuitionist–constructive mathematics. Certainly his ship, which one could name 'the non-constructive realist grammar of argumentation,' is shipwrecked. However, Hahn, in keeping with his commitment to mathematics in economic theorizing, could be rescued by the ship named 'the intuitionist–constructive mathematical grammar of argumentation.' This new ship is, as Hahn expects of any new ship, fitted out with novel sophisticated equipment, which hopefully will enable the economic theoretician to navigate into unchartered waters.[10] Whether this equipment will be up to the many tasks facing the theoretical navigators we cannot say. Wittgenstein, of course, would quickly remind us that attempting such a forecast is certainly not the business of philosophy.

9 Economic theory and Hahn's virtues of understanding

> For what I am centrally interested in is the enterprise of theorizing in economics. By this I mean the undertaking to gain understanding of the particular by reference to generalizing insights and in the light of certain abstract unifying principles.
>
> (Hahn 1985: 3)

Introduction

Throughout the previous chapters we have, on various occasions, used the phrase 'Hahn's methodology.' However, as outlined in Chapter 3, Hahn is hostile to economic methodology. Aside from this hostility, the term 'methodology' in contemporary usage is closely aligned to scientific disciplines and, as we saw, according to Hahn, economic theorizing is not scientific. Given this, and in conjunction with his openness to philosophy, perhaps a change in terminology would be appropriate. One could call Hahn's analysis and reflections on economic theorizing and economic theory his philosophy, not his methodology, of economics. For the later Wittgenstein, a philosopher is like a spectator at a game, with which she or he is not familiar, who attempts to understand the moves of the game by attentively observing them. Hahn, a major player, not a spectator, enables non-economists to understand economic theorizing and simultaneously either enriches or challenges the understanding of other economists of theoretical research in their discipline. In particular, he enriches our understanding of economic theorizing by showing how economic theory is not like scientific theory. Unlike scientific theory, it is not centrally concerned with prediction. Neither is it concerned with explaining by reference to hidden mechanisms. To read neoclassical economic theorizing as a quest for scientific laws akin to the laws of physics, is to utterly misunderstand that distinctive activity. Rather, economic theorizing and economic theory, like philosophy and history, is centrally in the business of understanding. It is a specific kind of understanding. By way of summary, one could claim that the *specificity* of economic understanding is given by its unique grammar of argumentation. In the philosophical spirit of Wittgenstein, rather than the scientific spirit of Newton, Hahn, a brilliant theoretician, takes a close look at economic theorizing and, in an incomplete way, identifies its specific grammar of argumentation.[1] In this final chapter, we briefly reflect on some of the key components of the grammar of argumentation as identified by Hahn. As we pointed out in Chapter 7, this is the grammar of argumentation of the 'new dawn (which) shone on those of us who came to economic theory after the last war' (Hahn 1991(a): 50). We approach his grammar of argumentation by focusing on what we call his philosophical virtues and his economic commitments. We name his philosophical virtues as follows: (1) Frege–Wittgenstein virtues; (2) Platonistic virtues; (3) Cartesian virtues.[2] These philosophical virtues are creatively woven into specific economic commitments. These virtues and commitments, we argue, are key informing principles in Hahn's philosophy of economics which enable us to obtain a richer understanding of that philosophy.

Hahn's intersubjective understanding

Hahn is well aware that there is much more to the discipline of economics than economic theory. His philosophy of economics is not an attempt 'to damn other endeavours in economics… there are "many mansions"… and in concentrating on one I do not wish to be taken as implying anything about the others' (Hahn 1985: 3). If we were to be very precise we should call Hahn's reflections his philosophy of economic theory and of theorizing. Be that as it may, for Hahn the aim of economic theorizing is to enhance our objective understanding of the economic world, including economic actions and their outcomes. As we pointed out in Chapter 4, for some scholars the humanities are also centrally concerned with understanding that which is not scientific. In the humanities human action is frequently seen as having an external, behavioural aspect and a private, mental aspect. Thus, to fully understand an action one must, as it were, enter into the private mind of its author. Precisely because of the specific privacy of this mental sphere, human action cannot be studied as one would study the human brain or any other purely physical system. In this subjectivist approach to understanding any rational human decision, the individual's decision must be located in the private depths of the individual's mind, to which she or he only has proper access through the non-linguistic process of introspection. Since any intersubjective understanding of that private, inner mental process is always, in principle, open to question, a central challenge facing the humanities is to find a key or set of keys *for others* to gain access to the private stream of consciousness of another agent. As we have seen in earlier chapters, this subjectivist notion of understanding had extensive influence on nineteenth-century post-Kantian idealism and nineteenth-century hermeneutics, as well as on Brouwer's philosophy of mathematics in the twentieth century.

Hahn is aware of this influential philosophical link between understanding and this private subjectivist mind, and is at pains to point out that the concept of understanding central to his philosophy of economics does not pertain to this subjectivist tradition. In line with the paradigm change in philosophy, accomplished by Frege and Wittgenstein, he emphasizes that the concept of understanding appropriate to his philosophy of economics is, public, linguistic and intersubjective. In this connection, it should be noted that the Frege–Wittgenstein linguistic turn does not push Hahn into the twentieth century behaviourist camp. Although in the Frege–Wittgenstein linguistic turn our cognitive rational abilities are intimately related to our linguistic abilities, there is no suggestion that the vast, sophisticated range of our cognitive–linguistic abilities can be understood in the stimulus–organism–response model of behaviourism. For instance, how could the Arrow–Debreu concept of equilibrium be explained by this stimulus–organism–response model? Hahn, as outlined in Chapter 4, emphasizes that, at rock bottom, economic agents are persons: beings with very sophisticated conceptual abilities. These conceptual abilities are displayed for us in an original philosophical way by the later Wittgenstein, without recourse to the notion of a private subjectivist mind on the one hand or to a reductionist behaviourism on the other. In this Wittgensteinian philosophical setting, rational decision making and choice is linguistically based and *ipso facto* intersubjective.[3] Thus, the understanding of economic decision making and choice is intersubjective, not subjective. In this approach to understanding, even what is frequently called subjective Bayesian decision making by an individual agent is intersubjective.

In addition to liberating the concept of understanding from this subjectivist psychologism, which was for some time very prevalent in the humanities, the Frege–Wittgenstein linguistic turn illuminates Hahn's emphatic demarcation between economic theorizing, on the one hand, and history of economic thought on the other. As we have already seen, Hahn, as an economic theoretician, is dismissive of the value of the history of economic thought. This dismissal is not based on the assumption that historical understanding is subjective. The understandings achieved in economic theorizing and the history of economic thought are, without doubt, intersubjective, but distinct. For instance, a good historian can make a novel contribution and thereby enhance the intersubjective understanding of the origins of the economic notion (more precisely notions) of equilibrium. In keeping with the later Wittgenstein, however, the discipline or language game of economic theorizing should not be confused with the discipline or language game of the history of economic thought. In particular, in the Arrow–Debreu language game, the historical origins of the concept of equilibrium is of no help in the correct understanding of how the concept equilibrium is actually used in Arrow–Debreu theorizing. In teaching Arrow–Debreu general equilibrium theory, the lecturer shows the students how the term 'equilibrium' is defined and used in that theory. Any reference made to similarities between Arrow–Debreu equilibrium and the concept of equilibrium in, say, mechanics may be psychologically helpful, but such references play no part in the grammar of argumentation of Arrow and Debreu. In the spirit of the later Wittgenstein, Hahn demands that students focus their economic attention on how the concept is used in Arrow–Debreu theorizing.

One may object that, while Hahn's demarcation is plausible, the history of economic thought could be useful to the theoretician in suggesting new problems. Hahn, we suspect, would not deny that challenging problems for the theoretician can come from a variety of sources, ranging from the history of economic thought to opponents, such as Simon or Kaldor. Hahn's point is that, whatever the sources, the theoretician's focus is on how the theoretical terms are, or can be, used in the theory and its grammar of argumentation. It is these which will enable the theoretician to understand and eventually solve the problem. In short, the foregoing Frege–Wittgenstein virtues enable Hahn to liberate the concept of understanding from its subjectivist moorings and, second, explains his emphasis on the demarcation between economic theorizing on the one hand and the history of economic thought on the other.

Fact and fiction in economics: a Hahnian perspective

In the preface to his edited work, *Fact and Fiction in Economics*, Mäki opens the discussion as follows: 'Fact or fiction? Is economics a respectable and useful reality-oriented discipline or just an intellectual game that economists play in their sandbox filled with imaginary toy models?' (Mäki 2002: xv). Rhetorical flourish aside, this issue has been an abiding concern throughout this work. Time and time again we encountered the question: does economic theorizing, *à la* Hahn's grammar of argumentation, illuminate the real world or is it a very sophisticated mathematical model which, in the end, turns out to be incapable of application to the economic world? In answer to his own question, Mäki concludes, 'as soon as one looks more closely, what one starts seeing is fact *and* fiction, in a variety of combinatory incarnations' (Mäki 2002: xv). Leaving aside the issue of economics being a science and narrowing the focus from economics to economic theorizing, Mäki's conclusion could be applied to Hahn.[4] By recourse to Hahn's Platonistic and Cartesian virtues combined to his economic commitments, we excavate both the fact and the fiction in Hahn's position.

We start with, what we call, Hahn's Platonistic virtues of understanding. We chose this name because these were, in the first instance, expertly and creatively exploited by Socrates in Plato's dialogues. The Platonistic virtues of understanding are (1) scrutinize the uncritical acceptance of certain categories; (2) make precise, via the quest for clear definition, what is vague; (3) be as explicit as possible – tacit assumptions can undermine a position. As we saw in Chapter 4 these Platonistic virtues are indispensable in economic theorizing. In relation to Mäki's fact/fiction issue, we argue that, just as Plato demonstrated how the application of these virtues enabled Athenians to see concrete ethical actions in a new light and thereby enhanced their understanding of the real world of ethical action, Hahn can maintain the same for his application of these virtues in economic theorizing.

As the history of philosophy clearly testifies, Socrates enhanced our understanding of the emerging discipline of ethics by creatively using these virtues. For instance, after Socrates we all know that terms like justice require further scrutiny. Moreover, after the Socratic application of these virtues Athenians influenced by him saw concrete ethical actions in a new light. They had a more enriched understanding of human action in the ethical sphere. This is true, even though Socrates used these virtues to suggest an ideal world of Forms, distinct from the real social world. Similarly, by adhering to these Platonistic virtues, Hahn can, with some justification, claim to have enriched both our understanding of economic theorizing and of the real economic world. In connection with economic theorizing, for instance, philosophers have a better understanding of how Debreu took the imprecise term 'equilibrium' and, *à la* Plato, gave it a precise meaning. Second, just as the Athenians saw concrete human action in the ethical sphere in a new and more penetrating light after Socrates, we can see concrete economic actions in a new light after Arrow–Debreu theorizing. According to Hahn, however, numerous methodologists, philosophers and economists, by assuming that economic theorizing is similar to theorizing in physics, misunderstand its proper function. They read economic theory, through the lens of scientific laws, which in turn are used for predictive purposes. As Plato appreciated, the use of his Platonistic virtues does not necessarily lead to law-like, scientific truths. These virtues, however, can enhance our understanding of the real world, without recourse to a scientific world view. This is one of their key functions.

In short, as we saw in the previous section, Hahn moves economic theorizing out of the specific domain of science into the broader realm of intersubjective understanding. In this non-subjectivist context, he can, *à la* Plato, claim that Arrow–Debreu theorizing, which is rooted in the above Platonistic virtues, enables economists to appreciate, in a way which did not previously exist, the real economic world, without being a scientific explanation or picture of that world. This is a unique gain in the economic understanding of the real world. This *prima facie* link to the real economic world, however, could be severed by Hahn's use of his other virtues and commitments. Of course it is equally possible that these may strengthen the link to the real world and thereby further enhance our non-scientific, but objective, understanding of that world. In this connection, we argue that Hahn's Cartesian virtues identify where the links to reality are both strengthened and weakened.

Hahn's Cartesian virtues introduced in Chapters 4 and 6 are (1) the necessity of a solid starting point in economic theorizing and (2) the value of the axiomatic approach. It is well known that Descartes wished to practice philosophy *more goemetrico*. To this end he radicalized the above Platonistic virtues into the fundamental principle that clear and distinct ideas are true. Hahn, while accepting the indispensable value of clear and distinct ideas in economic theorizing, does not accept this Cartesian principle – hence we preferred to call these values Platonistic rather than Cartesian. In his famous Cartesian method, Descartes introduces a systematic, methodic doubt to guarantee a solid starting point. In the domain of intersubjective understanding, Hahn also attains a solid starting point for economic theorizing, without, however, the extreme measure of a methodic doubt. As we saw in Chapter 4, he finds this solid starting point in Debreu's existence proof of equilibrium. Plato failed to give us an absolute compelling proof of his world of Forms, but Hahn has a logically impeccable proof for his starting point in the theoretician's quest for the intersubjective understanding of the real economic world, namely Debreu's existence proof. The *prima facie* understanding of the real world furnished by the Platonistic virtues has a logical proof as its starting point. This is certainly a significant 'plus' in establishing the objectivity of the *prima facie* link between economic theorizing and the real world. Once again, as claimed by Hahn, to read Debreu's proof as a piece of theoretical science, like Einstein's general relativity theory or quantum physics, is to utterly misrepresent the theoretical value of the project.

Descartes, as we already noted, wanted to model his philosophy on Euclid's axiomatic method. As we discussed in Chapter 6, Hahn also favours the axiomatic method. Indeed, because his economic theorizing presupposes Debreu's proof, we saw how he favoured the more traditional approach to an axiomatic system to either Debreu's strict formalist or Hausman's implicit definition approach. In this traditional approach, the distinction between economic axioms and economic assumptions, emphasized time and again by Hahn, is significant. In the Mäki fact or fiction debate, this distinction is crucial. However, as we saw, for Hahn, economic axioms are rigorous formulations of consensus truths. As we have already seen vis-à-vis the Platonistic virtues, being rigorous does not imply a lack of understanding. On the contrary, being rigorous *à la* Plato may enable one to see the world in a new and significant light. Thus, the economic axioms, being both rigorous and grounded in truths such as economic agents are persons, tighten the grip of the theoretician's logically based, intersubjective understanding on the real world. Economic theorizing, by its use of the Platonistic virtues combined with real world grounded axioms, is well down the road to the enhancement of the economist's, logically based, intersubjective understanding of the real world.

Assumptions, as distinct from axioms, however, cause difficulties for the realization of the task of a comprehensive, logically based, intersubjective understanding of the economic world. As we discussed in Chapter 4, some assumptions cover up gaps, which require closer scrutiny, in our economic understanding. Other assumptions are even more problematic: they loosen the grip that theoretically based understanding has on the real economic world.[5] Of course the critical question is whether or not some of these assumptions merely loosen or actually break the connection to the real world? To see why Hahn maintains that these assumptions do not break this link, we turn to what we called his economic commitments.

In this connection, two such commitments are crucial. These are (1) relaxing the assumptions by taking on board real world issues and (2) to reformulate, or more precisely, improve on Debreu's starting point. As we discussed in Chapter 7 when responding to Kaldor's uncompromising critique, Hahn's research into learning, etc. fills in some of the gaps in understanding concealed by assumptions. Moreover, other efforts are made at weakening assumptions by taking on board, for instance, Keynesian demands. Indeed, the outcome of this theoretical work is a better concept of equilibrium than that initially furnished by Debreu. In short, in this Hahnian perspective, theoretical research tightens some of the existing links to the real world and even creates additional ones. However, this theoretical research is not itself assumptionless. These assumptions may loosen other links or add on additional very loose links to the real world. Overall, however, Hahn's thesis that economic theorizing enhances in an ongoing way the objective understanding of the real economic world retains its plausibility.

Mathematics in economic theorizing: a Trojan horse?

Thus far in this chapter, based on Hahn's own analysis, we have reconstructed his defence of the claim that general equilibrium theory makes a unique contribution to the correct understanding of the real world. In this section we turn to another central neo-Walrasian commitment, namely the exploitation of the most powerful mathematics available in that theory. In this connection we ask: does this commitment have a negative impact on Hahn's claim? *Prima facie*, there is no good reason for not using the best mathematics available in the logical analysis of any domain. Although it is generally acknowledged that the Frege–Russell logicist programme which aimed at reducing pure mathematics to logic failed, no one questions the intimate relationship between logic and pure mathematics. Hence the P–K thesis, introduced in Chapter 7, which claims that Debreu's existence proof cannot be given an economic interpretation precisely because of its recourse to 'the best' mathematics available, is, to say the least, astounding.

In our view, although the P–K thesis is, *prima facie*, surprising, when one examines more closely the difference between mathematical existence and economic existence, one can see its force. As we argued in Chapters 7 and 8, the P–K thesis is based on (1) the difference between the domain of mathematical existence and the more restrictive domain of economic existence, and (2) the appropriate method for proving existence in these distinct domains. In what we called realist mathematics – the mathematics used by Arrow, Debreu and Hahn – the domain of mathematical existence can be imagined as one which is much more vast than the domain of the potentially infinite, which in turn includes the domain of the finite. The domain of economic existence, however, is limited to real historical time, and thus is finite: its outer limit, as it were, is the potentially infinite. An existence proof in realist mathematics establishes existence either inside or outside the domain of the potentially infinite. If the proof is constructive, as understood in intuitionist mathematics discussed in Chapter 8, existence is demonstrated to be within the domain of the potentially infinite, and thus is capable of economic interpretation. However, if the proof is non-constructive and cannot be turned into a constructive one, then what is proven to exist is outside the domain of the potentially infinite, and thus is not, even in principle, open to economic interpretation. Debreu's existence proof, however, falls into the non-constructive side of this crucial divide for economic theorizing. In response to Mäki's question of the last section, namely fact or fiction, Debreu's proof, though mathematically attaining the highest standards of rigour, is an economic fiction. Despite the initial success of the philosophical virtues and the economic commitments outlined in the previous sections in clarifying how economic theorizing *à la* Hahn can enhance our appreciation, and thereby our understanding, of the real economic world, it is truly ironic that these significant gains are undermined by the neo-Walrasian economic commitment of recourse to the best, i.e. the realist, mathematics available. The Arrow–Debreu understanding, so creatively enhanced by Hahn's own economic research and so originally defended by his philosophy of economics, because of its recourse to a particular kind of mathematics with its non-constructive proof of mathematical existence, cannot be given any economic interpretation which pertains to a world with, however vast but nonetheless, a finite time horizon and populated with bounded economic agents. This, as we saw, was Kaldor's fundamental insight.

As was pointed out in the last chapter, this negative result has a positive side to it. The P–K thesis does not imply that economic theorizing cannot be conducted in a rigorous, mathematical way. On the contrary, the P–K thesis points to the kind of mathematics to be used in such theorizing, namely intuitionist–constructive mathematics. This mathematics opens up the possibility of a new research programme compatible with Hahn's Platonistic virtues, virtues which require the economic theoretician to critically re-interrogate and to rigorously recharacterize rational decision making and rational actions along with their consequences.

Concluding considerations

Arising from his hostility to economic methodology, Hahn's analysis of economic theorizing has, on the whole, been neglected by methodologists or philosophers of economics. In our opinion, this is regrettable; his analysis is highly original and challenging. Economics is perceived by numerous economists, philosophers and methodologists as being, *par excellence*, the social science. Indeed, various social scientists look on the success of economics as a science with admiration and perhaps a degree of envy. Hahn, however, is very unique among orthodox economists. He argues that, whatever about other aspects of economics, economic theorizing is not a piece of empirical science. In particular we have demonstrated how his defence of neoclassical theorizing differs from Friedman's defence on the one hand and Hausman's on the other. In this vein, Hahn is emphatic that economic theory has nothing causal to say and that it does not as such tell us anything about the history of the world. Yet he insists that it is the key to the economic understanding of the world. For those who view economic theory as an exercise akin to theorizing in physics, this claim is, to say the least, perplexing. However, once one recognizes that economic theorizing is not like theorizing in physics, and once one appreciates Hahn's Frege–Wittgenstein, Platonistic and Cartesian virtues, Hahn's thesis that economic theory enhances the objective understanding of the economic world ceases to be perplexing. On the contrary, it is challenging, particularly for those who tacitly assume economic theorizing is scientific.

Moreover, Hahn's originality is evident in the manner in which his approach to economic theorizing differs from that of Debreu on the one hand and that of Friedman on the other. We hope that we have given the reader some appreciation of the very different philosophico-methodological stances of these major contributors to orthodox economics. As we discussed in Chapters 3 and 7, another brilliant economist, Kaldor, called for a major act of demolition of this orthodoxy. We saw how Hahn has little time for calls of crisis, especially at the hands of methodologists who approach the issue in a prescriptive way based on their own preferred philosophy of science. Hahn's response to Kaldor, however, was not that simple. He took Kaldor's critique very seriously. In a sense, the clash between these two outstanding economists reconstructs the so-called crisis debate in an original and challenging way. In our opinion, it clearly illustrates the fundamental difference between Hahn's commitment to the intersubjective, Platonistic approach to understanding and Kaldor's commitment to the intersubjective, Aristotelian approach. The ancient conflict between the Platonic ideal and the Aristotelian empirical approaches to understanding is given new life in the Hahn–Kaldor conflict.

Clearly Hahn's analysis of economic theorizing has major implications for current debates in economic methodology. In addition to those just mentioned, his philosophy raises key issues in the realist/anti-realist debate explored by Lawson, Mäki, Mirowski and McCloskey, to mention but a few, as well as for the extensive debate on economic modelling. One could say that, in general, the Hahn–Kaldor conflict moves the debate on the formalization of economics away from the question of the fruitfulness or otherwise of the mathematization of economics onto the question of the specific kind of mathematics to be used in economic theorizing. This issue is the Cinderella of economic methodology and has major implications for both the realist/anti-realist debate and for the discussion of economic modeling.[6]

Throughout this study we have adopted a Socratic approach to the methodology/philosophy of economics. In opposition to the so-called 'naturalization' of methodology,[7] which claims that economic methodology itself should be scientific, our Socratic approach views methodology as a critical dialogue, aimed at enhancing our understanding of economic practice in its full richness and complexity, ranging from economic theory to applied economics. In this work we have attempted to give voice to Hahn's challenging and original contribution to that dialogue. We are confident that the ensuing dialogue, in which the voices of all participants both economists and philosophers receive sympathetic but critical hearing, will be both exciting and rewarding. As Donald Davidson reminds us, 'it is only in the context of frank discussion, communication and mutual exchange that trustworthy truths emerge' (Davidson 2005: 240).

Notes

3 Hahn's hostility to economic methodology

1 Hahn is consistently opposed to schools in both economics and philosophy. Writing eight years earlier, he notes that in economics one

> is encompassed by passionately held beliefs... in almost anything that has ever been tried. In fact all these 'certainties' and all the 'schools' which they spawn are a sure sign of our ignorance. Perhaps something like this is needed to spur us on but I regard it simply as *trahison des clercs.*
>
> (Hahn 1984: 7)

2 In his conclusion, Darwin says 'I look with confidence to the future – to young and rising naturalists, who will be able to view both sides of the question with impartiality' (Darwin (1866) 1971: 456).

3 We will discuss the Kaldor–Hahn 'debate' in Chapter 7.

4 In fact, the debate about the role of mathematics in economics is much older. This is evident from the Walras–Poincaré correspondence at the turn of the twentieth-century.

5 It is instructive to compare Hahn's 'evolutionary picture of the possibility of mathematics being driven out of economics' (Hahn 1992(b): 5) with Solow's 1954 evolutionary argument for the formalization of economics.

> Why is economic theory becoming more not less mathematical?... As a good Darwinian I believe that this is no accident... Survival in the literature is a test of fitness if an imperfect one. If mathematical techniques continue to produce good economics then, still as a Darwinian, I predict that long before the appendix has disappeared from the human digestive tract most people interested in economic theory will as a matter of course learn some mathematics.
>
> (Solow 1954: 373–4)

Although Solow's Darwinian metaphor does allow for Hahn's possibility, it is used to legitimate the role of mathematics in economics. Thirty-five years later, there is no need for Hahn to make the same case.

6 See the next chapter for a more detailed discussion of assumptions.

7 One may well feel that numerous European economists share this view, but perhaps not the specific Friedmanite reading of science.

8 In earlier work we adopted a later Wittgensteinian approach to the issue of whether or not economics is a science. For more details, see Boylan and O'Gorman (1995).

9 Hahn is explicitly using a rather simplified theory here for the purposes of illustrating how the pragmatics of forecasting come into play in successful forecasting in the domain of action.

10 In a footnote he points out that 'modern macro models are more disaggregated,

numerical models containing 20–30 commodities being quite routine these days' (Dasgupta 2002: 84).

11 We discuss Hausman's Millean view of economic laws in Chapter 5.

4 In defence of economic theorizing

1 Hahn's attitude towards the later Wittgenstein appears to have hardened over the years. In his Jevons Memorial Fund Lecture he notes that his concept of understanding brings one into 'deep Wittgenstein waters' (Hahn 1985: 3). In 1993, however, he remarks that Wittgenstein 'had a number of poetic things to say' in connection with understanding (Hahn 1993: 85).

2 In this connection, for instance, Hahn, referring to Mr Benn, Mrs Thatcher, President Reagan and others, remarks

> all these people take it for granted that somewhere there is a theory, that is a body of logically connected propositions based on postulates not wildly at variance with what is the case, which support their policies. *It must be of some significance to enquire whether this is in fact so.*
>
> (Hahn 1982(a): 112; italics added)

3 This suggestion for, as it were, getting vague concepts off the ground is used by van Fraassen (van Fraassen 1980: 16).

4 In this approach one, of course, may debate the aptness of a specific example. However, once one furnishes some clear examples and clear counter-examples, one has shown that the concept is not incoherent.

5 Methodologically, this issue is not as straightforward as it may first appear. Gödel's theorems are certainly lurking in the background. After Gödel, one may say that it is not possible to axiomatize the whole of pure mathematics in a consistent way.

6 A later Wittgensteinian approach to philosophy would not accept this challenge. It is not the job of a philosopher to find such a definition. Defining, *à la* the suggestion of Hahn, the concept of understanding would do violence to its depth-grammar in our language-games.

7 These indispensable constraints distance Hahn even further from contemporary hermeneutical readings of economics, where these constraints are not acknowledged.

8 Hahn immediately adds that by 'knowing what he wants' economists mean 'the agent has a proper preference ordering over a relevant domain' (Hahn 1985: 5).

9 There is no evidence to suggest that Hahn is toying with a consensus theory of truth.

10 Hahn maintains that 'in the first instance then the axiom says that economic agents are persons' (Hahn 1985: 6).

11 This preliminary thesis will be qualified in the next section when we address Hahn's analysis of economic assumptions.

12 There are intriguing philosophical problems of identity lurking here. One could draw on a different analogy to buttress Hahn's position. The analogy is found in Hume (1985: 306). If an old church is restored, beams replaced and so on, we still identify it as the same church.

13 To illustrate this he refers to his own research on the Solow growth model with many capital goods in which the steady state turned out to be a saddle point, with the consequence that many divergent equilibrium points over finite time existed. According to Hahn, the 'Chicago economists' responded by simplifying even more than what Solow had done by assuming 'that the economy followed an equilibrium path over infinite time.' With this silly assumption of infinite times, these economists have swept many interesting challenges under the carpet (Hahn 1994: 251).

14 Philosophers of science are well aware of difficulties with counterfactual conditionals. We all readily have recourse to them but their logic has proven to be a minefield.

15 We call this quasi-Humean to indicate that this is not a scholarly exegesis of Hume.

Hahn indeed endorses such an approach. 'For people like me to invoke old heroes never implies deep knowledge of their oeuvre, but rather a general bow in the direction of a popular conception' (Hahn 2005(a): 6).

16 We further explore this issue in Chapter 7.

17 The perceptive reader will realize that these headings used to categorize the various limitations have Kuhnian origins.

18 One might feel that there is an inherent subjective element in any methodological use of the word 'aim.' Individual economists have aims, disciplines don't. These aims could range from mammon to metaphysics. While one would need to be either silly or stupid not to acknowledge the variety of aims of individual economists, disciplines also have aims. As van Fraassen asserts 'what the aim is determines what counts as success in the enterprise as such; and this aim may be pursued for any number of reasons' (van Fraassen 1980: 8).

5 The core of neoclassical economics?

1 Such a reading may be found in Backhouse (1995), Mäki (1996) and Reuten (1996). According to Hausman himself, however, 'readers have seen me as an apologist for equilibrium economics. But I am not' (Hausman 1997: 402).

2 This list is by no means complete. A quick glance at his *Essays on Philosophy and Economic Methodology*, as well as the elaboration of his major thesis in his *The Inexact and Separate Science of Economics* would prove fruitful for anyone who wants a more extensive list.

3 We have borrowed the metaphor of 'portrait' from Mäki (1996).

4 It is difficult to know whether or not Hausman would agree that this claim is controversial. He is certainly aware that 'many economists regard it (general equilibrium theory) as the fundamental theory of contemporary economics' (Hausman 1992(b): 168). In this context, he adds 'this seems a mistake,' whereas in his 1992(a) text he remarks that 'the disagreement here is only terminological' (Hausman 1992(a): 52, footnote 8). We will discuss this and other methodological issues concerning general equilibrium theory later.

5 This list is also used by Hausman in summing up his fundamental theory in Hausman 1997.

6 Hausman's objection to Kuhnian paradigms rests on his claims that such paradigms are 'notoriously ambiguous' and that they suggest 'an unreasonably irrationalist view of scientific development and change' (Hausman 1992(b): 31). These objections are developed in Hausman 1992(a).

7 While Hahn welcomes clearly defined terms, we will see that his methodological position implies the rejection of Hausman's reconstruction of equilibrium economics. Moreover, while Hausman's definition of 'fundamental' or 'core' is clear, its usage has bizarre consequences. Suppose that a number of economic research programmes had recourse to a majority of core axioms of equilibrium economics but that these were *in a minority* in comparison with the other axioms used. Let us further assume that the majority of axioms *in* these research programmes are taken from PKE (Post-Keynesian Economics). One might be tempted to identify such a research programme as a PKE one.

8 Hausman tells us that 'dogmatism is sometimes justifiable' (1992(a): 234), but that some methodological rules are 'objectionably dogmatic' (1992(a): 207).

9 This permanence, of course, is subject to Hausman's definition of fundamental, outlined in the previous section.

10 Indeed, it could be argued that Mäki is understating Hausman's position here. Hausman's position entails something approximating to a resolute reluctance to reject fundamental equilibrium theory when faced with negative evidence. Thus, he claims 'since the simplifications and *ceteris paribus* clauses needed to derive predictions

concerning uncontrolled market phenomena from equilibrium theory are the weak links, mistaken predictions *never* wind up disconfirming the theory' (Hausman 1992(a): 208, italics added). Later, he tells us 'indeed it becomes almost impossible to learn from experience. This is the situation in economics' (Hausman 1992(a): 307). This is more than a mere reluctance.

11 A good deal, as distinct from a great deal, of truth would lessen economist's confidence in basic equilibrium theory. A good deal of truth could not protect an empirical theory from never being refuted. For instance, the classical theory of the atom had a good deal of truth to it, but it was replaced by a better theory. We will see later how Hahn's defence of mainstream economics avoids these Hausmanite difficulties.

12 J.S. Mill's methodological writings are the historical source of Hausman's thesis of the inexactness of equilibrium economics. The extent to which Hausman's own analysis is faithful to Mill may be a debatable issue. Reuten (1996), for instance, challenges Hausman's interpretation. The pursuit of these intriguing historical influences is beyond the scope of this work.

13 One should not think that there is something paradoxical to the claim that one can speak in an exact manner about inexactness. If one is tempted to think in such a fashion, one should remember the basic logical lesson that logicians can and do speak consistently about the notion of inconsistency. A good logical mind will attempt to speak exactly about inexactness. It is to Hausman's credit that he effectively undertakes this analysis – this is so whether or not one accepts his analysis.

14 For a number of technical philosophical reasons, Hausman also does not favour reading inexactness in a probabilistic or statistical sense (Hausman 1992(a): 129). Without the appropriate technical specification, saying economic laws are statistical is just another way of saying that they are inexact.

15 In this connection Mäki makes the perceptive claim that Hausman's reading of *ceteris paribus* is very broad, and adds: 'Anything – not just violations of equality – that might interfere with what the theory says happens in the world becomes covered by the clause' (Mäki 1996: 21). If Mäki's addition is a correct reading of Hausman – we certainly agree that Hausman reads *ceteris paribus* in a broad way – then Hausman's explanation of inexactness will necessarily prescribe the refutation of the basic axioms: all possible countervailing instances are shifted to the complicating factors. The laws are telling us what would happen and what tends to happen in the absence of these various complications. The fact that Hausman maintains that, except for the philosopher's qualms about possible worlds, there is little difference between a counterfactual construal of inexactness and his vague *ceteris paribus* qualification view (Hausman 1992(a): 128, 132), could lend credence to Mäki's addition.

16 It should be noted that, in this connection, Hausman the philosopher is in good company. Hahn also accuses Kaldor of being too influenced by the textbook account. We will address this in Chapter 7.

17 The Kuhnian account of the role of textbooks in science is independent of any kind of relativism which may be lurking in some of his work.

18 One would expect methodologists, like Hausman, who view economic methodology as an empirical science to conduct a proper survey of neoclassical economists to ascertain whether or not they subscribe to the commitment of separateness. The results could be very interesting.

6 Economics and axiomatization

1 Hahn is not maintaining that logic is a part of empirical, cognitive psychology. We presume he is claiming that humans, if they wish to avoid inconsistency, must be logical. Logic is a prescriptive, not a descriptive, discipline.

2 The second interpretation is what we called the Hilbert–Bourbaki formalism. We will address this interpretation when discussing Debreu's methodology.

3 We will elaborate on this in the next section when we contrast Hahn's approach to the axiomatization of economics with that of Hausman.
4 For instance, according to Frege, Hilbert initially held this view in 1899 but quickly changed his mind (Frege 1971(b): 25). Whether or not Frege is correct is an issue for Hilbert scholars. For our purposes, we simply wish to note that some mathematicians, philosophers and logicians hold that an axiomatic system is an implicit definition, and others hold that the axioms, being propositions, cannot be definitions.
5 Recall that this kind of definition is called implicit, in contrast to *explicit* definitions used within the deductive system. As Frege perceptively noted, Hilbert does not use explicit definitions at all in his Festschrift.
6 This is a very abridged presentation. A classic detailed account may be found in Church (1956).
7 For a more detailed discussion of this point see Boylan and O'Gorman (2007).
8 It would take us into a detailed discussion in the philosophy of mathematics to see whether or not the role of the Fregian propaedeutic impinges on Hilbert's purely formalist reading.
9 Prescriptively, the question is the following: given the nature of the proof, what restrictions are logically imposed on any correct economic interpretation?

7 Kaldor and Hahn on equilibrium economics

1 It should he noted that Hahn's central focus is what he calls Arrow–Debreu equilibrium, whereas Kaldor largely focuses on Debreu's *Theory of Value*. Given that we are, in this chapter, centrally concerned with Hahn's critique of Kaldor, to simplify matters, we focus on Debreu. This should not be read as suggesting that Arrow was just a minor figure in the development of general equilibrium. Any such suggestion would be a travesty of the truth.
2 See the next section for our reasons for calling it Platonic.
3 Hahn, in response to Hausman, asks philosophers to address the issue of the variety of concepts of equilibrium. In response to this challenge, we introduced Quine's notion of explication. In our view, this is methodologically speaking, a more fruitful notion than that of definition when dealing with 'concepts which are not rigorously formulated' (Hahn 1996: 189).
4 Hahn could legitimately assume that a Cambridge audience would appreciate this reference to Wittgenstein.
5 In this connection, for a historical account of the relationship between Debreu and Arrow in the early nineteen fifties see Ingrao and Israel (1990).
6 Debreu presupposed what is technically known as Brouwer's fixed point theorem in his proof of the existence of equilibrium. However, this theorem cannot be proven in non-Cantorian, computable mathematics. Moreover, efforts by Scarf and others to render equilibrium constructible also fail. For more on this see Boylan and O'Gorman (2007 and 2010).
7 We will discuss constructive mathematics and its positive significance for economic theorizing in Chapter 8.
8 Brown (2002) provides an interesting and readable introduction to these topics.
9 As Poincaré notes, the number of steps 'is greater than aleph zero' (Poincaré 1963: 67), the first of Cantor's transfinite numbers.
10 Velupillai is well aware of the efforts of Scarf and others to develop constructive general equilibrium. Velupillai shows how non-constructive, fixed point theorems are used in these efforts.
11 We will discuss this in more detail in Chapter 8.
12 We are not suggesting that methodologists occupy some cosmic exile from which they can, in a God-like fashion, lay down infallible commandments. Clearly, methodologists have their own commitments. They are well known for washing their dirty

linen in public. Indeed, various economists not disposed to methodology are quick to point this out.

8 Economics, mathematics and rationality: a new grammar of argumentation?

1 This is a simplified articulation of Frege's position. Frege distinguished between ideas and concepts – a crucial distinction for Fregian scholars. However, his distinction is not crucial for the purposes of distinguishing between subjective ideas in the individual mind and non-mental reference.

2 Brouwer is probably best known among economic theorists for his (Brouwer's) fixed point theorem. It should be noted that this theorem holds only in realist mathematics. It is a *bogus* theorem in Brouwer's intuitionist mathematics, i.e. it is not a theorem at all in intuitionist mathematics.

3 We briefly addressed Poincaré's position in Chapter 7, when we introduced the P–K thesis.

4 The same 'logic' applied to Debreu's non-constructive proof of the existence of equilibrium. For the realist mathematician Debreu's proof is logically impeccable, for the intuitionist it is a bogus proof. For us the question is whether or not it is *economically* impeccable? We argue that it is not.

5 According to some scholars, Dummett himself did not espouse anti-realism. This conclusion is based on his remark:

> I personally have no unshakeable commitment to anti-realism in any of these cases even the mathematical one… I have urged the claims of the anti-realist position only because it seemed to me that, in most cases, philosophers unthinkingly adopted a realist view without noticing that it required substantiation.
>
> (Dummett 1978: xxxix)

Of course, as we will see later, we also do not require theoretical economists to adopt *the philosophy* of anti-realism. Our thesis is that only some anti-realist claims, including, however, anti-realist mathematics, are relevant to economic theorizing.

6 In tune with these remarks we suggested calling the Arrow–Debreu–Hahn theorizing 'theological economics' (Boylan and O'Gorman 2008).

7 Hahn, of course, does not identify his grammar as realist. In point of fact, however, because of his usage of non-constructive, realist mathematics, his grammar can be legitimately characterized as realist.

8 Dummett wishes to develop a comprehensive theory of meaning, whereas our focus is much narrower, namely the meaning of theoretical terms to be used in the mathematical modelling of economic decisions, actions and their social outcomes.

9 As we pointed out elsewhere (Boylan and O'Gorman 2010) our target is the set of theorems of realist mathematics which cannot be given constructive proofs. As Zambelli points out, among these non-constructive theorems are 'the Bolzano–Weierstrass theorem… the Hahn–Banach theorem and the fixed point theorem' (Zambelli 2010: 34). Those parts of realist mathematics that are constructive do not pose difficulties for economic theoreticians.

10 Of course the mariners on board this ship will salvage parts of the wreckage which they find useful – namely those parts that can be explicated via constructive techniques.

9 Economic theory and Hahn's virtues of understanding

1 As we saw in Chapter 4, Hahn characterizes his grammar as incomplete.

2 These names do not imply a commitment to all aspects of the philosophical programmes of the original philosophers.

3 As the later Wittgenstein demonstrated, there is no such thing as a private, purely subjective, language.
4 If our reading of Kaldor is correct in Chapter 6, Mäki's thesis does not apply to him. As Hahn notes, Kaldor saw neoclassical theory as 'science fiction' (Hahn 2005(b): 17).
5 As we saw in Chapter 3, Hahn, unlike some of his colleagues, imposes limitations on possible assumptions.
6 For a more detailed discussion, see Boylan and O'Gorman (2010).
7 Since Quine's famous 'epistemology naturalized' (Quine 1969), the project of transforming methodology into a chapter of the book of science gained momentum. We saw in Chapter 4 how Hausman, for instance, is sympathetic to that project. In our opinion, Hahn would not share that sympathy: economic theorizing, never mind philosophy, is not a chapter in the book of science.

Bibliography

Arrow, K.J. (1951) *Social Choice and Individual Values*, New York: Wiley.

—— (1974) 'General economic equilibrium. Purpose, analytic techniques, collective choice,' *American Economic Review*, 64: 253–72.

Arrow, K.J. and Debreu, G. (1954) 'Existence of an equilibrium for a competitive economy,' *Econometrica*, 22: 265–90.

Arrow, K.J. and Hahn, F.H. (1971) *General Competitive Analysis*, San Francisco, CA: Holden Day.

Backhouse, R. (1992) 'Should we ignore methodology?' *Royal Economic Society Newsletter*, 78: 4–5.

—— (1995) 'An empirical philosophy of economic theory,' *British Journal for the Philosophy of Science*, 46: 111–21.

—— (2002) *The Penguin History of Economics*, London: Penguin Books.

Benacerraf, P. and Putnam, H. (eds) (1983) *Philosophy of Mathematics Selected Readings*, 2nd edn., Cambridge: Cambridge University Press.

Black, R.D.C., Coats, A.W. and Crawford, C.D.W. (eds) (1973) *The Marginal Revolution in Economics: Interpretation and Evaluation*, Durham, NC: Duke University Press.

Blaug, M. (ed.) (1985) *Great Economists since Keynes: An Introduction to the Lives and Works of One Hundred Modern Economists*, Brighton, Sussex: Wheatsheaf Books.

—— (2000) 'Ugly currents in modern economics,' in U. Mäki (ed.) *Fact and Fiction in Economics*, Cambridge: Cambridge University Press.

—— (2003) 'The formulist revolution of the 1950s,' in W.J. Samuels, J.F. Biddle and J.B. Davis (eds.) *A Companion to the History of Economic Thought*, Oxford: Blackwell.

Boylan, T.A. and O'Gorman, P.F. (1991) 'The critique of equilibrium theory in economic methodology,' *International Studies in Philosophy of Science*, 5: 131–42.

—— (1995) *Beyond Rhetoric and Realism in Economics: Towards a Reformulation of Economic Methodology*, London: Routledge.

—— (1997) 'Kaldor on Method: a challenge to contemporary methodology,' *Cambridge Journal of Economics*, 21: 503–18.

—— (2001) 'Causal holism and economic modelling: theories models and explanation,' *Revue Internationale du Philosophie*, 55: 395–405.

—— (2003) 'Economic theory and rationality: a Wittgensteinian interpretation,' *Review of Political Economy*, 15: 231–44.

—— (2007) 'Axiomatization and formalism in economics,' *Journal of Economic Surveys*, 21: 426–46; reprinted in D.A.R. George (ed.) (2008) *Issues in Heterodox Economics*, Oxford; Blackwell Publishing.

—— (2009a) 'Holistic defences of rational choice theory: a critique of Davidson and

Pettit,' in T.A. Boylan and R. Gekker (eds) *Economics, Rational Choice and Normative Philosophy*, London: Routledge.

—— (2009b) 'Kaldor on Debreu: the critique of general equilibrium reconsidered,' *Review of Political Economy*, 21: 447–61.

—— (2010) 'Resisting the sirens of realism in economic methodology: a Socratic Odyssey,' in S. Zambelli (ed.) *Computable, Constructive and Behavioural Economic Dynamics: Essays in Honour of Kumaraswamy (Vela) Velupillai*, London: Routledge.

Bridges, D.S. and Richman, F. (1987) *Varieties of Constructive Mathematics*, Cambridge: Cambridge University Press.

Bridges, D.S. and Vîta, L.S. (2006) *Techniques of Constructive Analysis*, New York: Springer.

Brown, J. (2002) *Philosophy of Mathematics*, London: Routledge.

Caldwell, B.J. (1982) *Beyond Positivism: Economic Methodology in the Twentieth Century*, London: George Allen & Unwin.

Cassel, G. (1918) *Theoretische Sozialökonomie,* 5th German edn, translated as *The Theory of Social Economy*, New York: Harcourt Brace, 1932.

Chamberlin, E. (1933) *The Theory of Monopolistic Competition*, Cambridge, MA: Harvard University Press.

Church, A. (1956) *Introduction to Mathematical Logic*, Volume I, New Jersey: Princeton University Press.

Clower, R. (1965) 'The Keynesian counter-revolution: a theoretical appraisal,' in F.H. Hahn and P.R. Brechling (eds) *The Theory of Interest Rates*, London: Macmillan. Reprinted in R. Clower (1984) *Money and Markets: Essays by Robert W. Clower*, Cambridge: Cambridge University Press. Edited by D.A. Walker.

Darwin, C. (1971) *The Origin of Species*, London: J.M. Dent & Son Ltd.

Dasgupta, P. (2002) 'Modern economics and its critics,' in U. Mäki (ed.) *Fact and Fiction in Economics*, Cambridge: Cambridge University Press.

Dasgupta, P., Gale, D., Hart, O. and Maskin, E. (eds) (1992) *Economic Analysis of Markets and Games: Essays in Honour of Frank Hahn*, Cambridge, Massachusetts: MIT Press.

Davidson, D. (2005) *Truth, Language and History*, Oxford: Clarendon Press.

Debreu, G. (1959) *Theory of Value: An Axiomatic Analysis of Economic Equilibrium*, New York: John Wiley.

—— (1960) 'Topological methods in cardinal utility theory,' in K.J. Arrow, S. Karlin and P. Suppes (eds) *Mathematical Methods in Social Sciences*, Stanford CA: Stanford University Press.

—— (1974) 'Excess demand functions,' *Journal of Mathematical Economics*, 1: 15–21.

—— (1983) *Mathematical Economics: Twenty Papers for Gerard Debreu*, Cambridge: Cambridge University Press.

—— (1986) 'Theoretical models: mathematical form and economic content,' *Econometrica*, 54: 1259–70.

—— (1991) 'The mathematization of economic theory,' *American Economic Review*, 81: 1–7.

Dummett, M. (1978) *Truth and Other Enigmas*, London: Duckworth.

—— (1991) *Frege and Other Philosophers*, Oxford: Clarendon Press.

—— (2000) *Elements of Intuitionism*, 2nd edn., Oxford: Clarendon Press.

Düppe, T. (2010) 'Debreu's apologies for mathematical economics after 1983,' *Erasmus Journal for Philosphy and Economics*, 3: 3.

Epstein, R.L. and Carnielli, W.A. (2000) *Computability, Computable Functions, Logic and the Foundations of Mathematics* (2nd edn.), Belmont CA: Wadsworth/Thomson Learning.

van Frassen, B. (1980) *The Scientific Image*, Oxford: Clarendon Press.

Frege, G. (1968) *The Foundations of Arithmetic* (2nd revised edn.), trans. J.L. Austin, Oxford: Basil Blackwell.

—— (1971a) *On the Foundations of Arithmetic* (2nd revised edn.), trans. J.L. Austin, Oxford: Basil Blackwell.

—— (1971b) *On the Foundations of Geometry and Formal Theories of Arithmetic*, trans. E.H.W. Kluge, New Haven CT: Yale University Press.

Friedman, M. (1953) 'The methodology of positive economics,' in M. Friedman (ed.) *Essays in Positive Economics*, Chicago: University of Chicago Press.

Gale, D. (1955) 'The law of supply and demand,' *Mathematica Scandinavica*, 3: 155–69.

Geert, R. (1996) 'Appraising Hausman's Mill-twist, Robbin-giest, and Popper-whist, *Journal of Economic Methodology*, 3: 33–67.

Golland, L.A. (1996) 'Formalism in economics,' *Journal of the History of Economic Thought*, 18: 1–12.

Hahn, F.H. (1950) 'The share of wages in the trade cycle,' *Economic Journal*, 60 (239): 618–21.

—— (1951) 'The share of wages in national income,' *Oxford Economic Papers*, 3: 147–57.

—— (1958) 'Gross substitutes and the dynamic stability of general equilibrium,' *Econometrica*, 26: 169–70.

—— (1960) 'The stability of growth equilibrium,' *Quarterly Journal of Economics*, 74: 206–26.

—— (1962a) 'On the stability of a pure exchange equilibrium,' *International Economic Review*, 3: 206–13.

—— (1962b) 'The stability of the Cournot Oligopoly Solution,' *Review of Economic Studies*, 29: 329–31.

—— (1963) 'On the disequilibrium behaviour of a multi-sectoral growth model,' *Economic Journal*, 73 (291): 442–57.

—— (1965) 'On some problems of proving the existence of an equilibrium in a monetary economy,' in F.H. Hahn and F.P.R. Brechling (eds.) *The Theory of Interest Rates*, London: Macmillan.

—— (1966) 'Equilibrium dynamics with heterogeneous capital goods,' *Quarterly Journal of Economics*, 80: 633–46.

—— (1968) 'On warranted growth paths,' *The Review of Economic Studies*, 35: 175–84.

—— (1969) 'On money and growth,' *Journal of Money, Credit and Banking*, 1: 175–84. Reprinted in F. Hahn, *Equilibrium and Macroeconomics*, Oxford: Basil Blackwell, 1984, pp. 195–213.

—— (1970) 'Some adjustment problems,' *Econometrica* 38(1): 1–17. Reprinted in F. Hahn, *Equilibrium and Macroeconomics*, Oxford: Basil Blackwell, 1984, pp. 88–110.

—— (1971) 'Equilibrium with transaction costs,' *Econometrica*, 39: 417–39.

—— (1972) *The Share of Wages in the National Income: An Inquiry into the Theory of Distribution*, London: Weidenfeld and Nicholson.

—— (1973a) *On the notion of equilibrium in economics*, Cambridge: Cambridge University Press.

—— (1973b) 'On transaction costs, inessential sequence economies and money,' *Review of Economic Studies*, 40: 449–61.

—— (1973c) 'On some equilibrium growth paths,' in J. Mirrlees and N. Stern (eds) *Models of Economic Growth*, London: Macmillan.

—— (1973d) 'On the foundations of monetary theory,' in M. Parkin and A.R. Nobay (eds.) *Essays in Modern Economics*, London: Longmans. Reprinted in F. Hahn, *Equilibrium and Macroeconomics*, Oxford: Basil Blackwell, 1984, pp. 158–74.

—— (1975) 'Revival of political economy: the wrong issues and the wrong argument,' *Economic Record*, 51: 360–64.

—— (1977) 'Keynesian economics and general equilibrium theory: reflections on some current debates,' in G.C. Harcourt (ed.) *Microeconomic Foundations in Macroeconomics*, London: Macmillan. Reprinted in F. Hahn, *Equilibrium and Macroeconomics*, Oxford: Basil Blackwell, 1984, pp. 175–94.

—— (1980) 'Monetarism and economic theory,' *Economica*, N.S. 47: 1–17. Reprinted in F. Hahn, *Equilibrium and Macroeconomics*, Oxford: Basil Blackwell, 1984, pp. 283–306.

—— (1982a) 'Reflections on the invisible hand,' *Lloyds Bank Review*, April: 1–21. Reprinted in F. Hahn, *Equilibrium and Macroeconomics*, Oxford: Basil Blackwell, 1984, pp. 111–33.

—— (1982b) 'The neo-Ricardians,' *Cambridge Journal of Economics*, 6: 353–74. Reprinted in F. Hahn, *Equilibrium and Macroeconomics*, Oxford: Basil Blackwell, 1984, pp. 353–86.

—— (1984) *Equilibrium and Macroeconomics*, Oxford: Basil Blackwell.

—— (1985) *In Praise of Economic Theory*, London: University College London.

—— (1989) *The Economics of Missing Markets, Information and Games*, Oxford: Oxford University Press.

—— (1991a) 'The next hundred years,' *The Economic Journal*, 101: 47–50.

—— (1991b) 'History and economic theory,' in K.J. Arrow (ed.) *Issues in Contemporary Economics*, Vol. 1 Markets and Welfare. IEA Conference Volume Series, London: Macmillan (in association with IEA).

—— (1992a) 'Reflections,' *Royal Economic Society Newsletter*, 77: 5.

—— (1992b) 'Answer to Backhouse: Yes'. *Royal Economic Society Newsletter*, 78: 5.

—— (1992c) 'On some economic limits in politics,' in John Dunn (ed.) *The Economic Limits to Modern Politics*, Cambridge: Cambridge University Press.

—— (1993a) 'Predicting the economy,' in L. Hoire and A. Lwain (eds) *Predicting the Future*, Cambridge: Cambridge University Press.

—— (1993b) 'Frank Hahn: autobiographical notes with reflections,' in M. Szenberg (ed.) *Eminent Economists: Their Life Philosophies*, Cambridge: Cambridge University Press.

—— (1994) 'An intellectual retrospect,' *Banca Nationale Del Lavoro Quarterly Review*, 190: 245–58.

—— (1996) 'Rerum cognoscere causas,' *Economics and Philosophy*, 12: 183–95.

—— (2003) 'Macroeconomics and general equilibrium,' in F. Petri and F. Hahn (eds.) *General Equilibrium: Problems and Prospects*, London: Routledge.

—— (2005a) 'General equilibrium for intellectual historians,' *Storia del Pensiero Economico*, Nuovo Serie, Anno II, N.2: 5–12.

—— (2005b) 'An interview with Frank Hahn on the occasion of his 80th birthday,' conducted by Marcello Basili and Carlo Zappia, *Storia del Pensiero Economico*, Nuovo Serie, Anno II, N.2: 13–18.

Hahn, F.H. and Matthews, R.C.O. (1964) 'The theory of economic growth: a survey,' *Economic Journal*, 74 : 779–902.

Hahn, F.H. and Solow, R.M. (1995) *A Critical Essay on Modern Macroeconomic Theory*, Oxford: Blackwell.

Hall, R. and Hitch, C. (1939) 'Price theory and business behaviour,' *Oxford Economic Papers*, 2: 12–45.

Hands, D. Wade (2001) *Reflections without Rules: Economic Methodology and Contemporary Science Theory*, Cambridge: Cambridge University Press.

Harcourt, G.C. (1988) 'Nicholas Kaldor, 12 May 1908–30 September 1986,' *Economica*, 55: 159–70.

Hausman, D.M. (1992a) *The Inexact and Separate Science of Economics*, Cambridge: Cambridge University Press.

—— (1992b) 'On the conceptual structure of neoclassical economics – a philosopher's view,' in D.M. Hausman (ed.) *Essays on Philosophy and Economic Methodology*, Cambridge: Cambridge University Press.

—— (1996) 'Economics as separate and inexact,' *Economics and Philosophy*, 12: 207–20.

—— (1997) 'Why does evidence matter so little to economic theory?' in M.L. Dalla Chiara, K. Doets, D. Mundici and J. van Benthem (eds) *Structures and Norms in Science*, Dordrecht: Kluwer Academic Publishers.

Hempel, C. (1965) *Aspects of Scientific Explanation*, New York: Macmillan.

Hesse, M. (1966) *Models and Analogies in Science*, London: Sheed and Ward.

Hicks J. (1939) *Value and Capital*, Oxford: Oxford University Press.

Hicks, J.R. (1937) 'Mr. Keynes and the classics,' *Econometrics*, 5: 147–59.

Hilbert, D. (1899) *Foundations of Geometry*, trans. L. Under, La Salle IL: Open Court.

—— (1926) 'On the infinite,' trans. E. Putnam and G.J. Massey, in P. Benacerraf and H. Putnam (eds) *Philosophy of Mathematics Selected Readings*, 2nd edn. Cambridge: Cambridge University Press, 1983.

Hoover, K.D. (1988) *The New Classical Macroeconomics: A Sceptical Inquiry*, Oxford: Basil Blackwell.

Hume, D. (1985) *A Treatise of Human Nature*, Harmondsworth, Middlesex: Penguin Books Ltd.

Hutchison, T.W. (1977) *Knowledge and Ignorance in Economics*, Oxford: Basil Blackwell.

Ingrao, B. and Israel, G. (1990) *The Invisible Hand: Economic Theory in the History of Science*, Cambridge MA: MIT Press.

Kaldor, N. (1972) 'The irrelevance of equilibrium economics,' *Economic Journal*, 82: 1237–55.

—— (1975) 'What is wrong with economic theory,' *Quarterly Journal of Economics* 89: 347–57.

—— (1985) *Economics without Equilibrium*, Cardiff: University College of Cardiff Press.

—— (1996) *Causes of Growth and Stagnation in the World Economy*, Cambridge: Cambridge University Press.

Kenny, A. (2000) *Frege*, Oxford: Blackwell Publishers.

Keynes, J.M. (1936) *The General Theory of Employment, Interest and Money*, London: Macmillan.

Kirman, A. (2006) 'Demand theory and general equilibrium: from explanation to introspection, a journey down the wrong road,' in P. Mirowski and D. Wade Hands (eds) *Agreement on Demand: Consumer Theory in the Twentieth Century (Annual Supplement to Volume 38, History of Political Economy)*, Durham, NC: Duke University Press.

Koopmans, T.C. (1947) 'Measurement without theory,' *The Review of Economics and Statistics*, 29: 161–72.

—— (1957) *Three Essays on the State of Economic Science*, New York: McGraw-Hill.

Koot, G.M. (1987) *English Historical Economics, 1870–1926*, Cambridge: Cambridge University Press.

Kuhn, T.S. (1970) *The Structure of Scientific Revolutions* (2nd edn.), Chicago: The University of Chicago Press.

—— (1977) *The Essential Tension: Selected Studies in Scientific Tradition and Change*, Chicago: The University of Chicago Press.

Lange, O. (1944) *Price Flexibility and Employment*, Bloomington, IN: Principia Press.

Lawson, T. (1989) 'Abstraction, tendencies and stylized facts: a realist approach to economic analysis,' *Cambridge Journal of Economics*, 13: 59–78.

Leontief, W. (1936) 'The fundamental assumption of Mr. Keynes's monetary theory of unemployment,' *Quarterly Journal of Economics*, 51: 192–7.

Lester, R.A. (1946) 'Shortcomings of marginal analysis for wage employment problems,' *American Economic Review*, 36: 63–82.

McGuinness, B. (1994) 'Time, Truth and Deity,' in B. McGuinness and G. Oliveri (eds) *The Philosophy of Michael Dummett*, Dordrecht: Kluwer Academic Publishers.

McKenzie, L. (1954) 'On equilibrium in Graham's model of world trade and other competitive systems,' *Econometrica*, 22: 147–61.

Mäki, U. (1996) 'Two portraits of economics,' *Journal of Economic Methodology*, 3: 1–38.

—— (ed.) (2002) *Fact and Fiction in Economics*, Cambridge: Cambridge University Press.

Mantel, R. (1971) 'Implications of micro-economic theory for community excess demand functions,' in M. Intriligator (ed.) *Frontiers of Quantitative Economics*, Vol. 3: 111–26.

Menger, K. (1952) 'The formative years of Abraham Wald and his work in geometry,' *Annals of Mathematics and Statistics*, 23: 14–20.

Mok, V. (ed.) (1991) 'Symposium: Has formalization in economics gone too far?' *Methodus*, Vol. 3, No. 1.

Moore, G.E. (1976) *Principia Ethica*, Cambridge: Cambridge University Press.

Morgenstern, O. (1968) 'Karl Schlesinger,' in *International Encyclopedia of the Social Sciences*, Vol. 14: 509–11, New York: Macmillan.

Nagel, E. and Newman, J.R. (2005) *Gödel's Proof*, London: Routledge.

Nikaido, H. (1956) 'On the classical multilateral exchange problem,' *Metroeconomica*, 8: 135–45.

Patinkin,D. (1956) *Money, Interest and Prices*, New York: Harper and Row.

Poincaré, H. (1952) *Science and Hypothesis*, New York: Dover.

—— (1963) *Mathematics and Science: Last Essays*, trans. J.W. Bolduc, New York: Dover.

Potter, M. (2000) *Reason's Nearest Kin: Philosophers of Arithmetic from Kant to Carnap*, Oxford: Oxford University Press.

Quine, W.V.O. (1960) *Word and Object*, Cambridge, MA: The MIT Press.

—— (1969) 'Epistemology Naturalized,' in W.V.O. Quine *Ontological Relativity and Other Essays*, New York: Columbia University Press.

Reuten, G. (1996) 'A revision of the neoclassical economics methodology appraising Hausman's Mill-twist, Robbins-gist and Popper-whist,' *Journal of Economic Methodology*, 3: 39–67.

Rizvi, S.A.T. (2003) 'Postwar neoclassical microeconomics,' in W.J. Samuels, J.E. Biddle and J.B. Davis (eds) *A Companion to the History of Economic Thought*, Oxford: Blackwell.

Robinson, J. (1933) *The Economics of Imperfect Competition*, London: Macmillan.
—— (1970) *Economic Philosophy*, Harmondsworth: Pelican.
Samuelson, P.A. (1947) *Foundations of Economic Analysis*, Cambridge, MA: Harvard University Press.
—— (1955) *Economics*, 3rd edn, New York: McGraw-Hill.
Scarf, H.S. (1960) 'Some examples of global instability of competitive equilibria,' *International Economic Review*, 1: 157–72.
—— (1967) 'On the computation of equilibrium prices,' in W. Fellner (ed.) *Ten Economic Studies in the Tradition of Irving Fisher*, New York: John Wiley.
Schumpeter, J.A. (1954) *History of Economic Analysis*, New York: Oxford University Press.
Shackle, G.L.S. (1967) *The Years of High Theory*, Cambridge: Cambridge University Press.
Smith, A. (1776) *An Inquiry into the Nature and Causes of the Wealth of Nations*, London: Methuen and Co., Ltd.
Solow, R. (1992) 'Hahn on the share of wages in national income,' in P. Dasgupta, D. Gale, O. Hart and E. Maskin (eds) *Economic Analysis of Markets and Games: Essays in Honour of Frank Hahn*, Cambridge, MA: MIT Press.
Solow, R.M. (1954) 'The survival of mathematical economics,' *Review of Economics and Statistics*, 36: 372–4.
Sonnenschein, H.F. (1972) 'Do Walras's identity and continuity characterize the class of community excess demand functions?' *Journal of Economic Theory*, 6: 345–54.
Sraffa, P. (1926) 'The laws of return under competitive conditions,' *Economic Journal*, 36: 535–50.
Starr, R.M. (1967) 'Quasi-equilibrium in markets with non-convex preferences,' *Econometrica*, 37: 25–38.
Targetti,F. and Thirlwall, A.P. (eds) (1989) *The Essential Kaldor*, New York: Holmes & Meier.
Thirlwall, A.P. (1987) *Nicholas Kaldor*, Brighton: Wheatsheaf Press.
Tohmé, F. (2006) 'Rolf Mantel and the computability of general equilibria: on the origins of the Sonnenschein–Mantel–Debreu theorem,' in P. Mirowski and D. Wade Hands (eds) *Agreement on Demand: Consumer Theory in the Twentieth Century (Annual Supplement to Vol. 38, History of Political Economy)*, Durham, NC: Duke University Press.
Van Dalen, D. (ed.) (1981) *Brower's Cambridge Lectures on Intuitionism*, Cambridge: Cambridge University Press.
Velupillai, K. (2000) *Computable Economics*, Oxford: Oxford University Press.
—— (2002) 'Effectivity and constructivity in economic theory,' *Journal of Economic Behaviour and Organization*, 49: 307–25.
—— (2010) *Computable Foundations for Economics*, London: Routledge.
Vining, R. (1949) 'Koopmans on the choice of variables to be studied and of methods of measurement,' *The Review of Economics and Statistics*, 31: 77–86.
Von Neumann, J. and Morgenstein, O. (1944) *Theory of Games and Economic Behaviour*, Princeton: Princeton University Press.
Weintraub, E.R. (1983) 'On the existence of a competitive equilibrium: 1930–1954,' *Journal of Economic Literature*, 21: 1–39.
—— (1985) *General Equilibrium Analysis: Studies in Appraisal*, Cambridge: Cambridge University Press.
—— (1991) *Stabilising Dynamics: Constructing Economic Knowledge*, Cambridge: Cambridge University Press.

—— (2002) *How Economics became a Mathematical Science*, Durham, NC: Duke University Press.

Wittgenstein, L. (1963) *Tractatus Logico-Philosophicus*, trans. D.F. Pears and B.F. McGuinness, London: Routledge & Kegan Paul.

—— (1967) *Remarks on the Foundations of Mathematics*, trans. G.E.M. Anscombe, Oxford: Basil Blackwell.

—— (2000) *Philosophical Investigations*, trans. G.E.M. Anscombe, Oxford: Blackwell Publishers.

Young, A.A. (1928) 'Increasing returns and economic progress,' *Economic Journal*, 38: 527–42.

Zambelli, S. (2010) 'Computable and constructive economics, undecidable dynamics and algorithmic rationality, An essay in honour of Professor Kumaraswamy (Vela) Velupillai,' in S. Zambelli (ed.) *Computable, Constructive and Behavioural Economic Dynamics, Essays in honour of Kumaraswamy (Vela) Velupillai*, London: Routledge.

Index